TO MARY ANN

A ROSE ON THE STEEL GROUND

THANK YOU VERY MUCH

JULIE JOAN KY ALEXANDER

11/24/2020

JULIE LOAN KY ALEXANDER

A ROSE ON THE STEEL GROUND

TATE PUBLISHING
AND ENTERPRISES, LLC

Published by Tate Publishing & Enterprises, LLC
127 E. Trade Center Terrace | Mustang, Oklahoma 73064 USA
1.888.361.9473 | www.tatepublishing.com

Tate Publishing is committed to excellence in the publishing industry. The company reflects the philosophy established by the founders, based on Psalm 68:11,
"The Lord gave the word and great was the company of those who published it."

Published in the United States of America

ISBN: 978-1-62994-625-2
1. Biography & Autobiography / Cultural Heritage
2. Biography & Autobiography / Women
13.11.19

Father, watch over me:
my boat is so small,
and the sea is so wide.

—International Children's Prayer

DEDICATION

This book would never have come to be without my father, the greatest person who lived on earth during my lifetime and who is always in my heart.

And I thank God for carrying me safely through every hardship I have faced in my life. I have much gratitude to you, America, my second home, because you gave me opportunities to reestablish my parents' fine reputations, which they had worked too hard to build and which were–almost overnight–taken away from them for over 30 years. I thank the U.S. Postal Service, who gave the opportunity to earn my fortune, to carry my whole family on my shoulders, and to fulfill a duty and promise.

To my husband, Richard Alexander; my son, Michael; and to my mother, Hoa Trang, from the bottom of my heart, I appreciate each and every one of you for everything you have given me during my long and complicated journey, and I will carry you in my heart for the rest of my life.

INTRODUCTION

I was born in 1965 in Cu Chi, Vietnam and lived there through high school. Cu Chi is twenty miles from the northwest corner of Saigon and right in the center of the area once known as "The Red Zone" during the Vietnam War: red hot with horror, blood, and "Reds" (communists). Cu Chi was famous during the Vietnam War because of the underground tunnel that the Communists dug from Cu Chi to Saigon; this tunnel became known as "The Cu Chi Tunnel" and was one of the largest hidden military bases during that war.

The people of our town who survived the war then began to think of Cu Chi in a different way from being the origin of the tunnel. They decided its name had grown to mean "The Rose That Grows on Steel Ground;" Cu Chi's land may have been ravaged and the life pounded flat out of it, like steel, perhaps, and yet people were astounded to find that roses miraculously survived the war, too, and they all went on to flourish.

If you have never been there or seen pictures of it, Vietnam is like a wild, over-grown jungle. Summers are extremely hot and dusty, and the jungle is wild and seems to be creeping slowly, day by day, toward town, as if to devour everything in the path of its creeping and to swallow it whole. Rice water fields were planted in some parts of the countryside.

Birds, snakes, geckos, rats—all kinds of wildlife lived with us. At nighttime, you couldn't sit outside too long because the mosquitoes would peel you raw, head to toe, in the dark.

My family was a middle class family with seven brothers and sisters. My father, Lien Hau Ky, was Chinese and had left China with several friends and finally decided to stay in Cu Chi in 1945 and put down his roots there. He was chubby, about five feet, eight inches tall. All of my friends thought he was the most handsome dad in town, as he always wore a beautiful smile that lit up his face like a lantern in the darkness. He had a wide forehead and big ears, which Chinese people call 'Buddha's ears.' He talked really loudly when he talked and laughed very hard whenever he laughed. No matter what was going on or where we had landed—in hell or on high water, he was *always* the first one to make us laugh. I remember Dad wore shirts and shorts almost all of his life because it was always so hot, and sometimes he would wear just his shorts, his 'Buddha belly' spilling over the waist of his shorts. When my father was angry, he had a quick temper; but we could always count on him to cool down very quickly.

Not my mother, Hoa Trang, though! When she got angry, she stayed angry for a long time. She was an average-looking woman with short, curly hair and dark skin. She had sad and beautiful eyes, which filled easily with tears whenever she got mad. When she was not mad, her voice was soft and sweet. She liked to wear black slacks and shirts with huge pockets that she filled with everything she needed to use at work in the dry goods store my parents owned. My mother had always lived very simply because of what she had suffered as a child. She figured out how to rise above the circumstances that had caused her to suffer and how to be very successful at a young age. She could work just as hard and as enthusiastically as my father. Mom simply had never been given my father's gift for laughter.

They had both lived through nightmarish childhoods due to the havoc created by World War II in China and Vietnam. My father, despite his childhood, remained kind and generous all of his life; he worked very, very hard at whatever he did and yet could not resist helping those in need. Perhaps one of the most important gifts he left all of us was to learn to laugh: laugh in the face of whatever might threaten us and laugh because life can be so good and because it is good simply to laugh. My father simply wanted peace of mind and peace in the world.

On the other hand, we thought of my mother as 'The Dictator,' often difficult to deal with. When she was a child, she had starved and had had to beg for food, and she was therefore determined that neither she, her husband, nor her children would ever have to live as she had had to live as a young girl. Mother was single-minded about achieving success, and my father would never have realized the success he enjoyed from his businesses without my mother. My mother was fixated on gaining and holding onto whatever advantages she could obtain. My mother struggled hard to beat all of their competitors in their businesses to the point of pushing her employees, her own children, even her own mother and relatives hard to maintain their highly respected accomplishments.

My father worked hard, too; but above all, he simply enjoyed having everyone around him, wherever he was. Townspeople loved my father and struggled sometimes with my mother's difficult ways. Maybe because of this, she always felt no one cared about her and worried that no one would ever help her if she were in trouble or crushed to the ground again, as she had been in her youth.

Though they were immensely different in some ways, my parents supported each other strongly, fought for each other, and were very faithful to each other all of their lives. It was God's idea to put them together, I am sure, and they were happy together, differences and all.

Right after they married, they began to bring all of us into the world, all seven of us! When I was very little, our family was the happiest family in town because my parents' dry goods store was so successful. In their store, they sold everything imaginable, any-thing *anyone* might need: hundreds of giant, two-hundred-pound rice bags lined the long walls inside the store next to sugar, oil, dried food, office supplies, nails: they stocked over 100 different items. You had only to name it, and if it weren't right there in the store at that moment for some strange reason, my father would find it for you. The store was fully stocked at all times, ready for all customers who crowded in from early in the morning until dark; delivery trucks were backed up to our store, loading and unloading products all day long.

My parents were clever at marketing, too: they organized the products in the store with a lot of thought: heavier items were placed near the door so customers could carry them out easily, and the smaller, lighter, and more expensive items–ciga-rettes, etc.–were kept under my mother's ever-vigilant eye, near or behind the glass doors of her huge work table: no one *ever* shoplifted in our store. My parents also placed tempting items not necessarily on anyone's list in places where customers simply could not miss seeing–and wanting to buy–them.

Our store's prosperity was, ironically and so sadly, greatly enhanced because of the Vietnam War, which had torn our coun-try into pieces for over thirty years. In 1954, the Geneva Accord had split our country into two parts, North Vietnam and South Vietnam. Soon after this happened, a military base was installed close to Cu Chi, so that my parents supplied our army, in addition to all of the townspeople, with whatever they required. Money flowed, non-stop, into their hands like a river laughing in its bed all the way down the mountain. Many people worked for parents, and they were also able to hire at least three maids to work in our house at a time. The maids treated all seven of us like little princes and princesses.

If customers didn't have any money to pay for what they needed, regardless of who they were, my father let them pick up rice or groceries for their family and pay back the store later. He didn't even worry if customers never came back to pay their debts. His heart was as open and wide as the sky above.

My mother's sharp intelligence was truly the engine that ran the store. My father was responsible for acquiring goods they stocked. He left home very early every morning in search of things he knew they needed to restock and hot products he came across in the big city, where he bargained with store bosses to buy what he wanted for the lowest prices possible.

I can still see in my mind's eye the beautiful, ten-foot long, mahogany table that glowed warmly in the middle of the store. This table served as my mother's desk or 'Command Central.' It was where she did all of the paperwork for father's store. The table was an heirloom that had been in my father's family long before he had met my mother. Inside it had been built several sets of shelves and drawers enclosed behind beautiful, handmade glass doors. On one set of shelves, my mother kept the most expensive goods they sold: tobacco, batteries, electronics, etc.; on the other side of the table, in several drawers she kept the money and papers she needed to keep accounts and place orders. She had a stool behind her massive station, but she was rarely ever sat on it, as she kept her hawk-eye out for shoplifters and also made sure she took good care of each and every one of the customers. Since her table was so tall and long, it was a great place for my brother and me to play hide and seek until we grew too tall. Sweet memory...

About fifty Chinese families lived in town. We all leaned on and supported each other so that we could survive and find success in this foreign country. We celebrated Chinese holidays together according to Chinese traditions and worshipped our forefathers and the heroes who established China throughout its history. The strong bond among us all created a community that felt safe, supportive, and enabled its members to prosper.

Children in our community attended a private school that was founded and funded by the Chinese people in the community.

We learned the Chinese language, Chinese history, and the values of our Chinese forebears: our elders thought this important in order to prevent our assimilation into Vietnamese culture by the Vietnamese who also lived in Cu Chi.

As a very small child, I was blessed in so many ways in my life, though I had also grown up with a war that had begun long before I took my first breath. It was made clear to us by our parents–*without a word*–that we had no choice but to face whatever happened and not blink, to be brave, to accept and adapt to our lots in life, no matter what they might turn out to be.

I had known much happiness as a child, but I had also walked through that time filled with raw fear. And though I did not know it back then, God had not even *begun* to test me.

CHAPTER ONE

JUNE, 2009

The flight attendant announced we would arrive at the airport in six hours and proceeded with her in-flight instructions, which nobody was paying any attention to.

My heart was thumping like a kid's sneakers, rhythmically—thud, thud, thudding—over a rapidly flying jump rope, and I felt feverish. This was the trip I had dreamed forever of taking, my destination the most meaningful and important one I had ever hoped to reach in my whole life.

It was going to be a long, long, *very* long flight, and I had been very nervous and excited for days and then, the day we were to depart, from the very moment we had approached the airport—more excited than I had ever been in my whole life.

I had worn myself ragged from passing so many hours filled with such strong emotions coursing through me. I was already exhausted and there was so much time to go! Gazing out of my little 'porthole' window so that I didn't miss a thing, I watched the darkness wrap itself gently around us, and eventually staring into blackness hypnotized me into a fitful sleep with crazy collages of dreams.

APRIL, 1975

BOOM! BOOM! *BOOM!* I was jolted awake that morning out of my customary, light, day-dream state and into what became a nightmare: thousands of hard-stepping, angry-sounding army boots were clomp-clomp-clomping right by our front door; patrol trucks ground their engines as they passed our house; and shouting blasted all the way from the radio inside the county office next door right through our walls and into my room! My parents were whispering hoarsely together in the front room of our house; their hushed and hasty words hissed like cats fighting, but I could not understand what they were saying. What was happening!!!??? It was only 5:30 in the morning!

I jumped out of bed, shivering in my favorite, pink silk pajamas, to try to find answers. Everything I wore was pink because my older sister had told me once that the color pink brought good luck. I was ten then, so I hung onto every word she said and believed someday that pink would bring me big luck!

First, I ran into the warehouse of my father's enormous store, but it was empty; no one was there, and my small, barefoot steps echoed as they slapped on the concrete floor. Every item my father sold in the store still sat where it had been carefully placed the night or day before. The top of my mother's beautiful worktable loomed quietly over my head.

Outside the store, I found my father and my oldest brother Ton heaving giant, two hundred-pound bags of rice into the back of my father's light blue pick-up truck as if they were in a mad race of some kind. My mother and my oldest sister Chau were struggling to carry cumbersome pieces of luggage and awkward containers of food out to the truck to be loaded, too. I suddenly remembered they had been cooking and preparing lots and lots of different dishes a couple of days ago. They were cooking for this? And why was everyone running around?

My little sister Le was awake but upset from having been wakened, crying and fighting with my mother because she did want to get up. I went to see if all my other brothers and sisters were awake and up. My older sister Ngoc was still asleep with my younger brother Tai, where my sister Le had also slept. My handicapped, older brother Toi was also asleep, his one arm flung over his eyes. Toi had had polio when he was three and had lost one arm because of it.

Toi quickly slid out of his bed and said, in a very serious way, "This is it. You better get ready because we are going to leave home very soon."

What should I do to "get ready?" He did not explain. Leave home?! I did not dare ask.

In the front room of our house, I heard my father's strong, firm voice urging my mother to "hurry, hurry," to gather enough clothes to last a few days, and to wake and get us all dressed before it was "too late."

Too late? I never wanted to miss out on anything!!!

My family sometimes took vacations to the beach to visit relatives or went on shopping trips to Saigon. But we were always told we would be going on such a trip at least a week or ten days before we were going to leave. This trip was so different! It was so sudden: maybe it was a very special surprise?

Deciding this had to be one of our trips to the beach, I began to copy the rest of my brothers and sisters and put on two sets of clothes, the nicest ones that my mom had bought for me. I packed up some books, toys, and my favorite personal things. Maybe this would end up being the most exciting, interesting trip that we had ever been on! Everyone was silent as he or she prepared for this mysterious journey, except my father who issued directions to my big brother Ton and my mom now and then in a loud voice so they could hear him over the chaos all around. The only other sound in the house was voice on our radio that was almost yelling something that I did not understand at all.

Over the past few weeks, I had noticed my dad listening to the radio all day and all night, non-stop. And everywhere else I had been over the past few weeks, people had had their radios turned on, the volume turned way up: at my school, at the market, even walking on the street, people carried boom-boxes over their shoulders with the volume turned way up and the speaker directed at one ear so they could hear what the radio voices were saying over the street noise. The only things that I could understand the radio voices saying were people's names, places, and "dead."

Outside, the terrifying noises began to get louder and louder, and they felt closer and closer, as they shook the floor under me sometimes. Gunfire, bombs, and rockets were being fired and blowing up, over and over and over, like fireworks above our whole town; the one thing I knew for sure now was that this was *not* a celebration. Some of the din outside was not unfamiliar to us. I had come to know their voices all in a way when I was still in my mom's womb. Before today, they had usually occurred at night and did not last all that long. On this particular day, however, the explosions were constant, getting closer and closer to our house, over and over and over, boom, crack, boom, crack! I covered my ears sometimes.

All packed. What should I do now? No one was speaking to anyone else, and so I decided to help my oldest sister Chau finish loading the food onto the truck with Ton. My mother grabbed some blankets off our beds and threw them into the truck with some pillows and a few extra pairs of shoes.

I began to suspect what really be going on: something to do with the war everyone had been talking about. I did not really know what 'war' was, but no one smiled when they talked about it. I prayed we would not have to walk for too long, if we were really leaving home. I hated walking in the heat and dust of the city. It made me so tired, sweaty, and gritty

My mom and dad had begun wrapping up all the gold and valuable jewelry they had and stuffing tons of cash in a huge handbag that my mother then slung over her shoulder and carried with her the whole time she worked to get us all ready to go. Mother made every single one of us wear every piece of our jewelry, too: 24-karat gold necklaces, rings, and bracelets, earrings that she used to bring home for us when she went shopping with my dad in Saigon. Occasionally, we wore a little bit of jewelry for holidays, ceremonies, or for fun; but this was no holiday, and we were not having fun. We all looked so eerie and shiny at five o'clock in the morning, wearing valuable, heavy gems over layers and layers of clothes, as if some very young child had dressed us, as if we were dolls, in very weird and heavy costumes.

Sunlight had backlit the blue of the sky. Peeking through a hole in the front door, I saw crowds of people hurrying by, in families or bigger groups, on foot, trying to carry a lot of luggage, boxes, and other objects. Some were heading north, and some, south. Men pushed wagons they had crammed full of as much as their wagons could hold. All the women carried long bamboo poles on their shoulders, and from each end of their poles hung big baskets, each basket brimming over with things they wanted to take with them from home, like we were doing.

Fear began to make people push and bump into each other, try to shove ahead of anyone in their way. The crowd swelled like a river overflowing its banks and filling the street. Green army trucks crept as fast as they could through the crowds, honk-honk-honking as they rolled along, trying to clear the road of people. Our normal peaceful and quiet morning had been replaced by all of this chaos and the unsettling hoards of strangers fleeing as fast as they could under their awkward burdens, trying to work their ways to some safe destination in crazy, divergent directions through the crowd.

I began to fight with my older brother Ton, who had shoved *me* out of the way so he could peek through the hole. Suddenly, an ear-splitting explosion tore a hole in the sky, pounded in my head. I screamed and covered my ears. I thought that the world had all fallen down; then I felt the earth shuddering and cracking into a million pieces under the soles of my feet. It was as if someone had hit my head with a giant, invisible shovel, making me see stars everywhere.

Then, the very worst thing we had ever experienced happened: another blast hit our house directly, and our poor house shook with terror like an old man standing alone in a fierce lightning storm. The vibrations from the explosion caused the ground to wobble under my feet again; the walls shuddered, and cracks spidered the ceilings. In the kitchen, glasses and pottery were shaken down off shelves and splintered all over the floor.

Trembling, terrified, my legs began to feel like a pair of melting candles under me. I went blind, collapsed on the floor, covered my head with both arms, and passed out. When I came to again, I opened my eyes.

My dad shouted an order at me from across the room, "Stay down!!!!"

I did not know I had been unconscious. Soon, my father rushed toward me and pulled me up, hurriedly dumping me like a small sack of rice flour onto the truck with the rest of my brothers and sitters. He was not being cruel: he was trying to save us all.

My little sitter Le was screaming and trying to jump out of my father's arms because she was frightened out of her right mind. He sat Le down next to my mother in the front seat and quickly jumped into the truck to start the engine, while my oldest brother Ton, who was also shaking, tried to lock the truck door behind all of us. He couldn't even hold onto the padlock; fear made it jump out of his quaking fingers, over and over.

Suddenly my father slammed on the brakes, leaped of the truck again, and sped back inside the house with Ton. Five minutes later, they both returned with long, very sad faces. My mother simply turned to my father and said, "Just leave."

Our dog had disappeared after the explosion: Ton and my dad had not been able to find him when they ran back into the house. No one said a word.

My father jumped back into the truck. He turned around and looked at us sternly, told us to stay calm and not to panic. "Follow the crowd, if we are separated for any reason."

'*Separated?*! *From my family?*' Numb, as if dying from all of these shocks inside and outside of me, I sat in one corner of the truck bed with the rest of my brothers and sisters; they were all very still, sad, and numb, as if dying, inside, too.

Our truck started to roll slowly down the street. It was about seven o'clock in the morning now. Outside the truck, the world I knew had changed entirely. The house across the street from ours was crumbling and being swallowed by huge, firey lips from a bomb explosion earlier. Why? The families who lived next door to the burned house were frantically gathering all of their furniture and valuable belongings and stacking them on the sidewalk, and, at the same time, they were trying to help our neighbors extinguish their fire. I prayed that no one would get hurt in the fire; the house had disappeared in the flames, and what was left of it was black smoke, circling up into the sky like an evil spirit. The children who lived in the burning houses would not have a place to live now. Goosebumps began to sting my back and neck. What if we came back, and our house was completely gone, too? Or worse: what if my whole town disappeared? I suddenly thought I should have brought more of my things, just in case.

Then, an image of my grandparents flashed through my mind: I saw them as they had stood that early morning at the front door of their home, waving good-bye to us as we left. My heart kicked at my ribs, and tears poured down my face. If a bomb were dropped on my grandparents' house, too, nobody would be there to help them. Why weren't they leaving? Why weren't we taking them with us? My body felt as if I were sitting in a freezer and soaking hot at the same time. Bombs rumbled overhead constantly; machine guns blasted into the sky, creating a thick umbrella of fire that rained slowly back down like the ending tail of fireworks over town. Battles and gunfire had never, ever been this awful, this constant, and they had never happened in broad daylight very often.

As my father continued to maneuver through the streets to get us out of town, the atmosphere around us thumped and thudded with the rhythmic pounding of those boots drumming on the ground, piercing screams from lost children searching for their parents, and mothers screeching out the names of their lost children. All human sound was smothered by sirens and the nonstop grinding of military trucks. It sounded as if my town were being destroyed by some heartless monster.

Ambulances raced wounded soldiers into town from the battlefield to our local hospital. Worse than that, though, were the GMC trucks slowly pulling into town, the back bed of each one covered by a black tarp thrown over the dead bodies it carried. We knew.

On the street, the river of people was getting deeper and thicker, seeming to carry people off the sidewalks with it as it flowed by. People were running and carrying anything they could on their shoulders and balanced bundles on their heads. Their faces wore stark fear: did a safe place even exist, as if the current of the river of people that was pulling them along might even leap over a steep cliff, pulling them down to a death they had not expected.

And people kept pouring from the alleys onto the main street. Mothers, surrounded by kids in bare feet, all panic-stricken, were heading toward the center of town. Their husbands were grimacing as they pushed their heavily laden wagons full of their earthly belongings...Where had all of these people come from? I did not recognize anyone. How many days had they had been walking? I did not know, but you could tell they were exhausted and about to collapse. They had to have been walking for at least a week or two in order to arrive in Cu Chi.

The little children dragged their feet along the road. Some tried to lean on the wagons their fathers were pushing; some people could only limp along. Their faces were smeared with dirt, sweat, mud, and smoke. Their hair was filthy. Their clothes were torn from having walked through the jungle and caught and ripping on underbrush and thorns.

In that chaos, hundreds and hundreds of older people were also shaking and trying to move slowly forward and keep up with the crowd. Their hands weakly grasped their canes. Fear, exhaustion, and lack of sleep from their long journeys had caused their eyes to look blank and far-away. Sometimes, one of the older people gave up and fell right where they stopped walking. They tried to get into the corner of a store, onto the front port of abandoned houses, or into the shade of a tree to lie down, while bombs were blowing up all around them.

And there was no help to give. People were fighting for their own survival; no one could care about anyone else, about whether the old man who could not take a step without his cane would continue on or about the old woman being trampled where she had fallen on the sidewalk.

Some mothers were holding newborn babies in their arms. They were trying to nurse their children, despite their empty stomachs and dried breasts. I felt awful about their starvation, especially when our truck was full of food. I wished my father could stop to give those babies some of the milk that I had seen my big brother loading onto the truck earlier. I wished my father could pick up some of the children who were about my age, ten, and struggling to keep up with their mothers in all of the chaos. I prayed to God that it was all just a nightmare that would be over for all of us when I woke up after a long sleep.

As my father's truck bumped slowly along the smaller, country road, I thought about how my father told me that our town had been relatively quiet and peaceful once upon a time, but not for many, many years. We had become accustomed to a little fighting, but it had never lasted for as long as it had on this day. As Cu Chi was located very close to our military base, we had seen army vehicles and soldiers all the time. I knew the names of every one of those vehicles better than any one else my age because they also stopped at my parents' store all day long to drop off or pick supplies for the base. We had had to learn to be very cautious on the street on our way to school and to watch out for those vehicles when we crossed the main intersection: those trucks were the cause of the most accidents in my home-town; so many children had been hit and killed by those trucks. One of my parents' employees had been hit by an army vehicle and was in the hospital for two years. He came home with a bro-ken leg and had to walk in a crooked fashion for the rest of his life. My parents also had to pay a large amount of money for this accident because the army wouldn't claim responsibility for it.

The army truck drivers rocketed through our streets, no matter how many people might be in their way. They made the road shudder, stirring up dust and immersing us all in a thick cloud of exhaust. They were hurrying to ship sol-diers and supplies to a battlefield somewhere in the jungle. Once, I remembered, on the third day of our Chinese New Year celebration, a rocket dropped out of the sky onto my grandpar-ent's house and killed my uncle immediately. My grandparents had lain, knocked unconscious, across my uncle's body. The sight of my uncle's dead body, covered with a blood-splattered sheet, haunted me as a child when I lay down at night and made me feel sick to my stomach every time I thought about it.

The fighting had begun to occur more and more frequently over the last four years of the war. However, even when battles began to happen every single night, none of our community's families considered moving away. We were all well prepared and didn't for one second think about looking for a safer place to live, even though someone had always been wounded or kidnapped in the middle of the night. We got so accustomed to being on "flight alert" that no one really slept until the sounds of battle had come and gone and even then, never really allowed ourselves to fall into a deep sleep after that.

My father and grandfather had built a cave under our house where we all hid during night raids, as every household in town did. Our cave's door was in the floor right under the bed in the main bedroom, and a stairway led us down into a single, big room. It was about eight feet wide, ten feet long, and about five feet tall. It was where we hid together during the worst battles. An oil lamp lit up the cave all day and all night. The cave was very strong, built out of solid concrete and some of the U.S. military's culvert pipes, and a tunnel led off the main room all the way to an opening in our back yard, approximately ten feet down from ground level; about thirty feet long and three feet wide, it was just wide enough for one person to crawl through.

As soon as he heard gunshots at night, my father immediately collected everyone and helped us to get down into the cave. Then he helped my mother to carry down the ones who were not able to get into the cave by themselves. My father was the last one to come down into the shelter after he had carefully replaced its top.

It was dark in the shelter and very stuffy because there was not enough air for all of us to breathe. The air came in through a tiny, tiny vent far away at the end of the tunnel. The stuffiness was so bad in the shelter that it made my little sister Le scream and cry to go back up into the house, even though the fighting was going on. The air was so tight that we could hear and feel each other breathing.

The cave smelled of moist concrete and muddy air from rain that had been absorbed in the concrete walls. Mold was growing on the floor because we did not dare let sunlight into the tunnel. It was cold and very dark. With the little oil lamp, we could just make out each other's shadows.

Sitting in the shelter one night, I was listening to noises in the ground above us: the footsteps of people running on the street in the stillness of night seemed to be a hundred times louder than they would have sounded in the daylight. Boots pounded on the ground, like monsters stamping on our heads, sometimes as if they were right on top of our concrete ceiling. Worse than that, gunfire competed with the footsteps, ripping the ground wide open around us and felling trees that then toppled onto some houses' roofs. If a canon's boom vibrated through the air, it was followed by an explosion somewhere nearby.

One night in the cave I remember vividly: my father pushed all of us even deeper inside the cave close to the tunnel to hide us from any blast. That scared all of us. My little sitter Le screamed louder in my mother's arms. My brother Tai was so terrified that he burrowed into my father's lap, trying to get even more protection. I crawled deeper into the tunnel behind my big sister Chau to hide from the noise. Upstairs, we could hear glass shattering on the floors, as if it were hailing inside our house, right over our heads.

Even though I had already crawled deeper into the tunnel, I could still hear my mother praying constantly for our family to be safe, while the bombs hammered the ground overhead. The vibrations sometimes were so powerful, I thought they would split my body apart. I thought my head would explode, my heart ached, and my limbs were uselessly limp with fear. The blasts sometimes lit up the tunnel so brightly that I could see my father holding my brother Tai tightly in his arms, while he was also using his body to block the opening to the cave. The rest of my brothers and sisters were huddled up together in one corner of the cave. Whenever we were down there, I was always terrified that our house would collapse on top of us and burn down with us trapped beneath it.

The maneuvers and battles over the past four years had never actually lasted for long, perhaps for half an hour; but to me, the chaos lasted an eternity. Besides the bombs, the gunfire, the sirens' incessant wailing, soldiers' footsteps chasing each other, and gunshots cracking, people sometimes shouted and cried for help for a wounded relative or screamed for shelter: their house had been set on fire.

We sat very silently in the tunnel; my father sighed often, my mother kept praying, and we were all desperate for a miracle, hoping to live our lives again or dreading that this might be our time to die.

Hiding deep in the tunnel, between blasts, I could also hear very clearly the scratching of a cockroach scurrying on the concrete wall, a lizard clicking along, and crickets cricking somewhere further down the tunnel in the dark. I often wondered if those tiny, little creatures suffered as we did.

When we heard the last few, scattered gunshots far away and dying, that was our sign that the fight was over. My father went upstairs first to make sure it was safe for all of us to follow. Then it was time to clean up the shattered glass, broken furniture, and many other loose objects that had been rocked onto the floor and broken from the vibrations.

Dawn slowly rose again on the horizon, as it always did after our noisy, alarming nights. Everyone in town woke up and began to work again right away, just as if we had all slept straight through the night, instead of having endured the terror we had experienced just hours before. Birds twittered, wagon wheels bumped and creaked on the road, and truck engines revved and chugged down the road.

We had no other choice: we had to move on. It was our way.

On the main road, people had begun to hurry as early and quickly as they could to the marketplace to get a head start on taking physical stock of their businesses so they could continue to try to prosper. The restaurants and the cafeteria opened right on time, welcoming their usual, early morning customers without showing any sign of fear or ill effects from the night's threat. It was so essential to them, too, that they all be open to any chance they had of making some money.

Just like all of the other families, my family didn't change our morning ritual, despite our nights in hell. My father and mother got up very early, as they did every day, to cook a big pan of rice soup for our breakfast. The rest of us hurriedly got ready for school and gathered at the dining table to eat before heading out the door. Though exhausted, no one complained. As soon as we had finished our breakfasts, we kids raced out the door to begin our days at school.

The only thing that terrified me each morning was walking to school through the center of town where soldiers had dumped a huge pile of dead bodies from the night's battle. I came to expect them lying there, only three hundred feet away from my school: this was our normal scenery on our way to and from school. Visions of the bodies haunted my dreams: bodies completely destroyed, limp, eyes lifeless; loose arms and legs flung every-where; torsos without heads or limbs; bellies ripped wide open like screaming mouths. Millions of flies buzzed madly all around the dead as if they were insane with hunger, filling the air with a horrible, chain-saw whining. The smell of rotting blood and flesh rose into the air from the heat of the sun and made me hold my nose so as not to breathe in that air.

My parent told us <u>never</u> to look at the dead bodies because they were so worried it would traumatize us. However, I was just a kid, and for some reason—and maybe <u>because</u> I was a kid and because my parents had told us <u>not</u> to look—my curiosity was greater than my parents' warnings. And then, I usually threw up, right after looking at the dead ones. Maybe the soldiers wanted to show off their might or remind those of us who had lasted through the night that we, too, could be lying in the pile. But the government certainly did not care about all the children who bore this every single day on their way to school.

As my father had done for years, after we had left for school and my mother had gone to open the store, he went to the caf-eteria in the town to meet his friends and get others' reports of the long night past and the battle, as each had experienced it. They tried to estimate their losses, damage done to their homes and businesses, and then each man shared his secret fears and the names of those he knew who had died. Once they had emptied their hearts and minds of the terror, now past—for this new day at least, they discussed business, politics, inflation, the price of goods, and other mysteries of the economy.

And Cu Chi was well on its way into another day. No time to waste. Our unflagging drive to survive and succeed: that alone was what drove all of us to resume working to achieve fortunes, even in the face of the town's having come so close to ruin the night before.

In the back of the truck, I was frustrated and exhausted from having been shocked out of sleep that morning, but sleep was usually only rest, anyway, a wish we all had for true sleep. I wanted a peaceful night, sweet dreams, no sounds of war, crying, and screaming. I never again wanted to hear those soldiers' boots, trampling my little town, grinding to dust all living things hiding in their shelters under the ground.

I was ten years old, and my dreams, when I had had them, were nightmares. A normal, happy child would have dreamed of the future and about good, simple things: I spent my nights praying simply to live to see the light of the next day.

No child—no human, no being alive on the earth—deserved this kind of life.

Still making our tedious way out of town in the long line of vehicles, my father's truck passed the county office and the police department; these two buildings were the center of my town. My house was located right next to the county office, police department, and the other government agencies. These buildings were the pride and joy of the people of Cu Chi. They represented the strength of our people. Twice each day, when I was going to school, I walked proudly by these buildings. Two tall policemen in uniform usually stood outside, guarding our buildings. Behind them was a big gate, which was always shut. I loved to look up and see our flag against the sky, no matter if it was windy, rainy, sunny, oppressively hot, or numbingly cold.

I knew we were going to pass my school next. It was shaped like a horseshoe of three long buildings, each with brick walls and sheet metal roofs. Each of the buildings contained several classrooms; since the buildings faced each other, we gathered for our morning ceremonies every day in the center of the courtyard made by the buildings around us.

My school was my other home; I spent so much of my day at school, and I loved being there. We could play outside at recess in our small schoolyard, which was big enough for all of us. A few huge trees shaded the middle of the schoolyard and kept us nice and cool during the summer time.

Even though once in a while, bombs used to explode over our heads while we were in class, our teachers simply showed us how to ignore them and continued having us do whatever we were all doing, which was learning, talking, and laughing together. We loved to run around in our schoolyard, chasing each other, even if sirens on army trucks screamed as the trucks went by, filled with more dead bodies.

My teacher was so old, she had taught in the school when my mother was a teenager. We were all afraid of her, maybe more afraid of her than of walking past the dead bodies in the town center in the morning! She made us lie on long benches and whipped us on the backside with a long stick when she needed to discipline us. I was whipped so many times for making trouble in the classroom because I loved to play tricks and make jokes; I've been famous for this almost since I could talk. But no parent ever complained about this form of punishment because it was allowed and so expected back then in Vietnam.

In spite of everything she did to frighten or discipline us, I actually loved my teacher. She lived across the street from us, and my oldest brother Ton and oldest sister Chau had had her as their teacher when they were in school. My parents respected her and her family, and they talked to her often in the street to make sure all eight of us were in good standing and doing well at school.

As we drove past my school, my heart tightened: My friends! I was devastated, thinking about my friends, either left behind in

Cu Chi with their families who were not going to leave or whose families were trying to find somewhere to hide, as we were. My friends and I had spent so much time together as students, and after school, they often came to our house to play because we had several berry trees in our backyard that bore fruit all year long. I had lost so many of my most special friends because of the war. But we were taught not to dwell on losses: my parents taught us to keep going, no matter what.

None of us had been allowed to go to school for almost a month, since the government had announced that our country was in danger, and the radio began telling everyone to stay alert, to prepare for a "big fight." We had also not been allowed to go to school because of so many students in other parts of our country who had been killed by bombs dropped on *their* schools.

On our last day of school, we had been terrified. Nobody said a word about anything to anyone, except my teacher, who gave us each good wishes to extend to our families.

As my father drove past my school, all of the school buildings looked empty, solemn, silent, and lonely; the big gates were shut out front and locked with a chain. The beautiful trees that had kept us cool in the schoolyard with their shade on hot days had all been cracked apart and shattered into wood chips by falling missles. The schoolyard was full of leaves. The custodian must have gone away with his family a long time ago; no one had taken care of the yard or mowed the grass.

A school without children has no soul.

My father had been inching the truck south, following the creeping, endless line of traffic. Then, as soon as he could, he took a quick right turn to try to get off the main road and head for the countryside.

My big brother Ton, who had been sitting on the edge of the truck earlier, now moved toward the inside of the truck bed with the rest of us. My others brothers and sisters were lying down on top of rice bags. My sister Ngoc had covered herself from head to toe with a blanket that my mother had thrown into the truck for us. My little brother Tai was already asleep, after a bout of crying and being scared. My big sister Chau's face was so heartrending, solemn, and anxious.

The only one who remained calm was my handicapped older brother Toi. He probably did not even care what was going on in our world; he was probably even enjoying the trip. The bombs and the gunfire did not bother him at all; he even got excited any time he heard a big explosion somewhere in town. He probably wasn't worried about anything, except his toys: he had never had any friends because of his disability.

My father sped up once we reached the highway, and that took us deeper into the countryside. I suddenly felt like I was made of lead, except my mind was whirling with images of all I had seen and heard and thought about as we had driven along, and with millions of questions. I wished I could sleep like my sister Ngoc.

Leaning my head on one of the pillows my mother had tossed in back, I prayed that someday soon, we would not have to live in severe panic every single day anymore.

Sleep of a bumpy, jumpy sort finally came.

I was violently shaken awake in the back of the truck when one of its tires hit a pothole in the road. I didn't know how far we had gone away from home or where we were or where we were headed.

My father was following the vehicles in front of us that were all turning onto a small road farther out of the village in order to try and find a safer hiding place. However, this decision ended up causing us more problems than we had had before.

First, we saw that the bamboo growing alongside the road had been slashed by bullets and gashed by metal objects flying by. That was not a good indication that there was safety. Then, up ahead of us a bit, right in the middle of the road, a mother had been shot and was collapsing awkwardly into herself onto the bloody dirt road, her baby tumbling out of her arms; when the little one fell hard onto the dirt road, she kind of bounced and landed five feet away from her mother.

I wanted to throw up; my stomach felt like there were a thousand ants biting me inside. I was sweating all over, from head to toe, and had a sudden, terrible headache. Then the worst thought crossed my mind: we might get killed just like the mother on the road. I started crying and screaming: it was all making me crazy. My father and mother did not turn around to look at or comfort me.

My father finally stopped the truck in front of what turned out to be my mother's relatives' house right on this road to look for shelter. He probably felt it was wiser not to drive any farther on the open road in plain sight: we had been warned by what we had just seen.

My mother's family's house was small and set right on the edge of a rice field. Inside, we found so many people, and our family managed to maneuver everyone in our family inside. The others had all had chosen to come here for shelter, too, because it was far away from the county office and the center of the city. Most thought the Communists' target would be the center of town, rather than any place in the country.

We started unloading our food and carrying it into the house. Then, more than 30 people ran out of the house and jumped onto the bed of my father's truck, pawing at all of our food and lifting off the enormous bags of rice. Some hacked up a big pole in the back yard for wood to make a fire over which to cook the rice. They had probably been starving for a long time and praying for food: we had arrived just in time to rescue them. They cleaned up all of our food in a very short time and then asked for more.

Tearing the silence into pieces, bombs and gunfire suddenly boomed and ripped through the air right over the roof of my mother's relatives' house. Talking rapidly to one of the men at the little house, my father learned that the army's supply station was located right down the road, so that it was probably one of the places targeted to be destroyed first! It had been bombed before we had arrived, and the station had exploded.

This was the worst place for us or anyone else to hide! The explosion had already killed many people and set off an enormous fire, which was spreading swiftly and lapping up everything in its path as it cackled: constant gunshot and the roar of the dragon-like fire continued grew louder and louder.

On hearing this news, my father jumped right from where he was sitting at this news, lifted and literally threw us all back in the truck, and turned right around and headed toward home.

"We can trust God to see that we live," I heard my mother pray out loud, up front in the cab. Nothing else was said. Not a word.

I guessed we were heading right into certain death by heading home. Despite all of the dangers possible, my father kept driving away from that tiny, country village and all of that destruction. We had been surrounded by it and had been so lucky to get out alive!

It was about noon when we finally reached the very furthest outskirts of Cu Chi again. The flood of people leaving town this morning had ebbed away, and our truck was the only one on the empty road at this point. Only a few gunshots cracked now and then in the sky. My oldest brother Ton had been listening intently to his radio the whole time we had been traveling. Suddenly Ton screamed, "The Republican President has declared defeat! Vietnam has fallen under Communist control!"

My parents suddenly looked happy, relieved, and calmer than they had in a long, long time. My father waved at all of us in the back of the truck and yelled, "We are safe now, at last! And we will be home again soon!!!!" That gentle, loving, bright light of a smile spread across his entire face. My mother's eyes pooled with tears, even though she, too, was smiling.

HOME!!??? They were *smiling*? I was terrified to go home! What could they be so excited about? What might have happened in town after we left? Would our whole town even be there? What if our house had burned down to the ground and was merely charred beams in a pile of dirt and ash? My grandparents! I was too terrified to even think about them. Had *they* survived? I curled into a little ball in the corner of the truck, like a snail burying itself deep inside its shell. Did our neighbors who had stayed die during the combat? I looked at all my brothers and sisters, trying to read their minds. I could not see anything in their eyes or faces. Who knew *what* to think? And, of course, silence reigned, as was the custom.

Ton kept listening to the radio. Finally my father sped up again once we reached the highway, and we drove ahead into town.

The traffic became much heavier as we drove into Cu Chi. I could not believe what I saw before me: our town had totally changed in significant, strange, and completely unexpected ways since the new government had taken over. So fast! Communist soldiers paraded up and down in the streets in their green uniforms, covered from head to toe with branches and leaves, and all wore red armbands. They were shouting, singing, and smiling at everyone. They didn't look any different from our soldiers, really, except they wore very interesting slippers that had been made from used tires.

Our truck had to slow to a creep again behind other trucks apparently returning home; the flow of people returning home on foot had thickened again, too, and congested the streets.

People, our neighbors, also stood on both sides of the street, cheering for the new government, waving their hands in celebration, and welcoming the newcomers who had made our town more crowded and noisier than ever.

I did not understand at all.

Because in another way, Cu Chi hadn't changed that much since the morning. All the buildings along the main street looked just as they had this morning as we had passed them on our way out. When our truck passed my school this time, soldiers had completely filled the schoolyard, each one wearing a backpack stuffed full of pots and pans. Some of their personal items had been flung everywhere in the yard on top of the leaves that no one had raked away for a long time.

The new government had already hung lots of their banners all over buildings to show their pride in their victory and new power. Through the gates of school, I could see a new flag–not our flag that I loved–but an enormous red flag with a bright yellow star in its center, flying high across our sky.

After only half a day, my school had become the new government's headquarters. The county office building and the military base looked like they were drowning in a sea because the area was chock full of soldiers in green uniforms, walking back and forth in waves.

Our people hopped like chess pieces in a game being played at lightning speed. They had already begun to put back all of the office furniture that people had stolen during the battle. And the new government's flags and banners had been hung all over the place–from the roofs of buildings, from the trees, and from fences! One huge banner read, "Peace, Independence, Freedom, and Happiness!" I kept repeating the strange words in my head.

We finally turned out of the traffic, and when we did, I closed my eyes as tightly as I could. I didn't want to see *anything or anyone else*. Soon, I sensed, just from having ridden in the same direction we were going then so many times, that my father had slowed to a stop right in front of our house. I did not want to look. I was paralyzed. Finally, I couldn't *not* open my eyes.

Thank God! Our house still stood in one piece, right next to my grandparents' house, which was also in one piece!! Our house was even in pretty good condition, except for a few small holes that bullets had flashed through the front door and a big hold on the roof of the second floor that had been opened by a rocket on its way by. I had prayed so hard throughout our nightmare of a day that they would survive. Yes! My grandpa was already waiting out on the sidewalk for us with a big smile on his face. He hugged us all many times with happy tears in his eyes.

I could finally breathe again! All of the hundreds of sensations and emotions I had felt over the course of our crazy morning had built up and begun to stick like a plum pit lodged in my throat.

But suddenly, I noticed, standing before my home again, it was gone! As we had crawled in our truck out of town this morning, I had thought–deep down–that maybe I was really going to die, whatever that might mean. I looked at everything all around me again, slowly; took a deep breath; and ran to hug my grandma really tightly again.

Out on the street, the river of people that had poured out of town this morning was coursing back into Cu Chi. Thousands and thousands were shouting, singing, and waving to each other and to the hundreds of soldiers marching by. The war had ended so quickly, the changes it brought had happened so smoothly and swiftly, and so they thought the end result of it all would open a new and prosperous era for our entire country. It ended the night fights that had terrorized us all since before I was born. There wasn't any major damage in town because our Republican Army had not fought back against the Communists. And my people had cooperated and supported each other, as always.

Excitement grew in the huge crowd getting larger and larger by the minute, and it was so contagious. Everyone was so thrilled about the possibility and hope in the air. We had never had such a big celebration or that much fun ever before in Cu Chi that I could remember, and I had never seen so many people outside at the same time! All of the children finally got a chance to run in the street freely without worrying! Dogs chased the children and each other and barked for their new freedom, too.

'We should have had a revolution a long time ago, instead of being afraid every single day and night!' I thought to myself. Soon, I had joined the people in the street, waving at the soldiers as they moved in formation, and I began screaming like crazy. It did begin to feel like almost *too* much fun: can a dream come true in *one morning?* But I, too, wanted so badly to have reason to feel hopeful, just once.

CHAPTER TWO

JUNE, 2009

The plane must have hit an air pocket or two and shook me awake.

Rick looked over at me–he could never sleep on airplanes–and smiled, "No problem. We're fine. Go back to sleep. We still have many, many hours to go."

That smile was all the reassurance I ever needed, and that allowed me to fall back into my busy sleep. Before I did, I turned and peeked over the back of my seat to see if Michael was ok. His long eyelashes covered half of his cheeks, and he was breathing comfortably.

I turned to face forward again and slid immediately back into a strange collage of dreams.

APRIL, 1975

Our celebration of the end of the war and the Communist takeover lasted for days. The last of our soldiers came out of the woods into the city, followed by their tanks, trucks, convoys, and army vehicles of all kinds. The vehicles were muddy and camouflaged with branches whose leaves shook as if they were clapping every time the tanks hit a bump in the street.

Neighbors brought pots and pans and tin boxes–anything metal–and spoons and sticks to the side of the road, and they began to sway, dance, and beat on their "instruments" to make festive music to which they sang, "Peace, Independence, Freedom, and Happiness!" These 'lyrics' rang out, over and over, like enormous, live, joyful bells everywhere, filling the celebrating air.

Overnight, high above town, looking down at us like a god of some kind, an enormous billboard had been erected at the center of town by the new government; it was so huge, it seemed to shout down at us, "Peace, Independence, Freedom, and Happiness!" Its hopeful message was supposed to distract us from what we were about to learn were the harsh realities of our new life under communist rule.

Almost immediately, my parents discovered to their horror and shock that they were in extremely dire circumstances financially: their business had gone bankrupt overnight–without a single warning. That store had existed forever, or it had seemed so to us kids, as it had been there before any of us had been born. The store had provided our entire community with what they required for their daily lives: from building materials to farming supplies, from groceries to military uniforms, from cigarettes to rice, and so much more.

But the government took it all away. No more semi-trucks lined up in front of our store to pick up or drop off products or goods. My parents had no more bags and bags of money that they used to fill and then dump on the storehouse floor each night for us children to count. From behind the store's closed doors, we temporarily lived on the rice and groceries that were left over from the store. And we quietly waited for something to happen, for our old life to return.

From behind the store's closed doors, we watched the other residents continue to celebrate their new lives. It seemed that they were so passionate about the glorious, new government that they couldn't have cared less about their daily activities, even though they had little food! They believed fortunes would pour into their lives, any time now.

The Communists took control of everything in Cu Chi. Our store couldn't reopen because of the very sudden–and what turned out to be brutal–changes in the currency exchange: the whole country was in crisis, and our business had simply been bulldozed, flat. My parents also got in trouble because of the new government's new monetary exchange policy: my parents had too much cash on hand, and the new government had set a very small allowance for every family. My parents split their money to the employees and send them home.

My parents' glory and pride were gone. It was quick and painful: no more incoming cash, no more store or customers coming to our store. We could not afford any housekeepers, cooks, or maids, as we had had before. My mother suddenly had to cook and do all of the housework with my oldest sister Chau's help. My mother no longer sat behind her glossy mahogany counter to collect money from customers and make sure everything ran smoothly, ordering everything the store needed to sell, the job that she had had for almost twenty years.

My parent's debtors had left town at the very beginning of the revolution, and that threw our family into an even deeper ditch. We had no income at all, so my parents started selling whatever we had left to get money for our daily needs: the metal roof of the pigpen, the wood we had stacked in the backyard, all of our beautiful jewels, even empty bottles sitting on the store's shelves. My mother sold all of her precious jewelry and gold that she had saved all her life, just in case our family needed it to survive. The time had come.

As my parents had taught us, we were not to stop living in the face of difficulties, even if the challenges were bigger than any we had faced before: we simply had to work harder than we had ever worked before to overcome them. So my parents started raising pigs in the back yard with some supplies still left in the store, and they started growing rice on a water field they had purchased many years ago. My parents believed that our good fortune would return as soon as the economy was re-established in the country. But they did not smile.

Their fortune never returned. Their investments in the pigs and the rice field didn't pan out; all of our money was gone, and we were completely broke. There was nothing left to sell. We couldn't afford to buy any new clothes or any of the decent food still available on the black market, so my parents were forced to buy low-quality items from the cheap, government store.

No other kids my age in our town worked harder than I did to try to help out my family. Every day, I got in line at the market beginning at four o'clock in the morning, waiting to buy a few stale fish at the government store. I had to learn how to fight with people in town—and win—in order to get food, clothes, kitchenware—even a pinch of salt! Every day after school, I returned to the store to get back in line to wait for a head of lettuce or a couple of pounds of carrots. This was how I worked harder to help my family get through this new and miserable, shocking way of life.

Behind our closed doors, we isolated ourselves from society and avoided all social activities. However, many shocked visitors, mostly my mother's relatives, came into town to stay overnight with us. They were returning from where they had hidden in the jungle during the revolution. When it was all over, they had adopted Communism. Some of them had literally crawled out of underground tunnels somewhere in the jungle or forests just to see daylight again.

These relatives used to come to my parents' store not that long ago. But now they looked so different in their black uniforms with red bands on their arms and military scarves around their necks. They even wore those weird Communist soldiers' tire slippers!

These relatives had come straight to our home, expecting a free meal and a room, not just to visit. We were desperately poor and miserable; seeing them made us feel even lower. But, my parents had no choice: as custom had it, these relatives were to be welcomed, if reluctantly, and treated like kings and queens. We had to share what little food we had and our rooms with these uninvited—and now "foreign"—relatives.

We all—including our pets—lived on vegetables; we were getting skinnier as every day passed. The dogs started killing mice, frogs, insects—whatever was food in their eyes, except my father's beloved, old dog. He began to suffer from very serious malnutrition, got weaker, and went blind in one eye. He could hardly stand up or turn around. Most of the time, my father shared half of his own meal with his dog, big tears in his kind eyes.

My grandmother required a few ounces of meat each day at dinner. We children only were allowed a taste of it from the leftovers, if there even were any. An entire side of meat or the delicious fresh fish and shrimp that we used to enjoy became a distant memory. We considered ourselves so lucky that we could even afford to buy some cheap, broken, dried, shrimp crumbs to use as protein. My mother lightly sprinkled those shrimp crumbs on top of a vegetable stir-fry to flavor every meal.

Our lives revolved around the government's new ways. At night, we were all required by the new government to go to a meeting in our neighborhood. Elders had their own elder meeting group; young people met in a separate group; and we children, of course, had our own activities.

I especially loved going to meetings where people stood up to fight and criticize each other. Some brought their families' problems to the meeting for sharing; but those very same people sometimes reported their neighbors to the government, if they felt suspicious of those neighbors for one reason or another. As they attended more and more of these meetings, people began to become more and more hurtful to and insulted each other.

We children were taught the same survival "skills" in our nightly meetings: we were now being taught to place our personal needs *after* the government's demands. We were even taught to spy on our parents and neighbors, and we were taught we must tell the government leaders about our own families' secrets. We were taught how to criticize ourselves and everyone else around us, including our own parents: we were told we needed to do this to create a better life for everyone. We were taught how to live above the material world so we could be more giving people.

I began to love the revolution because what I understood then was that those in charge saw young children–like me!–as small owners of the country, too. One of the meeting leaders had said just that to me one night.

The theories also seemed so beautiful and so perfect to me *as a child* that I almost cried any time the leaders taught us a new theory or principle. I was too young to understand the harm of or to analyze this new information and the rules of conduct we were being taught. I absorbed everything I heard and saw around me like a sponge and wanted so badly to live the way I was now being taught to live.

I loved to tell my parents how beautiful the new government was, and I was so proud to spread the leaders' teachings that I learned in my young children's meeting every night. I had faith in the new government and convinced my parents to be patient. "We are going to have a very bright future! The leader promised us," I told them.

They did not smile.

I decided, 'It's too hard for the adults to believe and understand.' I began to feel very important to everyone around me at school, in my family, and in the community. I liked to talk and speak in public places to praise the communist party. I joined the music band at school and the county band, and we went out to sing everywhere about the new government. I could spend hours arguing and trying to convince people who didn't believe and have faith in the communist party that there were good reasons they should believe.

Instead, neighbors called me the "little red Communist;" my friends called me a traitor. But being called names didn't bother me at all. I simply continued to carry out my Communist leader's words. I was so optimistic and looked forward to a beautiful, new life, which I believed with all my heart would appear somewhere on the horizon, sometime soon. I proudly wore a red scarf around my neck every day to school that I had received from the Pioneer Communist Youth group the day I became a member.

"Little, red communist!" they yelled.

'Yes,' I thought to myself proudly, 'I am.'

The revolution did bring my family something incredible that shocked everyone else in Cu Chi, too. One morning we children were playing in my grandparents' front doorway when a stranger turned off the road and walked right toward the house, just as if he knew where he was headed. He looked so strange: he wore a beard that covered his whole chin and face, a dark green suit with an old, striped scarf around his neck, and wore those tire slippers, just like the ones I had seen on every single Communist in town. The man looked very worn out, thin, and raggedy, like a cave man who had just crawled out of the jungle. He carried a filthy, ancient handbag on his shoulder.

Without saying a word to any of us, he walked right past us children and walked right through the doorway and into the house, as if he had done it a million times before. We were so shocked. We had no idea who he might be or what he might do!

But my grandpa took one quick look at him, and with no doubt whatsoever in his face shouted out to my grandma, lying in the hammock in the living room, "Our son is home!"

I did not understand what grandpa meant by "our son." Then my grandma yelled back, "Whose son!? You are so confusing sometimes!" she complained.

Then I saw my grandpa, for the very first time in my life, cry like a baby. My grandma still hadn't moved out of the hammock. I learned later that she and my grandpa had apparently argued often about the man, who turned out to be my youngest uncle! He had once lived with them, and she had probably assumed my grandpa was just talking what she called "nonsense" about that uncle, as if what he was saying couldn't possibly be true.

I looked at this stranger who was hugging my grandpa! I had never seen him before, and he spoke in a weird dialect with a heavy northern Vietnamese accent and didn't sound like a local resident at all. It was very hard to understand what he was saying, and I saw nothing to prove he was our relative, except that my grandpa was crying and hugging him.

Then the stranger walked further inside after greeting my grandpa to see my grandma. She jumped right out of the hammock, wrapped her arms around him, and burst into tears. Sobbing and crying, my grandmother said, over and over, "Son, is that *really* you!? I am so happy to see you! You are *alive*!! I thought your crazy, old father was just being himself–plain crazy."

I finally decided that this *had* to be one of my uncles. I had never met him before. My grandparents were *not* crazy, after all, neither of them, and there they were, hugging this bearded Communist over and over and crying until they were cried out!

The reunion with everyone else in the family was emotional, too; my grandma and my mother cried because they had all begun to believe they would never, ever see him again. All the grownups kept saying it was beyond comprehension–a miracle–*that* he was still alive: he had been away during the devastating war between the North and South.

Soon enough, my grandparents' faces were rosy and blooming with great relief and happiness again. And my grandma could finally tell the heartbreaking story that she had carried locked up in her own heart for all of those years. Once a long time ago, she told us, my uncle had been a stubborn, wild child. Then he had left home at seventeen after a big fight he'd had with my grandpa. My grandparents had not heard from him nor seen him since. He had gone north, without a word to my grandparents for 30 years. And then, like magic: presto! There he was, standing upright, in one piece, in their house! Suddenly, they were so proud of that same son who had been lucky to have survived the war and returned to Cu Chi, a hero, a real Communist.

Just like my grandma, my mother was happy to see her oldest brother again. His name had been erased from our family register because we did not have record of his death and had just assume that, after this long silence, he was dead. Mom thought it was a miracle from God, and she went to all the temples in town to pay her appreciation to Buddha, who had brought her oldest brother home safely, as she had always secretly hoped He would. She would have pulled her heart out to give to her oldest brother, if she had been asked to do that.

Soon, family and relatives all gathered at my grandparents' to celebrate my uncle's return home. People brought groceries, vegetables, fruits, meats, or whatever they could find in their own backyards for the party. They stayed to share the food and talk to my uncle; they wanted to see a real Communist who had come back from the north.

Throughout the party, my uncle was surrounded by people who begged him to tell them his stories, over and over again.

"I got on a boat that night I left thirty years ago heading north. I had never dreamed that the trip would be as long as it was!

"I joined the Communist forces, fought on the battlefield, and killed many enemies during the war. Once I was almost killed in the jungle on the central highlands. I was wounded when my company was attacked one night on a mountain somewhere in the country. Lots of times, we had no idea where we were! It was terrifying.

"I finally got out of the army, got married, and worked in northern Vietnam as a coal miner."

My uncle had hundreds of war stories, and he hypnotized his constant audience. They asked many questions, congratulated him, cheered for him, and sympathized with the pain he expressed about leaving his family thirty years ago, never knowing how everyone had fared or if anyone was even still alive.

My grandpa stayed up with everyone all night to praise his son and to enjoy his whole family's big reunion. My grandpa was rapt, listening to his son's stories, and he remembered every single word of every single story my uncle told. Once in a while, he stopped my uncle, mid-story, to remind him of a detail that my uncle had left out of a story he was telling! With pride and a smile crinkling his face, my grandpa sometimes said, "You forgot to tell them you were arrested because someone stole the money you were in charge of when you were the treasurer for the army!" or "Oops! You forgot to tell them about the time you fell into a cage when you were on a raid!"

My mom stayed with them all through the party, sitting right next to my uncle all night. She didn't want to miss a single word her oldest brother had to say.

My father stayed home from the celebration. He didn't like to be in a crowd, first of all. He also didn't understand too much of what my uncle said, as he wasn't at all familiar with my uncle's dialect, and my father just wasn't very interested in the celebration. He did greet my uncle every, single morning, but that was it.

At the time, I didn't think that it was strange for my father to behave that way. I knew he was a shy man.

My uncle stayed at my grandparents' house for one month and then went back up North to bring his wife and three children back home to Cu Chi. My mother packed up so many presents for him to take along to his family up north.

After he left, my grandma continuously received letters from him, telling her to keep all of the valuable things she had on earth for him. My grandma was so innocent and trusting of her own children, she didn't hesitate to question his request or listen to what her morality might have otherwise told her about her Communist son. She cried over those letters because she thought what he was asking for was his mother's pride in her son's noble, Communist life. She didn't see that all he wanted was gold, the gold he assumed they had saved for him all these years.

One night, my uncle suddenly returned to Cu Chi with all of his family. During dinner that same night, grandma suddenly understood exactly what my uncle had been referring to in all of his letters: he stood straight up, pulled his gun out of his pants pocket, put it on the dinner table, and demanded that my grandma give him the gold he had been waiting to receive from her.

The truth was that my uncle had been jealous of all of us who had lived in the south during his thirty-year absence. He was extremely angry that he was only a poor Communist, compared to my mother, whom he assumed was living in a big house and enjoying a luxurious life. He claimed he and his family were dying of starvation, poverty, and misery in the north. He demanded that my grandparents give whatever they owned to his family, since he lived so far away from home.

My grandparents and my uncle, his wife, and all of his wife's family–all North Vietnamese–argued every day about my uncle's demands. Happiness left our house as quickly as my uncle had returned. My Communist uncle wanted his share of the house that my grandparents owned and also his share of my parent's house because he thought that my grandparents had given the house to my mother. His plan was to get the money, jewelry, and gold that he had expected my grandparents had saved for him. He felt entitled; he thought somebody had to pay him back for all the time and pain he had suffered in the war.

My uncle sometimes pulled out his gun, threatening to kill everyone if he didn't get what he wanted. My grandparents became terrified for their lives and for having lost their oldest son, once again.

What my uncle didn't know was that my grandparents had been extremely dependent on my parents since I was very little because they were old and sick. My uncle's demands only worsened their suffering, and then, my grandpa finally passed away from carrying all of these burdens in early June, 1976. It had been one year since my uncle had come back home.

My uncle quickly filed paperwork with the authorities that donated my parents' house to the government because he believed his capitalist sister did not deserve to live in the big house. My uncle tried every way he could to set himself and his family up to live a life of luxury.

My parents were shocked when the city office's inspectors knocked at their door and asked to interview them. They were even more shocked when they learned the reason for the inspectors' visit: they asked my parents why they wanted to give away their house to the government and where we were all going to live, if that occurred. They told my parents to think very carefully about what "they" were doing.

I suffered a great shock and came face-to-face with a grave reality from all of this, too: my Communist uncle's immeasurable greed finally destroyed my belief in what I had perceived to be the noble ideals of a Communist. As Communists, we were supposed to live very simple and generous lives with fidelity and honesty, and I had come to regard Communist members, who were Ho Chi Minh's partners, as the very best examples of such a way of life. I began to wonder how many other Communists in our country were like my uncle, robbing others and ripping the country apart solely for their own personal gain? How many more families in Vietnam were facing a tragic situation like the one our uncle had put us in?

In his true heart, my uncle was nothing more than a crook and a greedy man. He placed his own personal desires before everything and everyone else. He had crushed his parents' hearts; it even seemed as if he had killed his own father and schemed to destroy his own siblings' lives–*without remorse* or even a sense of gratitude to them for his very life!

CHAPTER THREE

2009

I must have been thirsty enough, though sound asleep, to wake up and ask Rick if he had something for me to drink. I felt as if I had lived three lifetimes and not slept at all!

Rick asked, "Are you all right? You are mumbling in your sleep; sometimes it even sounded like you were crying. And sometimes you called out for your father! What's wrong?"

I was quiet, staring into the blackness beyond my little "port-hole" window. I knew I had been dreaming, but I didn't remember any of what I had dreamed and was puzzled about the way he said I was acting in my sleep.

"You're usually such a sound and still sleeper!" Rick said, holding out a water bottle to me.

Finally, after drinking very deeply of the water he handed me, I told him, "I must be wild and excited about the trip and had some crazy dream because of that. You know me! I'm fine! Sometimes a little crazy, yes, but I'm fine. Don't worry, please." And I smiled, and he smiled back, relieved.

Then, I rearranged the tiny, flat, navy blue, wafer-thin thing they call a pillow on airlines, and I was soon deep in another dead sleep.

197-?

One morning, my mother woke up and said the most surprising thing: she said she suddenly saw our Communist way of life in a different light. She had become more realistic and very wary of the values and methods of our new government and its members' operations. She gathered us all together to prepare us to fight the next battle we would most certainly face, ironically one our own Communist uncle had begun.

The government had started attacking all the big businesses in the country very soon after this, declaring that all capitalists were enemies of Communism. They declared martial law overnight and targeted rich people in the south who used to own and run businesses, as our family had. Soldiers started searching every single house for hidden money, gold, and valuable possessions. They drove huge semi-trucks around town to haul away the tons and tons of possessions they found in our people's homes.

Since the government had already shut down our store, my parents thought the worst was over. However, we had remained on the Communists' list of businesses in town that needed to be prosecuted. As soon as the reforms were enacted, my parents began to experience severe anxiety and paranoia.

This second economic crisis brought Cu Chi to its knees. People began to feel very depressed, scared, even more vulnerable than they had been feeling, and completely helpless to defend themselves against the new regime. All of the businesses in town were shut down. The government controlled everything from heavy industry to trade, handcrafts, and agriculture. People withdrew, hid, and avoided getting involved in any of the new society's activities. They stayed alert and tried to anticipate and prepare for yet another one of this new government's storms.

Our poverty was intense: supplies in general were already short; now they were almost non-existent, and anything that was available was much more expensive than anyone could afford. The government promoted its new economy as fast and as hard as it could. No one's life was getting any better. The local authorities put Communist members, like my uncle, who had participated in their cause during the war, in charge of the economy. He was given an important position in the local government, managing local businesses.

Our family's financial situation grew even worse, day after day, and we could never, ever have imagined that that was even possible. My father's rice farm had used up all the money and gold that my mother had saved for so many years to cover my father's farm's start-up costs. Then, the water field never produced any rice, as my parents had hoped, despite the hard work my father, my oldest brother Ton, and my oldest sister Chau had done at the farm every day.

We had nothing left to sell: we were completely bankrupt and had slid down into the very bottom of the deepest ditch. Our big family of eight children, ages one to eighteen, and my parents were reduced simply to foraging for food every single day.

The only thing we *did* still own of value was our big house, which was especially valuable because of its location right in the center of town. The only thing my parents could do to survive was to sell that house to get some money, so we could move away to the countryside.

This decision was just about the last crack I thought my heart could ever bear.

But luck often knocks at your door when you least expect it to happen, and it came in the form of financial help and encouragement members of our small, Chinese community: our friends put together some money so that my father could open a new business. And that was how our family's restaurant, Nha Lau, opened in 1978, saving all of us from starving to death and losing our home.

By relying on his excellent skills as a chef, my father wound up helping everyone in town, as he always did. He loved to cook

Chinese gourmet dishes; all his life, he had often been asked to cook for wedding banquets, parties, and many special occasions in our Chinese community. He was so proud and relieved that he could use these skills to rescue us from what had looked like our dead end.

My father's stir-fry was one of the most delicious dishes in the whole country. The smell was so heavenly that it brought people who had just entered town straight to the restaurant. The sweet smell of pineapple, bell peppers, seafood, green onion, cilantro, and lots of other ingredients, and he cooked it all quickly over the high heat of flames burning fat in the frying pan. My father's stir fry was famous throughout Cu Chi.

Hot pot also was one of our customers' most favorite of his dishes, one that they did not want to miss if it was on the menu because only my father could create it with his magic. We called the dish The Island Meal because the tool my father used to cook this dish looked like an island. In the middle of the pot was hot, bright red charcoal surrounded by a delicious, boiling broth. Fresh meat and seafood, such as shrimp, fish, clams, fresh mushrooms, green-leaved vegetables, and carrots were all served on a huge platter with fresh noodles, along with the broth in the pot. The customers dipped the fresh ingredients into the hot broth and then topped it all with hot sauce, one of my father's very secret recipes.

For some reason, food businesses weren't targeted by the local government; as we were untouchable under the government's newest economy reforms, my father's restaurant opened at just the right time and played a very important role in my town. It became a very famous landmark for anyone traveling between the Saigon and the Cambodian border. Fortune somehow was smiling on us again.

Our restaurant had an excellent location, too, in the very center of town on the main artery that ran across the entire country to the Cambodian border. It was extremely convenient for those traveling back and forth on that route to stop and get delicious nourishment before they continued on their way.

The restaurant was also so beautiful, so spacious, and its menu so extravagant that no other restaurant in the area could compete with us. The food was so very delicious and affordable, and–its biggest plus–my father was such a welcoming and honest chef and owner. All kinds of people gathered together at our place, and my father was the heart of its comforting atmosphere. As soon as a customer walked in the door, he smelled amazing aromas, heard the clickity-clicking of busy chopsticks, and the happy chatter of our delighted customers.

Many of our customers were local government officers and Communist leaders who had just moved into town. They held private lunches and dinners at Nha Lau. The officials enjoyed the fact that they could make a reservation for a local conference party or school board meeting whenever they wished.

Best of all, our restaurant satisfied people of all classes across town, from important presidents who were in town on business and who ordered big and expensive dinners to local laborers who could buy only very inexpensive but satisfying lunches. All the sergeants and generals loved my father's cooking, too.

Our restaurant was always well-stocked with food: we had enough to serve our entire army or all the residents in town on short notice and smoothly! My father, head chef, was assisted by several prep chefs. Dad worked every single day, day after day, from four o'clock in the morning until midnight, seven days a week, nonstop, rain, shine, or unforeseen disaster with that beautiful, welcoming smile wide on his face, no matter how hard or for how many hours he had been creating hard at creating his magical dishes.

My father loved to chat with his old business partners who stopped at the restaurant often to see him. He could talk about the weather and the harvest with farmers who had come to town to shop. He could laugh (really loudly, as he always did) with the local officers at a good joke. From businessmen making deals with their partners to workers getting a few drinks with friends after a long day at work, everybody loved our place.

Nha Lau became also "Information Central:" people looking for a good carpenter, needing a referral for a good job–whatever they were looking for, they usually found an answer there. Sometimes, young people wanted a romantic and private place for a date or party, and they, too, found it there. People who had missed buses back home at night stopped at our restaurant to see if they could find a ride from one of the other diners.

Sometimes, people asked my parents for a free meal, if they had no money for food, and he was only too glad to prepare some food for them. My father was born to run a business, as many of his friends told him over and over, and they admired him for his very special knack at it.

The business received another incredible windfall when the war between the Vietnamese and Cambodian governments exploded on the Cambodian border. Every day, thousands of new customers passed through our town: from army troops to regular residents, everyone chose to exchange messages, business, war news, and gossip at our place. Thousands and thousands of the soldiers, who had just been ordered out onto the battlefield, stopped at our restaurant on their way out of town. The soldiers tended to spend their very last pennies on good food, cigarettes, and alcohol, and Cu Chi was the last town in which they could fill up on fuel, supplies, and personal items. Our place might even have been the last stop some of them ever made in civilization.

My parents showered the convoy drivers with extra attention to ensure that they never passed our town without stopping by, and the drivers always tipped us grandly. My parents gave them extra food, free side dishes, and my parents told them to feel free to knock on our door at night, if they needed us, even if the restaurant was closed.

None of the journalists or news reporters ever passed through town without enjoying and spreading the word about the fine food my father created and served. Soldiers who had just finished their tours and were lucky enough to return home from the war were so tired and hungry that they usually collapsed in the woods before they even reached town, placing themselves in yet another life-and-death situation. The ones who were able to return safely rewarded themselves with a big celebration at our place. And they ate as if they had never eaten before: they always completely cleaned our pantry stock out! They didn't mind if the soup had less flavor or if the rice had a burnt taste from my parents' trying to cook it fast enough to keep up with all of their orders. Dad would put smaller portions of meat than he normally would put in a serving to make sure everyone had a share. My parents were careless, doing that, but at least they had something left to serve.

The soldiers stood in long lines, waiting to get their food. If the restaurant didn't have enough tables to seat them all, they didn't care: they sat on the floor, on the sidewalk, and in our neighbors' yards: they sat anywhere to enjoy their very first meal back in "real life."

The soldiers' business doubled the profits my parents had enjoyed from their regular customers. When soldiers didn't have any money, they paid us with gold and valuable stones that they had found right on the battlefield in Cambodia.

War is a horrible thing; but, ironically and sadly, its effects literally saved my family's lives back then. We were able to resume our normal lives. We kids were growing up and getting ready to confront the realities and harshness of life on our own, and my parents' restaurant carried us comfortably through what might have been the biggest nightmare we had lived through yet. We had lived right in the crossfire of the first war, which was a nightmare; I knew we could survive this new war, as long as there were no gunshots or bombs in our town.

I was ecstatic that my parents didn't have to sell the house, and we didn't starve to death. Instead of having to share a handful of dried shrimp tail crumbs every night, we had all the food we desired.

The war between Vietnam and Cambodia lasted for more than three years. The end of the war was even more exciting because although no more army troops were being sent into or out of battle and passing through Cu Chi on their way, our business didn't slow down. The Vietnamese government was trying to help the Cambodian people recover their economy and shipped tons and tons of goods to them every day right through our town.

Very early in the morning, before the restaurant had even opened, customers were already waiting at our front door, and trucks were lined up along both sides of the street, waiting for their first meal of the day. Truck drivers, business people, and highway workers, getting ready to head to the border, stopped by our place, and they all had a lot of money. In addition to their normal cargo, these truckers also were smuggling illegal products across the Cambodian border: cigarettes, medicines, fabric, electronic parts, cosmetics, and hundreds of other things. The truckers spent money freely and lived very luxurious lives. They sometimes ate half of what they ordered and sent back the other half, not even taking the uneaten portion with them, when most people in the country were starving to death.

I found their behavior utterly selfish and despicable. And this very behavior is what got our restaurant in some trouble in the neighborhood because beggars began lining up in front of the store and fighting with each other to be the first to get leftovers from these rich and wasteful customers on their way out of the door.

When the war ended, luck remained with us. The Communists' military base was located right at the corner of the main road in Cu Chi. Every day, soldiers came to our restaurant to eat and to chat with the waitresses and with my parents. They mostly had come from the North and hadn't seen their families for a long time. Homesick and lonely, they looked for a place that made them feel at home. They shared all the war stories they had with us, from tales behind the wounds they got during the fighting to the sad passing of parents, and even to talking about their anxiety about girlfriends who were waiting for them to come back home. Those customers gradually became like family members, not only for business purposes but also because of the caring they received from my parents and grandma, but also the caring that they gave back, even to us kids. And, of course, they brought us a fortune, as well.

We kids all helped our parents at the restaurant. Every day, I got up very early in the morning to help set up the tables. Then, I hopped on my bicycle and headed for the market. The farmers had harvested all of the fresh vegetables on their farms in the middle of the night and brought them to the market, which opened at three in the morning. Their booths were lit with tiny oil lamps, which gave off just enough light for them to set their merchandise on the deck and for early morning customers to be able to see their produce.

There weren't many people awake and out at the market at this time of day, except for me and the vendors. They all knew me; if they couldn't see me in the dark, they recognized my voice even from beyond the kiosks. As soon as I showed up, the vendors hurried to put bundles of lettuce, green onions, carrots, cucumbers, basil, cilantro, peppers, garlic, and sometimes special things into the basket that was attached to the back of my bicycle.

Then I moved on to the booth selling fresh noodles and bread. By the time my baskets were full, my bike weighed a ton. I had two giant baskets hanging on the front of my bike and a huge basket set up on the carriage on the back. I couldn't even ride my bike to the restaurant but had to push it along the road. I was a very tiny girl of about ninety pounds, but the produce and other foods weighed more than fifty pounds! Many times, I thought it was impossible for me to make those trips, even for one more day. But the next morning, I woke right up and hurried to get back on my bicycle so I could get down to the market on time, at usual.

Once I got to the restaurant, I gave all of the food I had brought for my dad and then pedaled right to school, without having had breakfast, to make sure I got into school before the gates were shut.

At lunchtime, I went home to the restaurant from school and helped to serve lunches; this was our busiest time of the day. From far away, as I pedaled toward Nha Lau, I could see vehicles parked up and down our street; hear the voices of the customers yelling out their orders; and smell the aromas of my father's magical, spicy food seeping out of the restaurant's doors and scenting the air over the town.

As I parked my bike, people had already formed a long line as they waited for a seat inside. Every table in the restaurant was taken, and the hungry people outside were getting more anxious and impatient by the minute to have their lunch.

Inside, it was sheer chaos. All the waitresses were racing back and forth between the kitchen and the dining room, while my older sisters and I hurried to clear dirty dishes from tables as soon as customers stood up to leave. Everything–bowls, plates, glasses, bottles–had to be removed in a flash so we could seat new customers as quickly as possible. We stacked piles of bowls and dishes as tall as mountains in our arms and carried them into the back room to be washed.

My older sister Ngoc liked to wear high-heeled, wooden slippers, which made it so difficult for her to maneuver in the crowded room. My parents were nervous that she might fall down and hurt herself, but she didn't fall many times. I never understood how she did that.

My sisters and I also were responsible for collecting money from customers as they left their tables. My parents were so busy cooking that they couldn't possibly watch the money, and customers were always in a hurry to leave. So we each had to keep one sharp eye on empty tables as they became available so we could seat new customers right away and, at the same time, keep the other eye on customers who were in the process of leaving to make sure they didn't take off before they had paid. When customers had finished their meals, my mom would tell us the total of their bill, so we could collect the right amount of money from them. I will never understand how my mom could remember what was served to each and every table when the place was so packed and such a madhouse. Beside that, some of the waitresses loved to collect the money and put it in their own pockets, instead of turning it over to my parents. I caught them pocketing money many times, but my parents just ignored me as if there were nothing wrong. That, I did not understand.

We could only work at the restaurant for a few hours during lunch before we had to go back to school, and we worked harder during those few hours than anybody else in town. So many hundreds of people had flowed in and out of our restaurant during lunchtime that we were exhausted through to our bones when the lunch rush was over. Then we girls ate quickly and returned to school in time for our afternoon classes, half asleep.

And then it was back to the restaurant again right after school, just in time to clean up the messes still left over from lunch, and we sisters were responsible for collecting and counting all of the money still on tables, while my parents began to get ready to cook dinner. We had no adding machines, credit cards, or cash registers back then to help us keep track of it all, and my parents simply kept the money in a small drawer at the back of the restaurant.

They were already sweaty and exhausted from the heat. My father's T-shirt was soaked from working in the hot kitchen, but that smile of his was still bright and wide as a watermelon.

My parents' business began to play an important role in my town's redevelopment, helping other businesses come alive again. Other shops and the cafeteria also stayed open later at night than they had before the war to make their contribution to Cu Chi's prosperity.

More than twenty kids between ages eight and fourteen wandered around our restaurant all day long, selling cigarettes, snacks, newspapers, magazines, lighters, and lotto tickets. Most of those kids' families had emigrated to Cu Chi from somewhere outside town during the war. The kids gathered in front of the restaurant and slept outside of it after we closed. My parents gave them a lot of the leftover food after the restaurant closed at night. The kids made money, sent it home to support the members of their families who had not immigrated with them, and bought cheap lunches from us during the day. Those kids had never gone back home, but their parents never came looking for them, either.

Business was going well, but my father continued to encourage all of us to focus on our educations, as well. My father was the only Chinese man in the community who paid a lot of attention to his children's education. He had never been to school at all, but he wanted his children to achieve a high level of education, to be intelligent, and to be useful and successful. He had learned a great deal firsthand during his life about how to survive and be successful without an education: becoming an educated person with a degree had always been just a dream for him.

My oldest brother Ton was at the university, working to earn his master's degree in economics. My father wanted each one of us to follow in our big brother's steps. He believed firmly that education assisted children in finding shortcuts to realize the goals they had for their lives and to live well, despite the overall economy's condition. He pushed us to concentrate on studying, not on making money. He wanted us to earn a degree, rather than to struggle as hard as he had had to do just to survive. He cared much more about our acquiring knowledge and setting goals, rather than seeing us having to pick up every penny we came across on the road. He was so happy and proud of us when we brought home awards from school.

Working at the restaurant and going to school every single day kept us so busy, we rarely got enough sleep at night, something we were unfortunately accustomed to from our sleepless nights during the war. With the restaurant open and running, we had to stay up late to finish our homework, once the restaurant had closed. The younger ones learned from the older ones' examples. We worked together and helped each other; therefore, the children in our family were well known among the teachers at school for being the best students, dedicated, obedient, and well-mannered.

My parents were far too busy at the restaurant to participate in our school activities. They could never leave the restaurant even come to conferences at school; but my father made every effort he could to talk to our teachers whenever he saw them on the street to find out how each of us was doing and to give them special delicacies when they came to our restaurant. Our parents had placed all of their faith in us, since they knew they could, watching us study hard every single night, and we never, ever skipped school. But we really were on our own; the only thing they could do for us was to encourage us and support us financially. We volunteered to work to help them, and in turn, they gave us their full hearts and greatest support. Our family seemed to be regarded as one of the model families in Cu Chi, one that everyone in town wanted to emulate.

Many people in town also regarded my parents with admiration and respect because of our restaurant's enormous success. They were so proud of my father, who was so talented that he could run Nha Lau, the most wonderful restaurant in town, after having run the most successful dry goods store in Cu Chi and surviving the starvation we faced once the store had been closed down.

And then, something happened almost overnight: a completely new, very subtle kind of war began to be waged against us in Cu Chi. My parents had had absolutely no time at all to socialize with anyone in the neighborhood or town. They didn't know how to behave with the government leaders and all the local officers when they met them outside of the restaurant, and my father spoke almost no Vietnamese, which crippled him in many such situations. My parents simply focused on their business, took care of their children and their parents, and paid no attention to their competitors. They thought that being good citizens and welcoming all of their customers–from the most decorated generals to the poorest of the poor–would be enough.

They were very wrong. Suddenly, they were targets of jealousy for the townspeople, especially those in the food business: my parents' huge success was like needles in their eyes. My parents were criticized for not having developed a stronger and closer relationship with the top government leaders, people who could have protected and supported their business when this all began, and as a result, they were destroyed by some of the community right around them.

Cu Chi was too small for our success. Our one little star had lit up, brightening the entire sky over Cu Chi. But, because we were the only ones to do that, we also then became the only target at which people could shoot.

Our neighbors began to threaten the convoy drivers who ate at our restaurant, and they also forced many of our customers to go to different places to eat. All of the other restaurant owners in town were so jealous of us that they paid the kids who had been living outside our restaurant and selling things inside during the day to irritate our customers instead of selling things to them. The kids began to break our customers' vehicles and steal parts off of them, as well steal my parents' personal belongings.

Business plummeted swiftly, day by day. Jealous townspeople even paid the police to threaten and give our customers a hard time, and we were attacked in other sudden and unpredictable ways. My parents tried to be very patient and simply focus on their business, to ignore and not react to the cruel things people were doing to them. They worked harder and harder than ever to try to recover what they were suddenly in the shocking process of losing.

And then, one night, once again, our lives fell completely apart. When the Vietnam-Cambodian war ended, the government transferred thousands of disabled veterans from Cambodia to live in Cu Chi. This new camp was located only a few miles away from our house. Every day, veterans from the camp came to town to shop, eat, and drink, and they were heavily armed with guns, knives, and grenades. They themselves were like bombs, ready to explode from within: no one dared to hang around these devils. When the vets came to our restaurant, usually they paid nothing or very little. My parents never once complained or showed their anger against these hostile veterans, ever.

The veterans were very angry about their new plight in life: they owned absolutely nothing in the world and had been given only a roof over their heads and a tiny bit of support from the government. They behaved horribly, talked very haughtily, and were very disrespectful to everyone. They swore impertinently in public. They scornfully teased and flirted with any woman they met on the street. They stopped vehicles in the middle of the highway to beg for money; if drivers refused to give them anything, they would beat up the driver or break his car's windshield.

No one dared to confront these angry, frustrated veterans; most of the time, everyone stayed behind closed doors at home.

And it was always even worse and more terrifying when the vets were drunk. They ripped Cu Chi apart, randomly firing guns, weapons, or throwing rocks–whatever those hooligans could find to use as weapons. The war was over, but a new form of warfare was being waged in our town: no bombs were dropped, but the gunfire began again: those disabled vets were the most ferocious devils alive.

Then, one night, they completely destroyed our restaurant: it was the worst horror anyone in Cu Chi had endured at anyone's hands. It began one night when they came into the restaurant and ordered some alcohol and food. Then, they stuck a rusty, old nail into their food and claimed my parents were trying to kill them. My mother apologized to them over and over, but they started screaming and yelling at her, and then they began to beat up my mother right at their table. All of our other customers ran out, in fear for their lives.

My father and a waitress pulled my mother away from the assailants, and my mother ran out the door and hid at a neighbor's house.

Almost killing my mother–even that act alone–wasn't even enough to satisfy these madmen. They began breaking glasses and dishes, hurling all of the chairs and tables around the room, and throwing bottles and silverware randomly all over the place. The noise was deafening, almost the same chaotic sounds as the ones we had heard overhead from our cave during the war. And in the end, they completely put out the light of our "little star," Nha Lau.

I ran to the county office and the police department to report the crime and ask for help. The officials called for troops from the camp. But by the time the police arrived at the restaurant, more than 60 new vets had come to join forces with their crazy vet "brothers" and were waiting in front of the restaurant, all of them just as eager to fight as those who had begun the madness. They carried all kinds of machine guns, shotguns, hand-grenades, even rockets. They went crazy: they laughed, swore, screamed, and threatened us. They shot their guns into the sky and started fighting all over again.

Cu Chi was completely shut down by order of the government because the vets would have destroyed the whole town, if they had had so much as a hint that anyone else would turn against them. Residents locked their doors, blew out their lanterns, and hid deep inside their homes: no one dared to get involved.

Down the street from our restaurant, masses and masses of armed, handicapped veterans marched or hobbled into town, primed to kill. And, beyond everyone's imagination, those inhuman and bestial vets became even more frenzied.

And then the worst possible thing happened: our local government's troops simply gave up. They had called Saigon for reinforcements when those veteran devils surrounded the local government office and the police department, stopping all vehicles and any pedestrians still out on the street: Cu Chi was under control of the insane! The veterans wounded some of the police officers right in the streets. With every incident of devastation they caused, the vets became more and more fueled by their unstoppable power.

All of the havoc and destruction they had caused already wasn't even enough to quell their fury. The wild men called for help from other vets at their camp. Now, Cu Chi was filled, not only with terrorists on foot, but in convoys, jeeps, and big GMC trucks, wheeling and squealing their ways into the center of town.

The big gates of the police department had been locked. The county office was completely shut down, and outside, surrounding these key government buildings, the insane soldiers were throwing rocks, destroying signs, and trying to break down the metal gates to get inside.

Somehow, the vets had learned that our local government had called for army reinforcements from Saigon and that those soldiers were on their way to rescue us. This enflamed them even more. Shouting, yelling, and swearing at the top of their lungs, they dared the Cu Chi police to come outside: the vets wanted to confront our policemen, face to face. They wanted yet another fight to prove how unstoppable they were, and they wanted to get even with our local army forces for treating them like mad dogs! They were also furious that our local police officers had never been on the battlefield and had never suffered the inhumanities they had suffered. Bitter and full of self-pity for having become disabled in the war, they wanted to get even with the government that had sent them to war in the first place and then returned them to civilian lives that were more miserable than the lives they had originally left behind. After returning from war, they were neglected and had all but been abandoned by their own people; even their families treated them as if they were orphans and forgot about them. These veterans hated everyone around them who were healthy and had happy families, anyone who was luckier than they were.

Their war on Cu Chi was an opportunity for them to release their fury, enmity, and rage at all people, and they rained those feelings down upon us and our business, and upon all of the town, like bombs falling over and over our heads, once again.

Six hours later, the battle had died down, and my parents and their friends went back inside the restaurant to try to clean it up. What we saw inside was sickening: food was spoiled and thrown *everywhere*, and pots and pans lay on the floor amid glittering shards of shattered glass. Except for the fact that the building itself remained intact, the whole place inside had been completely ruined.

This almost killed the spirit of our entire family. We grieved our losses, though we were also glad that none of us had been seriously hurt and that we still had a place to live. My mother burst into a torrent of tears she had been holding in for hours since being attacked and terrorized. My father was, for the first time in his life, shocked into silence, quiet, and depressed. He sat in a chair in his filthy tee shirt and shorts, bent his legs, and rested his lowered forehead in his upturned palms. I could not bear to look at my dear, strong father this way. He was our light and leader. Cu Chi had been turned upside-down and smashed to pieces. Compared to the war before the revolution, this war had almost been worse because it was so personal for us. My parents had fought and worked so hard to raise themselves and all of their children back up again from the ditch into which we had been forced to slide after the war; we rose, happily and with a lot of work, and then, in what felt like a wink, we were all crushed to nothing, flat.

Outside the restaurant, we could hear sirens shrieking when the rescue teams from Saigon finally arrived. The vets halted all fire trucks, ambulances, and police jeeps by throwing themselves into the street, guns raised and cocked, yelling out that if one single policeman took a step toward any one of them, they would kill every, single person in town.

Night had fallen; darkness surrounded us. We were terrified and prayed for a solution. Another big fight could destroy Cu Chi, once and for all.

Negotiations between the vets and the police went on for hours.

Finally, we heard a single, hoarse veteran's voice yell at the crowds of officials and police, "If you will all apologize to us, we will cease our fighting."

We were shocked and disgusted: *they* should be the ones apologizing! *They* were the ones who had ignited this enormous firestorm, fed it for hours and hours, destroyed our restaurant, and maimed our police officers and others in their wake.

And then, the unimaginable happened: our head government official stepped forward and said, through a loudspeaker, "We apologize for your situation." Our head leader then continued talking quietly for a while with the vets' representatives. Finally, the vets' representatives returned to the hordes of vets waiting for orders. Suddenly, they all turned and began to walk back toward their camp, proudly and loudly celebrating their victory. It was over, and so was our life.

That night, as my father sat at the table, staring at it or at something far beyond it that none of us could see, and my mother sat on a pillow, holding her disheveled hair off her dirty, exhausted face with one tired hand and crying uncontrollably, there was a knock on the door.

We were terrified. Could the evil ones have returned to town—to *our house?* No one spoke, but we stared at each other, eyes wide with fear.

My father rose, terror whitening his face, and he slowly shuffled to the door. When he opened it fully, we could see the police chief and a head city official standing outside on our doorstep. They asked my father if they could come in.

My father gestured them in and toward the sitting room.

My mother leaped up, smoothed her hair, dried her face with her filthy apron, and invited them to make themselves comfortable, ever the perfect hostess.

"We've been to the restaurant," they began, "and it is a heartbreaking, shocking sight to see. Your fine restaurant has been the center of our town and has served us all in so many more ways, beyond your serving us all such wonderful food." I knew they were simply offering empty words.

They continued. "We will make it our priority to get you enough money to cover the damage and rebuild. You are the heart of our town, and we cannot thank you for all you have done nor ever repay you enough. But we will do everything we can to work toward that."

My mother's lips first made a circular, shocked 'O,' and then they spread across her face and met in a smile. My father's beautiful smile lit up his whole being. The men all stood and shook hands and bowed to each other, over and over and over.

"This is our solemn promise, and we will not stop until we have made sure you have been repaid. Our solemn vow," said the Chief of Police, again, pulling nervously at the shiny button on the cuff of his jacket, but trying to sound as earnest as possible. My father showed them to the door, and they all shook hands and bowed again, and then father closed the door.

And we all went crazy with joy! We jumped and danced around the room, hugging each other and laughing. My mother began to cry again, but this time with a smile on her face. And my father was smiling and crying, too, which we had never seen him do before.

Once again, we had been spared.

Time flew: one month, three months, then a year passed by. Even after two years, we had still not heard a word or received a penny from either of the officials who had come and made their solemn vow to us. This was the second, most important lesson I learned about life under our Communist government's leadership: they were simply not to be trusted. The first lesson had been learning about my inhumane, heartless, Communist uncle who had believed in Ho Chi Minh and his brutal regime.

My parents slowly withdrew into themselves like snails. They seemed to give up completely, which they had never done before, and it was as if their broken hearts would never heal again. They had been beaten down so many times, fought their way back up again, and had been beaten back down again. Their confidence and optimism in the face of this trouble were crushed this time. My family's very tight team had not only fallen apart under pressures from the government—despite the government's promise of help, which turned out to be empty words—and from other residents of town. We were victims of revenge, envy, and brutality. We all learned an unforgettable lesson: it changed our once-positive outlook on life and made us much more cautious about the world. The life and death of our restaurant was the experience that affected me the most deeply in terms of trust, and I will carry that scar in my heart for the rest of my life.

It took my parents a very long time to regain their strength and attempt to live their lives again. I was very worried that it would never happen, but finally, they somehow summoned enough courage to try to rebuild the restaurant, to try to recover their business. Another lesson for us kids.

However, both of my parents continued to suffer from loneliness and ostracism by people who had once been parts of their close and community. There was no place for my parents to hide and raise their family without feeling heavy sadness and abandonment. My parents freely fell into a big black hole of this rejection.

And just when we thought life could not get any worse, as a result of the war between the Chinese and the Vietnamese government, our family suddenly became a target of the local government. We were at the top of their list of Chinese capitalists who needed to be destroyed. We became the enemy in Cu Chi. The local government sent inspectors to our restaurant, and they watched our every move, every day, from early in the morning until we closed. They wanted to find out how much we made each day and how much the expenses of the restaurant were.

That was not all: they made my mother go alone to the county offices to investigate her for hours. They harassed and threatened her, just to learned about our profits from the restaurant. My mother almost had a heart attack from being so scared and frightened. Besides that, they sent undercover officers to spy on our restaurant; these men were disguised as customers to verify the information that my mother had given them. They overwhelmed my parents psychologically on purpose.

Then they sent strangers to our house at night who searched every corner of our home thoroughly, upstairs and downstairs, in the bedroom, kitchen, cabinets, closets, and dressers. They squeezed and shook all of our clothes, underwear, socks, and towels; they even tore apart all of our Tampax to look for illegal entertainment products. They were determined to find my parents' hidden treasures.

Unfortunately, they would never find what they wanted, no matter what they tore apart because we had been broken right after the revolution. We didn't have any gold, diamonds, or jewelry, which they had expected to find. The restaurant was making just enough to cover our living expenses and our schooling.

The government was disappointed and infuriated, since their investigation was unsuccessful. They grew more angry and ruthlessly closed down my parents' restaurant, forcing them to the edge of bankruptcy. They dramatically increased our taxes so that there was no way our business could survive. The officials went back over my parents' tax returns for the three prior years and came up with a random number that they estimated that my parents had underpaid them and blamed my parents for miscalculating their taxes. They forced my parents to pay back these mysterious, back taxes they seemed to owe the government. Then they closed down the business.

They finally broke my parents' wills and convinced them to let the government take over the restaurant and made them work in their own restaurant for the new government owners. And the government not only wanted ownership of the restaurant but of our house, as well, the very roof over our heads. They decided to take the house away from us, just because they were furious they hadn't found any treasure or valuables they had once believed my parents were hiding.

And, as if that wasn't enough, on our resumes, each of us children were stamped 'Chinese capitalists,' a damning classification: it meant we couldn't get a job anywhere in the country. Our family was now regarded as belonging to the very bottom class of society; we were equal with prisoner-of-war families, who had participated with the Republican Army before 1975.

My parents could not stand all of this. They signed a document at the county office, swearing they would never open a business again. Our big doors were closed for the second time in 1982, when I was in the twelfth grade.

My father simply returned to working his rice farm and prayed that his children would be able to change our own destinies ourselves. He had no hope left for his own life. Every day, he rode his little moped out to the farm early in the morning to work in his rice fields. He enjoyed sharing stories and chatting with all the farmers in the countryside. Once upon a time, he had loved all people, and the farmers at least boosted his spirits and reinforced a bit of his belief in the fact that there good people on earth.

My mother very gradually recovered from her terror of the government's relentless attacks, but she remained full of pain and lost her desire to work and support her children until we graduated from high school. She tried to convince my father to look for a different career or business because she saw no hope for herself. A dead end.

My oldest sister got married after years of fighting very, very hard to find a job and career. Her new husband was the son of one

73

of my father's closest friends. The son had worked for my father, and he had also lived with us since he was very little. My new brother-in-law very quietly stepped up to shoulder the extremely difficult responsibility of trying to support our family while we were all still in school.

My father had a pick-up truck that had been parked, unused, in the garage for years. My brother-in-law started using my father's pick-up truck to deliver goods he picked up here and there around the city, and on his way home, he brought fertilizer to sell to the local farmers. He worked very hard every day, from four o'clock in the morning until midnight. Sometimes, he didn't sleep at all. He gave all of the money he made to my parents to spend on us as they saw fit.

We were all so grateful to our brother-in-law; he willingly volunteered to sacrifice so much to support all of us at a time when we were helpless and without resources of any kinds. He never asked for anything in return for his help. He never complained about working too hard or showed any jealousy of us kids, all of whom were getting an education. He treated us as if we were his own blood relatives; we looked to him as if he were our oldest, revered brother; and we believed God had delivered him to us, the greatest blessing from God that we could have received. He was our own special star in our black, black sky. Lots of times, we heard him crying alone in his bedroom because our family was so poor.

My father liked to go with my brother-in-law on his deliveries around the city. They had great fun together, and that helped my father forget the pain of his past. Although the delivery business didn't bring very much profit, we were at least surviving, and that was a great gift. At year's end, we didn't have any money to celebrate the Chinese New Year. My brother-in-law, even after a whole year of working so very hard, hid at home, avoiding his friends because he didn't have any money to celebrate with them.

In the meantime, we waited patiently for an opportunity–any opportunity–trying, just as my father had once done–to look at life optimistically. But we saw no road opening for us to take on our way toward a better way of life. We lived in extremely draining conditions, not only in need of food but continued education, health care, and other very basic needs. We had gone back to eating vegetables, instead of meat. We spent very little of our money and only then when it was very urgent. We could breathe but just enough to take short breaths or very short sighs.

CHAPTER FOUR

JUNE, 2009

Rick shook me, and I opened my eyes and turned to him.

"Look out the window," he smiled and pointed.

Pale washes of water-colored light were beginning to erase the blackness from our window, and the clouds we rode above were pink! My favorite color! I knew this journey was going to be so special, and there was more proof of it: a sky filled with pink signs.

I gave Rick a quick kiss and thanked him for waking me up to see it. "How much longer do we have before we arrive?" I asked, yawning.

"We're about halfway there, Loan," he replied.

I sighed. "A long journey, for sure!" I said over my shoulder to him, snuggling back into my "pillow," and fell away from him into dreams, once again.

197-?

Because each member of our family's resumes had been officially stamped 'Chinese Capitalist,' getting jobs or even enrolling in a vocational school was impossible. We would never have denied our Chinese heritage; at the same time, that heritage put success far out of our reach.

My older sister Ngoc had just finished high school and had been denied entrance into vocational school. She was a smart student and had graduated from high school with very good grades. She now wandered around the house with no job, seeing no promise in the future. I was one year younger than Ngoc. Next year, it would be my turn to graduate from high school. I was terrified to fail, as she had, and to wind up doing nothing but waiting helplessly for sheer luck.

But I simply refused to give up that easily: my brother-in-law had shouldered the complete burden of and responsibility for taking care of all of us for so long. He needed help. Moreover, three of my young brothers and sisters were close to graduating after I did; they still needed to be protected and cared for, and, at the same time, to learn to become successful on their own.

My father's strength was deeply rooted within me and helped to hold me to a steady course: I decided I was the one who had to break through whatever horrific barriers were thrown in my way and that nothing would ever obstruct my path or prevent me from being successful: my plan was to take my turn at supporting my family. I was sick of being sheep, walking meekly behind 'our Communist masters,' like trained dogs, as my parents had finally done, letting their lives be controlled by the government, and losing everything.

My experiences had been harsh teachers about the real world 'out there.' Nowhere within me anywhere, anymore was a shred of that little girl who had once listened raptly to and believed the Communist leaders talk about Ho Chi Minh as if he were an angel. Life had done nothing but constantly pound us down, and our pain had begun with Communism. That truth motivated and stimulated my deep-set, natural instincts to rise up, which my father had given to me—no matter what the cost—*and* to go higher.

I also wanted to get even.

So, I came up with a plan. First, I did some research in order to create a list of all people who had ever come to my parents' store to pick up money, medical supplies, and clothes for the Communist forces when I was little. During the war, my parents had donated so much material support to the Party, though they never volunteered to do so, and their out-of-pocket cost was not insignificant. The Communist regime had actually swallowed a good part of my parents' income before 1975. My parents had indirectly and involuntarily acted on behalf of the Communists, who were hiding in the woods, jungle, and underground back then, and they wouldn't have survived without my parents who kept them supplied and saved them from being wet and cold and getting sick from deadly diseases carried by mosquitoes in the tropical forest where they were in hiding. Their bodies would now be rotting under the grass on the battlefields without their help. My parents had not only paid taxes to the republican government but also to the Communists, solely in order to enjoy in peace in our home.

Unjust. Inhumane. Abusive.

I could not bear any longer the losses my parents had suffered. I had to help them, and, after all, I was in the twelfth grade, a young woman now with personal resources, and I was driven hard to restore our family's good name and regain for them adequate acknowledgement of their many good deeds for our country.

In order to carry out my mission, first I needed to find people who would bear witness willingly to my parents' contributions to the communists' victory. My mother was the one to give me my first lead; she told me of an old couple I did not remember as a child; she said they used to come to the store whenever the Communist troops needed money or supplies.

My mother told me this old couple lived deep in the jungle, so I set out one day on my bicycle across town and then followed a footpath that first led me deep into the still-dangerous countryside. I rode my bike for hours and hours, following a thin trail, some parts of which disappeared in thickets of thorny bushes and some parts of which disappeared under water. I rolled my pants up to my knees; but even rolled as high as they could go, they dragged in the water, becoming heavier.

My little bike became felt heavier and heavier from gravity, mud, and the water I had trudged through with it. When I tried to lift the bike up, it seemed to pull me down into the muck even further. My body was soaking wet, and the path, which had been created through the brush and undergrowth solely by the footsteps of those few souls who still lived in this wild place as they headed back and forth to and from town, seemed to go on into infinity. I could see no end to it.

No addresses were posted in the area either. The path was the only way to get to my destination. The sun shining hard down on my face was blinding and burned me all over. I was hot from struggling through the mud puddles with my cumbersome bike. My eyes also blurred from being exhausted and thirsty, yet there was no water to drink on the rice field, which was ironically full of water.

I sat down to take a quick break on a patch of dead grass. I was close to giving up, hoping somebody would come along the path and help me. There was no breeze, and no motion, except a few dead leaves that fell on the ground next to me.

I was torn between giving up and going home or moving forward. Though the path didn't look any easier moving forward, I thought perhaps my destination would bring me some hope. Going back home would be far easier, but then I would have done nothing to try to brighten our future. I had taken on this responsibility myself. Precious hope pushed me on.

I stood up, carrying my bike across the water field, and continued looking for the house in which an old woman named Batu and her husband lived in.

And soon after that, my grueling work paid off. I came upon a tattered, forlorn, tiny shack with a coconut leaf roof and decaying bamboo walls. A good gust of wind could easily have picked it up and carried it into the sky. It was just as my mother had described it to me; it looked as if it had been thrown together hurriedly in the middle of a dead land that no one dared to enter.

We had heard that dynamite and traps had been hidden underground throughout the area. Thousands of Republican soldiers had lost their lives in this desolate area during the war, and Vietnamese Communists had hidden here, prepared to fire at and kill anyone they came across. I guessed that the few residents of the area had learned how to survive by watching their every move; they could lose their lives with one single misstep. Only Communist Party members and relatives of their comrades were guaranteed safe access to this place and return to civilization alive. Why, I wondered, would Batu and her husband continue to risk their very lives working for the Communist troops under such impossible physical and emotional conditions? Perhaps they were already dead, zombies, or angels, now beyond pain.

I took a deep breath and stepped right up to the front door of the little shack and knocked. The door was a rotten piece of plywood, barely attached to the outside wall of the shack but obviously hanging there solely to give the shack's residents some privacy.

Footsteps very slowly scuffled across the floor inside. And then, a skinny, decrepit woman, coughing and wheezing from an obviously untreated, bad cold or bronchitis, opened the door. The old woman and the shack looked to be in the same condition, merely holding themselves together by sheer will.

The woman invited me inside, offered me a seat, and went off to get me a glass of water.

In a dark corner, I saw a wasted old man sitting at the end of the table with a big bag of tobacco that he was rolling into cigarettes. His hands rolled the tobacco while he stared at me. The old man had been born and lived all his life in the jungle, my mother had told me, and his skin was very dark from having worked for so long and so hard in the rice fields. His face and eyes were so gentle that I knew he was a very honest person. His teeth were stained from drinking tea and smoking tobacco constantly. When he smiled, his eyes disappeared because they were so small.

Batu's husband rarely spoke. I watched him roll another small, thin piece of paper around a big hunk of tobacco. Then he lit the cigarette and remained sitting at his end of the table, smoking like a chimney, once in a while looking up at us, nodding his head to indicate his agreement with some part of our conversation.

When the old woman finally sat down and joined us, I quickly introduced myself by telling them my parents' name. They both burst into happy tears! They were so happy to hear they were all right. They were also shocked that I had located them 'in the middle of nowhere,' a place in which you could find a fallen bird's feather on the ground much more easily than a human being's footprint.

Soon, this old couple began to look more and more familiar: I *had* seen them before. I was trying to remember when and where I had seen them when an image of the barn behind our old store popped into my mind. Ba Tu and her husband had often come to our house to sell their pigs to my parents' pig business, which they ran on the side, and to visit and talk with my parents after delivering the baby pigs. Our pen always had over thirty pigs in it at a time. This small side business was very convenient, an easy way for my parents to realize a huge profit, since the feed and farm supplies were cheap and always available in their own store. My parents also fed the pigs with wasted and spilled food from the store.

Then Ba Tu revealed to me a shocking secret, and her eyes grew large and round, like two wise moons rising, as she told me a story I could not have dreamed up in a million years: my own parents had made many, enormous, and extremely risky contributions to support and enable the Communist party's victory. They had not only given huge sums of money to the party but also had played a very critical role in maintaining its survival and growth. Those baby pigs had been a front for so much more! Ba Tu said the Communists had also chosen my parents' store as an informal, regional base, as their headquarters were somewhere far away. In addition, my parents were charged with providing safe shelter to undercover Communists traveling in our region of Vietnam. We had fed so many "relatives," which was how my mother introduced the strangers around our table to us kids during the war; I just assumed they were starving and had come from far away to us for help. *Relatives? Ha!!*

In addition, the Communists had used my parents' store as an enlistment station for young people who wished to join the party. They waited in our pig barn for someone to arrive from somewhere deep in the forest to take them back into the forest to the Communist army camps.

My parents probably didn't know too much about this last part of their underground activity; they were only following the instructions of a decent, old couple who were selling them baby pigs, who were friends, and who seemed trustworthy. What even my *parents* didn't know is that this kind old man and woman, too, had been coerced by the Communists to serve as their liaisons to my parents and anything they could make possible.

My parents' own business was so busy with hundreds of people stampeding in and out of the door every day that, as a result, the undercover assignment wasn't too difficult for them to fulfill. Our barn was a perfect, protected place from which the Communist agents could manage their undercover activities secretly. My head was spinning with old images from childhood that suddenly made sense, as Ba Tu revealed more and more.

However, Ba Tu wanted to assure me, that my parents *never, ever* volunteered their services but were involuntarily "drafted" to assist the Communists in their very dangerous and brutal war affairs. My parents could have been arrested, given prison sentences for life, and lost every single thing they owned overnight, as well as their own children.

Why had my parents done this? No one was more important to them than their children! No one! We were raised with a doubt about that. And that must have been why.

Ba Tu seemed to understand my head was bursting with a million questions and fears by reading my eyes. "They had no choice, child," said Ba Tu, softly. "No choice. *You must understand this.* They had merely assumed the covert relationship that your grandparents had had with the party over thirty years before, during the war between France and Vietnam. When your grandparents had lived in the village, which was Communist-controlled, your grandma was a member of the party and had had held an important position among local party members."

'*My grandma*!?' I could hardly even hear this information, on top of what I had learned about my own parents! My grandparents, too?! My grandma was one of the sweetest and kindest, little, old ladies in town! But apparently, after eating at my parents' restaurant, the soldiers used to walk next door to see my grandma, and that became a routine for all of them. They would stay with her, chatting until really late at night because my grandma would never tell them to go home.

The soldiers didn't hesitate to share their feelings with her. She used to burst into tears when a soldier showed her a wound on his shoulder that he had received during battle. He insisted with pride that he had been a hero to fight back when his company was attacked in the middle of the night in the woods somewhere in Cambodia.

My grandma rubbed his wounded shoulder with some ointment used as a cure by some elders in town, and she told him," It will take awhile to heal, grandson. It *was* a great thing for you to perform your duty on the battlefield."

The wounded soldier's eyes would light up, and he continued telling her about the most horrible war experiences that he had had in his life.

Another soldier cried to my grandma about his girlfriend who lived in northern Vietnam and who was going to get married to someone else. He didn't know how long it might be before he could get back to her and try to do something about the situation.

Then my grandma quickly told him, "Grandson, do not worry. I know so many good girls in town. I will find one for you in a very short time. Keep moving forward and try to be happy."

My grandma: a Communist with a leading role??? I could never have even thought once that this was going on around me and could hardly take it all in!

Batu let me think quietly for a while, and then she resumed her story. "Then in 1954, when France gave up and left Vietnam, your grandma quit her job and moved into town with all of you. However, her name was still on the list of Communist comrades, and so she became a target of the new republican government."

As she spoke, I became more and more aware that not only were my *parents* in great danger, but my *grandparents* were in danger, as well! If they had not cooperated with the Communist government, the Communist government leaders would have forced them—in terrible ways—to keep secret their roles in the party. Goosebumps prickled across my neck and down my back as I realized the weight and extraordinary danger my parents' and grandparents' secret lives had forced them to bear.

After telling me this incredible tale, the two old people began to complain about how badly *they* had been treated by the government after the revolution. Ba Tu's eyes glossed over with a wash of tears as she tried to describe how much anger and pain she felt for being mistreated. "The new government squeezed me and my husband dry like discarded wedges of lemon; they got the juice they needed from us and tossed us in the garbage pile.

"We had <u>given up our lives</u>" and she pounded her fist on the table to emphasize each word she spoke, "to fight for *our* country. But after the victory, someone else marched into town, took over, and stamped all over us!

"They called me a hero *to my face* to appease me for our having spent over 40 years of our lives assisting them, always struggling and living in dead-end poverty. We had nothing! They gave us *nothing* in return."

She paused and looked into the weak fire, then watched her husband's rolling hands as he made yet another cigarette.

She took a deep breath and continued. "They appointed me Vice President of the Women's Club, but the pay wasn't enough to enable me to feed us. All those promises the Communists made before the revolution were nothing but emptiness," she said bitterly. "Even though I was still a member of the party, I had no health care and suffered an illness for which I could not get treated. Twice a month, I dragged myself into town for meetings, and I was always invited to party anniversaries and to Chinese New Year, Independence Day, or Labor Day celebrations. "And after 40 years of working and dying for the that party, that was all I ever received: invitations to parties I could barely hobble to. That was not nearly enough in return for all we gave and gave, just like your parents did." she said bitterly.

All of this new information and her stories shocked me and made me feel even more sorry for my parents, but now also sorry for Ba Tu and her husband. They were tragic casualties of the war, risking their lives and livelihoods only to be used and betrayed in return. Abuse, again.

"I had no education or degree," said Ba Tu with great hurt in her eyes, "and that was the reason I lost the work I had been doing for my country during the war. Young people have no idea what dangers we lived through and risked our very lives for. They don't appreciate our sacrifices for them, their futures, and Vietnam. It's disgusting.

"All we have are memories and our pride in what we accomplished. That is all that keeps me going."

I had to find words to say to these heroes. She had served as the essential bridge that enabled all of the army bases to maintain good communication with their leaders and thus win the war. Although she disagreed with the Communist ideology and saw no way of moving out of the miserable conditions in which she lived, she was still a Communist. She was still faithful to them and swore she would be a comrade of Ho Chi Minh forever.

"As long as I may live, I will continue to fight for justice," she proudly declared, her eyes regaining tiny sparks of light again.

Then it was my turn to talk about the reason for my visit with them. I told them about all the troubles my whole family had had since 1975, and then I told Ba Tu we were turning to them for help. I made sure Ba Tu and her husband understood that this was not my parents' idea, but mine and mine alone. I simply refused to see our future destroyed by someone else's hostility and discrimination. The war between the two governments had nothing to do with us: we were merely its victims.

"The Chinese boycott policy has put all of us, my parents' children, in straight jackets, incapable of working toward hopeful futures and achieving new lives in any way. I need to find someone who can wash the black marks off our foreheads so we can be treated as equals to all the other children in the country."

It was unsettling the way Ba Tu rolled her eyes when she listened to my stories, one after the other, and I wasn't sure what she was thinking. Then she explained that she regretted having been disconnected from my parents after the revolution. She thought my parents had contributed so much to the country that they should at least be honored as heroes of the nation.

I told her I had the same thoughts and feelings about her and her husband! Ba Tu's eyes then filled with tears, and she apologized for not caring more about my parents, who had stood hand-in-hand and back-to-back with her and her husband on the devastating and dangerous battlefield during the war.

I decided, after hearing all that I had heard and seen what I had seen, that Ba Tu would not be able to help at all since she, herself, was still in trouble, only held a very modest position in the Communist Party, and her voice would probably not be heard. My hopes plummeted and I doubted my plan altogether.

Then Ba Tu completely shocked me. She stood up, told me to go home, and then to meet her at her office early Monday morning. She told me no more than that. We all exchanged heartfelt goodbyes, and I left her little shack with a sad and heavy heart. My eagerness had disappeared, together with my beautiful plan to free my family from the corruption of the society. Then I felt ashamed to have even bothered the old couple, when their lives weren't any better than our family's was.

The bike ride home seemed even longer and more arduous than it had that morning. I was soaked, muddy, scratched, and bleeding, and my feet were so sore. However, I reminded myself that visiting them had been better than having done nothing. I had also learned shocking and amazing things about my parents and grandparents, the war, and had met two elderly people who had lived underground in the forest in the most deadly area of the war zone so that the Communists could achieve victory, which they did. And what had they received in return for their sacrifice: nothing but empty promises, degradation, and a disgusting lack of gratitude for their work from the younger generation. They felt invisible, the most helpless and painful way anyone could feel.

I knew.

My parents were at the door, waiting for me when I arrived home. They were so worried about my having gone into such awful territory, and they wondered if I had even found Ba Tu and her husband. I told my parents every detail I had learned from Ba Tu's stories, except my feelings about it all. I also was discouraged to say that I wasn't sure if Ba Tu could do anything to help us at all when she herself wasn't doing well at all.

My parents only asked me one question about the old couple's health. They were happy when I told them that the old couple was doing well, despite their living conditions, and still surviving such harsh living conditions.

My parents had lost all hope and faith in almost everything, but they still encouraged me to follow through with my plan.

That night in bed, images of everything I had seen and learned in the forest and in the little, collapsing shack ran 'round in my head like a movie or merry-go-round. Ba Tu and her husband had no children to take care of them. They had only each other to watch over and lean on for survival. Their tiny home was located a painfully long and dangerous distance away from and back to civilization, even for *me*, a young person! No hospital or nurse's station was nearby. Their little shack could collapse at any time, and then where would they live, I worried? They would be unprotected, right in the forest, with no roof or walls for protection from wild animals, snakes, and the drenching rain! Perhaps they could make a home closer to the water fields? They needed so much more help than my family did! Ba Tu had coughed and coughed, her lungs wheezing like leathery, old billows. They needed nutritious food, medications, and safety.

I fell asleep that night, crying with helplessness.

The next morning, despite my heavy heart, I did exactly what Ba Tu had told me to do: I had no other choice. I walked into the county office in the town hall at eight o'clock in the morning. Ba Tu was already there, waiting for me with a handful of documents. She had probably had to get up really early in the morning just to get to her office and prepare everything for me.

She thrust the paperwork at me right as I walked in the door. She told me to follow the instructions, fill out the papers, and return as soon as possible. She said she would wait for me to come back.

I had no idea what the papers were, but a very tiny beat of hope skipped in my heart. I left her office, the harsh sounds of her coughing and wheezing trailing behind me. I also felt terribly guilty for asking her to get involved in my family's seemingly hopeless situation when hers was no better—or worse! But it was too late now to stop or back out; I reluctantly had to launch my arrows at the targets she had set up. I had opened what might even turn into a can of worms that I would have to clean up.

The paperwork was easy to fill out, and I found her waiting for me, as she had promised, when I returned it. She was very excited to see me and immediately grabbed the documents I had brought and poured over them very closely, her eyes rolling up and down with her eyebrows as she read.

She wasn't very happy at all with the way I filled out the paperwork. I was embarrassed, but she did not complain about it. She just told me that she needed more details. She told me I needed to write a long, emotion-filled essay about my parents to emphasize all the work they had done, not just mention some of it. She stroked my head gently and said, "You can do this. You cannot give up now."

I was shocked. In front of me was not just an old lady who wasn't able to spell her name correctly, but one whose mind was still so sharp. I had misjudged Ba Tu. She had given me so many thoughtful ways to present my parents as leaders in the movement, not just partners of the party.

She pulled out a chair and gestured for me to sit down at her desk to re-do the paperwork on a creaky, little table that was just big enough for her to store a few notebooks, a pen holder, and a few other things.

Ba Tu had placed her desk in a corner of the office next to a small window so she could enjoy daylight shining in. Behind her desk, on top of a file cabinet was a statue of Ho Chi Minh, a party flag, and flowers.

As I looked around at her office, she smiled and said, "This is all I was given after thirty years of working for and being prepared to die fighting for our country." She sighed. Nothing could be done. Again, helplessness.

I hurried up to finish my job so she could go home and rest. I had always been a good writer; therefore, it didn't take too long for me to reorganize what I had written, following all the suggestions that Ba Tu had given me.

And she smiled with more satisfaction after she read my second stab at the essay. Then she didn't say another word. She told me to go home now and say hello to my parents for her.

That was it? Walking out of the county office, I grumbled to myself sarcastically, "Good luck, Loan." Doubt once again filled my head, despite that one teeny, tiny glimmer of hope Ba Tu had sparked. I had felt hopeful so many times in the past, only for those hopes to be crushed. I imagined the paperwork I had filled out for Ba Tu being shoved into the "untouchable cases" files where it would sit for the next ten or twenty years as soon as the county officers saw my parents' names. I could hear them laughing about how stupid we were, trying to erase the black marks on our foreheads, like crows trying to change the color of their black feathers. I imagined they would laugh at Ba Tu's thinking she could change the whole system with that one stubby pencil she had given me to use. They would dismiss her as an insignificant, little fish, trying to swim against the current.

I suddenly wished Ba Tu would just forget the whole story about my family and go home to take care of her bronchitis, instead of trying to fight all the Communists in town for us. I sighed heavily.

But I *was* grateful to her for trying to help us and for having had the opportunity to know her, a wonderful woman who had treated us with respect–different from the way the rest of the community and the Communists in town did.

I was going to graduate high school in a couple months. It was finally time. Just like the other high school students, I filed to take the entrance exam we all were required to take in order to compete for a space at a university. I didn't even expect to be allowed to take the exam because I was sure my resume–with my blackened name on it–would make me ineligible to take it.

A few days before graduation, my parents were stunned to see in their mail a letter from the city office. The letter delivered the shocking news that my parents had been declared heroes of the nation! The award commended them highly for their immense contributions to the victory of the communist government during the war, and they received the second place hero medal order from Hanoi, the headquarters of the party and capital of Vietnam.

My mother was invited to the county town hall where the government planned to celebrate her for her achievements. Further, they declared my mother would receive money every month and that the government would pay for her medical expenses for the rest of her life, plus the cost of her coffin, if she were to die.

How did something like this happen to us? Nothing had ever happened to us like this before. Out of the clear, hot, blue sky!

I immediately took the letter all the way to Ba Tu's house to share this miracle with her.

And to my total surprise, she just smiled gently at me and said, "I already knew."

Ba Tu revealed the secret behind her making our victory come true. First, she had taken a shortcut with my paperwork by filing it directly with her boss, who was at a level higher than the local government officials but somewhere far away in the country. It was the trump card, her having done that, and she had made it possible for my family to rebuild itself and for our reputations to rise back up shining out of the black ashes of our past.

Ba Tu then told me an even bigger secret: she used to be in charge of all spy activity in the region. She knew that trying to fight with the local government wouldn't help regain my family's respect in the community. She had been incredibly impressed with me, she said, in her quiet and calm way. She acted silently and bravely, using all the tricks she had learned about manipulating those in charge, to enable our family, and especially the children, to anticipate brighter futures.

Ba Tu had given my family the most priceless gift of all: our rightful freedom, which the local Communists had taken away, and she made me feel safe again about competing with all of the students in my country for a university spot: no one could ever discriminate against any of us any more. She was an angel who gave me back my strength and confidence to stand up straight and proud. I was so excited, thinking about my younger brother and sisters' brighter futures. The path before us opened up, one more time, and it was wider and straighter than it had ever been before. Incredible things had resulted from my hard work and Ba Tu's magic to overcome our last disaster. Everything seemed to be falling into place.

I graduated from high school, earning top scores and was awarded high honors: I was the school's best student. I was intelligent, and my teachers had always complimented me on my work. I was good at all subjects, but I was especially skilled at and loved math and physics.

Because of my scholastic achievements and because of Ba Tu's magic, I knew I could expect to be accepted by any university to which I applied—medical, engineering, or business school. However, I chose to study at the university in Saigon known for its economics of finance and accounting classes. Choosing this focus would give me an advantage in terms of winning the contest because it was not a popular major, and it would be easier to get a job in Saigon, if I graduated with from this program. The particular school to which I applied only accepted the top three hundred students from among the thirty thousand students throughout Vietnam who were competing for a spot at this school.

The entrance examination competition was held only once a year in July. The university required that its applicants had taken math, physics, and chemistry during the last three years of high school.

I worked so hard in the six weeks between high school graduation and exam day, studying harder than I had ever studied in my entire life. I got up very early in the morning and stayed up very late every night to study. I had to earn my next opportunity to move forward. Period.

And the course of my life did move forward in 1983 when the university in Saigon informed me that I had been admitted. I had done it! At the same time, my older sister was admitted to academy school to become a teacher! My parents were so happy and proud of us. That news lightened their burdens, both financially and emotionally, as <u>two</u> of us were on our way to independence and would soon be in positions to support them.

My father called me "the soul of the family," and my brothers and sisters admired me: I had raised our names up so that we were finally regarded as equals to all other children in Vietnam, and it was my effort that had put the shine back on our family's name.

Very soon, I would live in Saigon, the huge city in which I had dreamed of living since I was a child. My grandma and my mother were very worried about my leaving Cu Chi to live in Saigon, as happy as they were about it at the same time. My grandma kept warning me about how complicated it was going be to live there, even though she hadn't lived in Saigon for one day in her entire life!

Only my heart of a father remained calm and confident. He trusted me and had total faith in my abilities to handle the huge changes ahead of me. He said, "You are stubborn, resolute, tireless, studious, and highly dedicated to your dreams and goals for all of us, no matter how far down we have gone." Then he chuckled, "And Saigon is not across the ocean but only twenty miles from Cu Chi!" and wiggled his hands in the air over his head, exasperated with my mother's worries.

My luggage was packed: my bag was small and lightweight; my dreams, responsibilities, expectations of myself, and hard-driving ambition were enormous. Ba Tu had cleared all of the debris and undergrowth in my path, and my family had encouraged me, supported me, and showered me with endless love, which I drank in like a budding rose thrives on water.

CHAPTER FIVE

JUNE, 2009

The tall man in the seat behind me kicked the back of my seat accidentally, as he tried to make his way out of his seat and shocked me awake. I stretched and thought how good it would feel to walk a while, and a trip to the bathroom would be one way to accomplish it. I didn't just want to walk up and down the aisle a hundred times like a crazy, nervous person and worry people that I was about to do something to endanger the flight!

So, I climbed over Rick, planting a quick kiss on the top of his head; he had actually fallen asleep, sitting straight up in his seat, and I tried to climb carefully over the lady sitting on the aisle beside him, who was out cold and wrapped up like a mummy to her chin in a thin, navy blue blanket, snoring like my father used to do.

After my walk up the aisle and back down to my seat, I was surprised at how tired I still was. Traveling stirs up a lot of emotion in me; I had made only a very few airplane trips in my life, and so I was not completely comfortable on a plane. But with Rick beside me and Michael behind us, his limbs still curled up into a strange, sleeping pretzel, I felt safe enough.

I climbed back over the navy blue mummy and Rick, somehow managing not to disturb either one (though I am a small person in size), pulled the little window down over the brightening sky outside my "porthole," and down went my eyelids again. Shut tight.

198-?

I was on my way to college! I could hardly believe my dream was beginning to come true.

I felt like Dorothy in *The Wizard of Oz* as my bus drew closer to Saigon. From its outskirts, the city looked beautiful–an almost magical place, full of possibilities.

Once we reached the heart of the city, I began to understand how enormous Saigon really was compared to my little hometown. At first, it was overwhelming and extremely crowded: more than four million people lived within 850-900 square miles. There almost wasn't enough air to breathe or room to turn around in without touching someone else.

The city had been constructed largely of brick buildings that absorbed the heat under the relentless sun, and the buildings turned into giant ovens, cooking the whole city–inside and out. Rivers of people poured through the streets, day and night, because the extreme heat would have cooked them if they stayed inside their houses. It was so hot and humid that I felt as if steam were evaporating out of every pore on my skin, even out of my ears! The city's multiple-storied buildings created impassable walls, so that even the tiniest breeze could not get in to cool us.

Deafening noises pounded in the air. I couldn't hear anyone talking to me on the sidewalk, even if they were standing right in front of my nose: old truck engines revved; exhaust pipes popped; busses honked constantly like herds of giant, yellow geese; and semi-trucks chased each other up and down the avenues. The cars, busses, and trucks emitted tons of smog and unburned fuel, all of which then polluted the air and made it so thick, it felt like trying to inhale cotton scented with the heavy, oily cooking odors from restaurants all around the city.

The city became even more chaotic when trucks full of hundreds of animals arrived in the city from the countryside at various markets around the town. Dogs, cats, birds, chickens, ducks:

all of these poor animals were taken out of their wild, natural habitats and caged on trucks heading to market. The city's noise scared all the animals terribly. The city's trees were empty of wild birds, who must have been scared away by the pandemonium, and though dogs barked at night, no roosters crowed in the morning; our roosters at home had been my alarm clocks. No insect could survive because of the vibrations caused by the street traffic. No crickets cried and no cicadas rustled loudly in the summertime. I was on another planet–or so it seemed to me at first.

And the streets were filthy, even though the street sweepers worked really hard to clean them up very early each morning.

In Saigon's markets, vendors sold anything anyone could wish for: rats, snakes, grasses, wild animals, very expensive jewelry, and even pieces of cheap rock!

On the other hand, Saigon was beautiful in certain ways to this wide-eyed newcomer. The French had designed and planted Saigon's national parks over a hundred years ago, and the parks were the city's saving graces. Its flowers, trees, and green space helped cool down the air a bit. The trees that had been chosen and planted actually grew well in the torrid heat and made the city look a little more attractive and alive. Once in a while, scents of living things floated into town from these parks and relieved my spirits.

Saigon residents were surrounded by what felt like thousands of police officers, and the police were armed from head to toe with long guns on their arms and green hard hats on their heads. I had seen armed police before, but the sheer mass of those in Saigon was more frightening than anything I had ever seen. But these men played an important role in this city: they directed traffic, gave residents directions, gave out traffic tickets, cleaned up the black market, and stopped crime. Solemn and watchful, they stood at the corner of every, single intersection; in shops; and in front of schools. They even hid in bushes, as if they knew somehow someone was sure to come along soon who was doing something for which they could surprise, catch, and arrest them.

However, the sheer size of the police force put a huge damper on any sense of freedom Saigon's residents felt. The presence of all of those police officers made people feel anxious and uncomfortable all the time, especially those of us coming to Saigon for the first time. Constantly, in the back of my mind, I thought, 'What will happen next? Will something blow up on us soon? Am I doing something wrong?' Cu Chi had had no any traffic laws, no one-way streets, or traffic lights. I didn't know what a crosswalk, an intersection, or a "pedestrian only" zone were. I had always just walked or ridden my bike wherever I wanted to go: no police followed my every move.

I got caught for violating some law or other in Saigon almost every single week at the beginning of my life there. Fortunately, when I showed them my ID, they would let me go immediately because Cu Chi was so far from civilization, they understood I just did not know. Perhaps they let me go because my hometown had been so famous during the war that no cop dared to bother any resident who had once lived there.

Though extremely overwhelmed and exhausted from the stress of adjusting to my new "home," I always wore a big smile on my face back then because my life was brand new and exciting, despite the enormous challenges Saigon required I face. And eventually, I caught onto the city's lifestyle very quickly. I began to feel more confident living there, grew quickly and learned how to cope as successfully as the city's other residents did. I observed people around me carefully.

My grandma and my mother had wasted their time, worrying about me in the city. The city wasn't as dangerous as everyone had expected. It began to appear beautiful, modern, and luxurious to me. It had a youthful look and healthy activities. Saigon's people were friendly and very fashionable, and the young people in Saigon were very active and opened-minded, working hard to stay in step with the city's changing economy and lifestyle. I felt no pressure or anxiety about living in the big city, once I got it, after all.

I was so excited to have finally become a college student, too. Students had come to my university from all over Vietnam, and I loved meeting and getting to know them. I did receive the promised government grants and scholarships I had been told I would receive. The government gave those of us on grants and scholarships money, food, clothes, and many personal supplies every month and continued to do so throughout my four years in college. They even provided us a place to live, if we needed one.

There was one hitch, of course: those of us who received grants and scholarships actually 'belonged' to the government; we were their 'possessions,' in a sense and had to live by their rules.

I was now completely independent of my family for the very first time. My parents didn't need to worry about me or support me financially. I took care of myself. Although my scholarship was small, I still could survive on it without any problem. I had actually made it: I had that new life that I had dreamed about for so long but didn't think would ever be mine.

I lived with my oldest brother Ton's family who lived in my sister-in-law's uncle's house; her uncle was in the military and lived in a foreign country. Ton was in Saigon because he had graduated with his Masters Degree in economics and worked for a big manufacturing plant in Bien Hoa. This house was about three miles from school, and it took me approximately ten minutes to get to school on my bike from home.

The house was located on a crowded and noisy highway right in the center of the city. Ten of us shared the house's one little bathroom, and that number did not include some of our unexpected visitors, who 'dropped by' and spent the night sometimes. Although our house was very tight because there were so many of us living in it, it was still so much better than the housing in the dorms. We worked and lived together peacefully. Each morning, everyone left the house early and did not return home until dark. That gave me plenty of quiet time during the day to study after school, and I didn't have to sleep by the bell, eat by the bell, or stand on line forever, waiting to receive my food at meal times.

The realities of the lives of all college students of my generation were horrifying because all of us were actually very poor and completely dependent on the government. I felt especially sorry for students who had to live in the dorms: they had to exist in inhumane conditions. Because their housing was free, the students were supposed to accept and deal with whatever they were given without complaint. Eight students were placed in one, tiny, little dorm room that should have housed only one person. The dorm rooms were dark, very filthy, and lacked electricity and water. One very weak light bulb hung from each room's ceiling so that students who lived in the room could tell where they were in the room, if they had to get up during the night. But no one could study or sleep very well in these dim rooms: students were stacked, one on top of the other, in funky, old bunk beds that made terrible, creaking noises anytime anyone stirred in her sleep.

Dorm food was even more disgusting. Every day, students waited in line after school to get their meals: buckets of rice mixed with weeds and flowers. Sometimes they also found surprises in their food: rubber bands or small rocks. They were forced to exist on a few stringy vegetables, a couple of slices of pig fat, and a bowl of vegetable broth. Starved for protein and other necessary sources of nutrition, most of my friends were exhausted from a lack of the nutrients good food would have provided them. They all looked very pale and came to class with empty stomachs or stomachs half full of sugar from their rice, which lacked any real nutrition.

I was so shocked: the university was destroying its own students' health, and one day, some of these very same students, whom the university had sickened and weakened, might earn accolades for the government! However, the government must have thought that they should be happy just to have been admitted and given free food, rather than having to stay home with their families, struggling day by day to find any food. The government expected them to be grateful because they didn't have to work for their food. The poorer students didn't have the money to buy a ticket to go home whenever they wished, so they were stuck at school, living in such awful conditions until there was a big celebration, like the Chinese New Year, when their parents could send them money to come home.

I felt so terrible about the living conditions of my classmates. Most of them had come from other provinces in central Vietnam, where people were called "dog eat rock" and "chicken eat salt." Those insults were intended to insult their poverty. Most of the rest of the students were from South Vietnam. None of them had a choice as to where they lived at school, and their parents were just like mine: poor and desperate. They probably were so happy their children had been given the opportunity to go to college and improve their lives.

Compared to my classmates, I was living in heaven. I could go home to visit my family every week, if I chose, because I lived in a private house. I cooked my own, wholesome food. I spent my freedom any way I wanted to. I didn't have to go to bed before the light bulb was turned off in each dorm room. Although my house was crowded, I felt so much more secure than my classmates. I didn't have to worry about my personal belongings being stolen, as students who lived in the dorm did. I could stay up late at night to do my work without being bothered by security patrols who made sure the students didn't over-use electricity.

However, in another sense, the stress all of us studying at the university felt was equal. We had been born in the wrong decade because the economy was so awful in our country; therefore, families exerted great pressure on and high expectations of all of us to succeed and thrive and rise above the levels at which they had had to live and raise us.

Agricultural accounting, my major, was considered to be at the bottom of the list of majors at the university that could lead to good career assignments. The major at the top of the list was tax and revenue, and all the students whose parents were Communists were allowed to choose this major. The second best major was industry and trade, but being allowed to choose this major depended on how perfect a student's resume was.

Those of us in agricultural accounting felt left behind, and not many of us were even interested in majoring in this field. We were essentially neglected, compared to the students allowed to major in the other fields. Those students majoring in the top tier fields were also luckier than us because they could also lean on their rich and powerful parents. Although our school careers had just begun, those students already knew where they were going to work after graduation. They talked constantly about the job options that were open to them, once they had graduated.

Although we all attended the same auditorium lectures every day, the students in my agricultural accounting class always sat in a little corner in the auditorium clumped together. The university's principal tried to convince us that there were equal opportunities for each and every one of us. But we knew we already bore those invisible marks on our foreheads that made us low-class students. We were on our own. No one was there for us to lean on.

I became careless about my agricultural major because I thought to myself, 'Oh, I have four more years to switch into something else." Bad idea. I was sitting on my pride of having been admitted to college. I just accepted my major.

I had been discriminated against in my hometown, and the material we were studying didn't mean as much to me as it did to most of my classmates. Still, I was determined to be happy and focus on my future, which was going to be the best I could make it, despite the lowly slot into which I had been stuck at school and despite the discrimination I felt as a result. Some of my classmates could not bear the discrimination, and they desperately wanted to switch to a different class.

Unlike them, I actually enjoyed sitting in the corner of the auditorium, listening to the privileged students from North Vietnam talking together. They boasted about their filthy rich, Communist families and of the big chunks of money they had to spend on their shoes and clothes. Learning about their luxurious lives, when I was wearing four-year-old hand-me-downs from my older sister, excited me. I loved to listen to their stories about the most expensive restaurants they had dined in with their friends in the city, while I lived on my meager, monthly stipend from the government.

I was still determined to survive and finish my four years in college without a problem. That would be my miracle, and I believed that if I could reach that goal, my life could be just as fascinating as those of the rich students. I knew in my heart I was more than equal to the hard work required of me, and I had the patience and drive I knew I needed to succeed.

There was only one hitch to my independence: I had shouldered and vowed I would honor that responsibility for the survival of my family. I carried that burden of responsibility in my heart, one that I taken on alone. What made it so hard was that, right then, I was so helpless to improve their situation: I was a brand new college student without an extra cent.

So I decided I should do the responsible thing right <u>now</u>: I would look for a job that would enable me to send money home to my parents. I couldn't ignore them all, who had stood behind me all the way, any more than I could ignore my family's tragic situation back home. The government had let my mother and the rest of the family down, too, once again.

As always, I came up with a great idea that involved the rich students in school. I simply took advantage of them: I bought rice and groceries from them every month to resell on the black market. Those wealthy students, who didn't need to take home rice, a couple pounds of sugar, laundry soap, or a pair of bicycle tires, needed someone who was willing to stand in line at the supply department to pick up their supplies and groceries for them. I fit the bill perfectly to handle *that* job, as I had done this kind of work ever since I was a child. I paid the students fairly for what I bought from them and still made a good profit for reselling these items on the black market. My main aim was to help my parents, which this job helped me to do.

I became popular in school because of my little 'trading post,' and more and more customers sought me out as the days went by. I was successful with my little business, and my classmates began calling me the 'trading specialist.'

Every single day after classes, I went right to supply department, waiting to buy goods from other students. The woman in charge of the office wasn't too happy to see me there: she knew what I was up to and wanted a cut of the sales I made. She always gave me dirty looks, as soon as I opened the supply room's front door. She raised her voice at me and rolled her eyes dramatically, trying to get rid of me. I simply offered a higher price, just to get more clients.

I discovered how thick a skin I had had to develop because of my life's tough experiences and because of my father's smiling example; my skin was thick enough to ignore every one around me, even those fighting with me to buy what *they* had to sell. I never gave up, even if I had to lose some profit. I kept a big smile on my face, even when I felt annoyed at the supply room lady. I bought everything I could throughout the school day until its end.

Then I repackaged the rice in forty-pound bags and loaded these onto a tricycle cart, which people used in Saigon for transportation around the city and which was propelled by a man who pedaled from behind. In the heat and dusty smoke in the city, I became filthy and exhausted. My clothes got dirty and soaked with sweat, and I myself was starving for food. But I dared not to leave my business area because some one else might steal my clients.

At the market, I sat on a tall pile of rice bags and packages of other groceries that I had bought at school. The black market wasn't too far away from my school. I looked at it as another battlefield that I had to fight my way through–and win! And I had won before. It wasn't considered appropriate for a college student to be hanging around the black market and dealing with the buyers there. But I had no choice. It was my plan.

I was so worried that friends might see me there, even though they knew I had been doing this for the entire school year. I always wore a big-brimmed, ugly old hat that covered my face, to prevent anyone from recognizing me.

It turned out that the people in the black market loved me! They always wanted to buy from me. They paid whatever I charged, without negotiating. They didn't want to barter with me because the economy was so bad that even rice and groceries had become very, very valuable. They treated me like a queen. I was proud of myself, but I also felt shame about doing something that no other student would think of doing. I was really good at making money, which I needed to send home, but I also felt regret for fighting with people at school because I was trying to be first in line to buy things before they could buy them.

I was very busy every day from early in the morning until dark. Unlike other students, I rarely had time to rest or hang out with my friends after school. I was always in a hurry to get out of class so I could get to my side job. Most of my classmates went to see movies or listened to music together; they were free enough just to enjoy spending time with each other, while I worked my hardest, both to succeed in college and to help my family to go on.

I was very careful about not buying things for myself. I lived happily on what I was receiving and with what things I already had. I saved every last cent I earned to give to my family to pay bills and buy food, and I didn't mind sacrificing for all of them; I knew someday, I, too, would live a better life. My whole family was much more important to me than my own needs. I was happy and proud of myself. My heart was full of love and so much hope for a greater future. And so, I didn't feel ashamed about sitting on top of a cart full of rice or standing in line just to buy a few soap bars at the store. I bet there were very few students who would have done what I was doing because they didn't want to lose face with their friends.

I went home every weekend to see my parents. I usually took the last bus from Saigon on Saturday afternoon. It was crowded, filthy, and very uncomfortable, but it was a lot cheaper than private transportation. It took almost three hours to get from the city to my hometown twenty miles away. The bus was also full of chickens and pigs, and bicycles teetered on top. Inside the bus, products of all kinds were stacked together with hundreds of people who trembled against each other. Lots of times I got home almost at midnight because the bus had broken down in the middle of nowhere, from being overloaded, or because it was just too old and just plain worn out.

Weekends were always the most exciting time for my family. I brought home not only the money that I had earned, but also a lot of groceries and dried fishes, which were my father's favorite food. I would never forget to buy my mother a few packs of her favorite seasoning, mushrooms, vegetables, and spices for cooking. My grandma loved fruits and sweet treats that you couldn't find in Cu Chi. Of course, I brought my little sister snacks, as well.

"You bring home more than dried fish, Loan. You bring great happiness and laughter to us all," my Buddha father said and smiled broadly at me. We would all stay up until midnight, talking and laughing together. My father loved to listen to my stories about school, the city, and what I had gone through each day. My father would not touch his dinner on Saturday evening until I arrived home. No matter how late my bus arrived, he waited on our doorstep, watching for it to pull into town.

"You are our center, Loan," my big sister Chau said to me. "The house is so quiet and empty of your laughter when you aren't here." My parents were so pleased to have a daughter like me; apparently, they told everybody about everything I was doing.

I spent most of my spare time at home in the summer. Usually my classmates took off and went camping or traveling together in different provinces, but things were different for me because my mother was so superstitious; she wouldn't let me go anywhere that crossed a river or a mountain. She didn't allow me to take a train or get on a boat to travel far away from the city with my friends from college. She told me that a fortuneteller had told her that I would not have good luck with traveling. My friends teased me for being over-protected, but they would never understand how important I was to my parents. If I lost my income or anything happened to me, that meant I could not continue to help them, and it would be catastrophic for them. So, in a way, I understood how they—especially my mother—felt.

Compared to my classmates, I began to see that I was a lot luckier than they were. When I arrived at the university, I thought my family was as poor as people could be. But listening to them talk about their lives at home, in fact, I learned that all my classmates' situations were even more miserable than mine. Their parents probably made enough money to feed the family, but it cost them a lot of extra money to support a child in college. The government scholarship was so small, and the cost of living in the big city was so high. The students who lived away from home needed lots more money for clothes, extra food, entertainment, and transportation.

I always had cash in hand to help my friends, too, when they were short of money, and I tried to help support my friends in college. They admired me for being so independent and so generous. But my friends never knew about the heavy burden of responsibility I carried in my heart.

I was getting close to earning my four-year degree, if everything continued to go as smoothly as it had been. It wasn't too hard during the first couple of years in college, as one professor had told us as we began our college years. Now I had more time to have fun, hone my strongest skills, and work my side job. I also took a sewing class at night, which was held right next door to my college, and I began making children's clothes that I sold in the stores. And I liked to sing and performed as a singer and dancer in some musicals put on for special school events or anniversaries.

I truly loved my new life as college student in Saigon. I was young and full of energy, and I simply kept one eye sharply trained on that bright and happy future I knew was waiting for me. The big city had its own kind of beauty that my little town didn't have. In Saigon, the horizon was punctuated with many majestic skyscrapers, which I could see from miles away; in Cu Chi, our house was the town's tallest building!

I lived in Saigon's sixth district, where most Chinese people who had come to Saigon from the country lived. At night I liked to walk down to Chinatown, which was located about a half-mile from my house. The stores were open all night long and sold everything in the world. (In Cu Chi, all doors shut right after dark.) All the Chinese restaurants were crowded, and the private retail stores were busy. All the farmers brought their produce, fresh fish, poultry, and meat from home to sell at the evening market in Saigon. I loved to hear the loud cries of Chinese vendors selling noodles late at night on the street or the interesting sounds they made by knocking two pieces of wood together in a certain way, almost as if they were playing musical instruments—a unique selling technique! I will never forget that wonderful, musical sound. I could buy all the groceries I needed for a quarter of the regular prices, since, at that late hour, people were trying to get rid of their goods and hurry home.

People poured out of their homes to get some cooler air at night after the heat had subsided. They shopped and enjoyed delicious food of all kinds in sidewalk cafes; food in the cafes was very cheap. If a breeze somehow miraculously had made its way to Chinatown, it carried the wonderful scents of Chinese food.

Chinese music and the cries of the vendors blended together, creating in Chinatown a very unique and special corner of the city.

At the very end of my day, I liked the quiet of night when the whole city was falling asleep. I could hear the footsteps and the whoosh of the street cleaners' brooms, sweeping the streets. I couldn't believe a big, crowded, noisy, and stress-filled city that had burned like a big fire ball just hours before could finally quiet and cool itself down to sleep.

Children who had grown up in Saigon knew the rush of the city. Young children, older children, and teenagers alike all went to school, not only during the daytime, but at night, as well; they took extra classes in English, math, science, and in other areas. Their parents paid more attention to their kids' future than to anything else. I realized the children who lived in the countryside, like those in Cu Chi, were missing out on too many opportunities. They were lucky enough to spend a few years in school so they could read or write but never thought about a career. The children in Cu Chi who grew up in farming families were stuck on their families' farms. The children who grew up in the marketplace would become storefront workers, just as their parents had. And of course, in the poorest families, the children tended to become servants to some rich family or handled the heavy labor work in town. The circle turned and turned, from generation to generation, without any progress or improvement being made. I felt so blessed by God and thankful to my parents, who had given me an opportunity to create my own future.

Living in the city for four years helped me eventually discover the person I really was. For a long time in my life, I saw myself at first as a pitiful, young girl who needed a little bit of time to adjust to her new environment; I felt back then a lot like an earthworm that had just crawled out of the soil: I needed a thicker shell to survive under the heat of the hot city sun. I also needed a big rainstorm to wash off the dirt of my past life from my body, so I could grow to stand up taller without the extra weight of the past holding me down. I did not wear fashionable clothes and sometimes suffered the stares or laughter of passersby. But, deep down, I always knew that it was the person I am inside that truly mattered.

On the other hand, I knew that people are complex. I had grown up freely, like grass, strong and healthy, even without cultivation; but it was wild and plain grass, nevertheless, without any character. My ideas were always different from anyone else's in the family and in the community. I was as stubborn as bamboo is to get rid of; I liked to argue, sometimes to defend my opinion, whether I was right or wrong, and sometimes just to argue; my father yelled at me constantly for arguing with my siblings over what was really nothing. I also loved to argue with my grandmother about religion because I didn't believe anything she said.

I could entertain people around me by making a joke but saying anything serious to get people's attention. I was intelligent enough to design my dreams, but I was not clever enough to make myself look normal like the rest of my brothers and sisters. I couldn't find a shirt and a pair of pants that went together well enough. There was nothing I liked that didn't make people laugh. I was eccentric and made no sense, as my sister always told me. No matter how hard I tried, I still couldn't get rid of the earthworm part of me inside. It was rooted in my thoughts, my behavior, and my personality, as was the young person I was growing into at school. But earthworms are also very necessary in enriching the ground from which so many things we depend on grow, I reminded myself; so maybe, somehow, I would find my special place in the world, even if I wasn't normal.

I was having the most wonderful time of my life with new adventures and discovering many incredible things. I loved Saigon, but I also loved my hometown. Each had given me such different experiences, all of which were so important and meaningful in my life. My four years in college were short, and it would soon be over, but I had enjoyed them and learned as much as I could from the entire experience.

CHAPTER SIX

JUNE, 2009

Rick told me later that I slept right through the coffee, tea, and "a little something to munch on" service; but he had taken something for me, just in case, and told me none of it was very good. Oh, how I yearned for my father's tasty, morning rice bowls!

1987

Out of the clear blue sky with no warning, my happiness plummeted like a rocket speeding through the atmosphere back into the ocean: my father had collapsed from a stroke. It occurred during my first summer break from college. The weather that day was so nice and warm, and my father had gone off to do errands with my brother-in-law for their business. My father would never guessed that that would be the last such trip he would enjoy. No one thought for a second that a strong, healthy, active, and very optimistic person like my father was walking along with a devil at his side.

My father was helping my brother-in-law unload fertilizer at the farm when my father suddenly fell into a heap onto the ground. My brother-in-law rushed him home, and then we took him to the closest hospital. He was immediately admitted to the emergency room, where our family gathered.

The doctor examined him and diagnosed my father with a serious heart problem and high blood pressure. My knowledge of anatomy and hearts was far too limited. I knew people could die from several serious heart diseases, but I never thought they died from the one that my father was suffering.

I was shocked into silence when the doctor explained how much danger my father was in. He told me my father might never get well again. The doctor also said that if my father were lucky enough, he would live but that he would be disabled forever.

The doctor *had* to have made a big mistake. Nothing felt real to me. My father wasn't supposed to get sick. My dearest father just could *not* be sick. That constant smile, encouragement, laughter...I decided that the doctor had no idea what he was talking about. No one on earth would get as sick as he was because of a minor fall. I would not allow it that my father had to give up his beautiful, active life because of a minor accident. They didn't know with whom they were dealing!

In the emergency room, my father was still conscious, but the left side of his body was completely paralyzed and numb. He was lay on the bed with his eyes shut. He looked pale and very tired; he breathed heavily and did not move at all. He opened his eyes when I called his name, but he couldn't say a word. His voice shook when he tried to talk.

My mother was unable to handle anything this serious and emotional; she was so stoic the rest of the time that something like this tested her ability to remain driven and goal-oriented: it simply opened a flood of all she had been holding in. She broke down, waiting at the door of the emergency room, and she cried and cried and cried.

The doctor's orders were that my father stay at the hospital for a while to receive treatment and so that they could watch him for complications for a while. Except for giving my father some sleeping pills, he did not receive any other "treatment" during the "treatment" process over the next two weeks.

We waited.

I stayed at the hospital every day to take care of my father after he had been admitted. They were able to give me a chair to sit on next to his bed so I could get some sleep at night; the hospital was so over-crowded, my father had to share a room with eight other patients, and a chair was all they could fit in the room for me. All day long, visitors flooded my father's room, coming in and going out again, as if they were in the public market and the patients were slabs of meat they were buying. Nighttime was even worse. Patients cried names out loud, called for help, whined, moaned in their sleep, and complained to the nurses about their needs or just in general about their problems. They were frightened.

My father's bed was so filthy: it had never been changed! It made me sick. Once, after a patient was released, I noticed that the nurses neglected to clean the bed or change the sheets before the next patient was brought into the bed. I started feeling uncomfortable and doubted the hospital's policies and "treatments." I finally demanded that the doctor let me take my father home, so he could recuperate at his own home.

Home is always the best place on earth, especially if you are low or sick. My father looked so much better the minute he walked through the front door of our home. The medication they had been giving him at the hospital was eating at his body and had only made him progressively weaker and weaker. Giving him a shower helped him feel refreshed immensely—more like a human being—instead of having to lie in someone else's filthy sheets or go without a single bath at the hospital for two whole weeks.

Slowly, my father began to get stronger, day by day. He started getting up, eating a little food, and saying some words. We lifted him up out of bed, helped him to stand, and got him to walk around the house in the morning. We helped him do some easy exercises the doctor had recommended.

And then his left hand began to work again after a few weeks! Another miracle. He could hold objects and squeeze my hand.

I was so thankful that I had been home–not at school–when he had had the stroke.

Besides making sure that he got his medication and exercise, I started looking for alternative treatments, such as acupuncture and Chinese herbs. I searched everywhere for the best physicians, anyone qualified to cure my father's illness. I wanted so badly for my father to be healed before I went back to school. I wanted to watch him riding his little moped to the farm every morning. I wanted to hear his loud greeting when I arrived home every weekend. I wanted him to be healthy, the cheerful, Buddha father he always had been to me.

By the time my summer break was finally over, my father's condition had stopped improving. I packed up my luggage, got prepared for a new school year, and I told my father I would find some good doctors in the big city, so he could finally recover very soon. In addition to researching the government hospital in Saigon, I looked for some private doctors. One of my father's friends introduced me to a heart disease specialist who happened to have an office not too far away from where I lived in Saigon.

I took my father for an appointment to see this new doctor, who gave him a "treatment" of some kind and prescriptions to control his high blood pressure. But he did not promise that my father would ever return to normal, since he said the stroke had damaged some blood vessels in his brain.

I didn't want my father to get discouraged by the doctor's diagnosis, and I simply refused to believe that doctor myself. I wanted my father to live happily and to hold onto and continue to follow his positive-thinking outlook.

My father told me after that visit, "There is only a little, tiny numbness on my head that bothers me a lot; but the rest of me is fine," he said, and it did begin to seem as if he were feeling better every day.

And suddenly, it was time for me to return to Saigon.

It was so difficult for me to concentrate on my schoolwork as deeply as I had all last year. All I could think about was my father's health. I looked forward to every weekend when I got to see him and make sure he was still doing well. I even skipped classes to help my mother to take him to the doctor. I was the one my whole family depended on, always; somehow, I–and no one else in the family–had earned my title, "The One Who Could" accomplish whatever needed to be done.

My grades began to drop, and then I failed the first class I had ever failed in my *life* that first semester of my senior year. The college's policy was that a student who had failed one course during the first semester would be dismissed and kicked out of school if she failed two classes during her second semester.

Panic set in. Panic about school. Panic about my father. Panic about graduation and my future! I tried so hard to focus solely on my schoolwork: my success at school was the only key I needed to ensure myself a solid future: if I were unable to support my family because I was unable to graduate and be qualified to get a good job, it would be a disaster for them–and me. It had been my dream for so long.

I decided that to try to rush my father's healing wasn't a good idea: only time would tell. I could not heal him. I tried to calm down and wait until my school performance became more stable. I quit skipping classes and spent more time at school and in the libraries to study. I was still making money with my business, but I cut back as far as I could on my expenses in order to save as much as they needed for my father's medications. I also decided not to go home Friday nights after classes but to wait until really late Saturday evening after I had completed all of my homework.

I spent every Sunday at home with my family, basically taking care of my father. I took him to see his acupuncturist on his motorcycle and to visit his best friend, just as he used to do before he got sick. I seemed to be the only one in the family who was able to get him up and get him out the house. I tried to keep him active and moving around, instead of lying in bed and complaining about his pain. I made him do some exercises to keep his blood circulating. I gave him a massage, as the physical therapist had trained me to do. I helped him to hold a bowl, use a spoon and chopsticks so he could feed himself. He never fought with me when I bothered him or told him what to do; but he did not comply with anyone else in the family who tried to do these same things for him. He was so cranky and became more and more difficult, but not with me. I think because he saw me only once a week, he probably tried his best not to disappoint me on that one day I was home, even if he wasn't feeling too good. He hadn't complained to me at all, even though my mother told me, "He can't take it any longer." as my mother told me. He complained all the time about headaches and the numbness, which tortured him all day and all night: never heard a word about either problem myself.

Time flew by. It had almost been one year since the day my father got sick, and now my second year in college was finally over. Two students in my class had been kicked out of school at the end of the year for not meeting the school's rules with regard to failing classes. Our class held a little goodbye party for those friends, who weren't as lucky as I had been in this challenging and troubling time. It was also the celebration party for the rest of us who were still moving forward for the next two years.

What ever would I have done if I had been in their shoes? I couldn't go back to my hometown because I had been kicked out of college, a big failure. I felt chills when I thought about that.

The next two years dragged on and on because of new challenges waiting ahead for me, but at least I could relax and spend a little more time with my family over the summer without being worried about losing my key to the future. School also was going to be easier from now on than it had been when we had just started learning our main subject, instead of beating around the bushes of Communist theories. The theories were definitely confusing, general, and complicated. Now, in my last two years, I finally was going to learn something real and something that would be helpful in my career.

The government wanted us to become "well-rounded," not merely experts in our respective majors. The university also required that we master more than coursework in our majors: we were required to work on a farm for eight weeks of each year and to take three months of military training each year, during which time we were trained to use an assortment of real guns and weapons and to fight on a battlefield, in case the government needed us to do so. We had had to agree to undergo this training before we were finally accepted into the university. Each one of us was "government property:" forever. No exceptions.

It was exhausting.

In my third year, our entire class was split into our four different majors, so I studied mostly with the rest of the agricultural accounting majors. I didn't have to watch the competition between the wealthy Communist princes and princesses. I had become more cranky, critical, and negative since my father got sick. I didn't want to listen to their beautiful life stories any longer when mine had been so sad and full of darkness and pain. Jealousy shot through every fiber of my body when I thought about how much luckier those people were than I. Their parents weren't sick on their deathbeds and suffering like my father was. They were rich and powerful enough to have access to good doctors and expensive hospitals for any treatment they might need. My family had been down and falling further and further down for so many years; now, their lives were only going to get worse if my father got any sicker.

The most beautiful time in my life, the one I had looked to enjoy all of my life, and my golden dreams seemed to be vanishing before my eyes. I wasn't interested in participating in school activities, as I used to do. I preferred to be alone and sit somewhere quiet after class. My family at home was on my mind constantly. I wanted to live an innocent life, one just like those students who had nothing to worry about but themselves. I wished I had a lot of money, just like they did, to find the best doctor possible and buy better or stronger or more appropriate medications for my father. My heart was breaking into bits, as I watched whatever small resources we had had disappear.

My mother started borrowing money from other people for the family to live on. Her debt became bigger and more and more impossible to pay off, since our income was shrinking at the same time. I felt sick at being so helpless; whatever I *was* able to do for my family wasn't even enough any more.

My father's condition remained the same, even after a year of "treatments." The medications didn't do anything to improve him. He still complained every single day about his headaches and the numbness on his head, which apparently had gotten worse and was making his life more miserable than death.

We didn't have access to any x-rays or scans so that the doctor might make a more accurate diagnosis. The doctor simply guessed his problem had been caused by a stroke that had prevented blood from circulating properly and regularly to his brain. Sleeping pills were prescribed to put him to sleep and soothe his pain. The drugs only made my father move as slowly and mechanically as a robot.

My sweet, positive father was disappearing before our eyes! He often got angry and refused to take his medication, and we began to worry more about his emotional condition than his physical condition. Something much more serious than heart disease and stroke had to be causing the changes we were witnessing in my father. Soon, my father became terrified of the doctor and eventually refused to see him. He only wanted to get out of bed and move around, not take pills that made him sleep all day. Eastern and Western medicine, modern pills, Chinese herbs, acupuncture, or physical therapy had all failed to improve his condition, even a bit.

Then my father became adamant about wanting to give up. He decided we should not spend any more money because what we had purchased so far hadn't helped him make any progress, and it was all dragging us down with him. Or sometimes he would say he just wanted to give up because he couldn't tolerate any more of the pain. He rarely ever talked to my mother, except to tell her how miserable he was. He rarely smiled or laughed. He had turned completely inside out and sometimes burst out in tears and cried from the early morning until night or for as long as he stayed awake.

My dear, smiling, "most handsome father in the village," who was my spine and guide, had lost his abundant enthusiasm for life and confidence. His personality wasn't his anymore. One thing—and one thing only—never changed in my father while he lived: he sat at the front door of our house every, single Saturday evening, waiting for me to come home from Saigon, regardless of how late the last bus was scheduled to arrive. The others told me that he looked forward all week long to listening to my stories about my `life in the big city. With my imagination, my father could feel the real world out there that he was now missing, could see a lively picture of the entire city, and remember the rush of a city lifestyle. My voice broke the silence in the somber house, and my laughter brought everyone together, as my older sister Chau used to tell me. I was my father's ears, eyes, and his heart. Apparently, I played a very important role in his life when he was disabled, depressed, and hopeless. It was then, and only then, that he laughed, smiled, and listened very closely to all of my opinions on political issues, our country's economic problems, the environment's being degraded by crime's increasing in the country. I tried to collect as many stories as I could over six days so I could entertain my father when I got home. He ate well and relaxed, but only when I was around.

One night, while I was telling Dad about the advertising that they hung in the trees in Saigon, on lampposts, and in school yards for everything from available housing to hemorrhoids, he even chuckled, reached out to hold my hand in his, and said, "You are a gifted child and the soul of our family, Loan." His eyes glistened brightly. He saw me as solely responsible for keeping him alive, and I thought I couldn't bear the painful weight of it all much longer.

One day, I noticed tears in his eyes; he was alone at the time. I suddenly had an inexplicable sense that something really serious was happening to my father that would gradually take him away, altogether, from us. I so desperately needed him to be alive with us: that was all I wanted.

My mother was almost hysterical about my father's dying. She went to all the temples in town to pray for my father's health. She looked for famous fortunetellers and masters: anyone who could explain my father's mysterious and constant headache; it had become so severe that all the doctors had given up on trying to treat it at all.

She continued to look desperately for any treatment she could find for my father's illnesses that we hadn't tried yet. Science, paranormal phenomena, or the magic of superstition: my mother tried them all. Relatives suggested that I go to the mountain to see a famous medium; the medium told me that somebody had put a curse on my father, and she gave me a voodoo to take home. This voodoo was a piece of paper printed with a weird symbol. At her instruction, I burned that piece of paper, rubbed its ashes on our chickens' eggs and rolled the eggs all over my father's head. Then I took the eggs back to the medium after three days, as she instructed. The next thing that happened sounds absolutely, impossibly impossible, but I cut that egg and found a curse inside! The curse was an old, green piece of paper, six inches long and two inches wide, covered with moldy spots and strange, black ink that had bled into the paper. It was rotten at one corner from the moisture in the egg. She said that curse had been buried under the concrete floor of our house for over thirty years. She was afraid it was now too late to save my father's life.

My heart froze.

I took the voodoo home to show my parents. I told them the medium had said my father was in danger. I tried not to believe what she had also said about the curse: that a heated fight between a carpenter and my father led the carpenter to place the curse on my father under the very ground of our house when the carpenter was building it! I was terrified because there *was* evidence to back the bizarre story up! I will never forget that medium and my experience with her as long as I live.

I resolutely believed that my father could be cured and become healthy again if only we could find a better doctor. But my father continued to decline, as our financial resources shriveled. Our family's pick-up truck had been our main source of income, but it began to break down all the time, stranding my brother-in-law in the middle of nowhere. It was so old it wasn't worth repairing or something we could even afford to repair.

And then, people stopped loaning money to my mother, as she hadn't paid back the first loans she had taken from them. My mother now had to fight the biggest battle she had ever faced alone: how to make sure our family survived. She was so stressed and cried every single day, feeling guilty for not being able to come up with a solution to save us all.

That was when my grandma made her decision to sell her half of the house to help ease my mother's broken spirit and heart. She said that she and my youngest uncle didn't need much space to live in. Since my mother was her only daughter, she was very worried about her. My grandma handed the four pieces of gold she received for selling the house to my mother, whose big eyes, full of tears, said "Thank you," so clearly.

The four pieces of gold my grandmother got from selling her house didn't last long, once my mother paid off her debts and fixed the truck. She spent whatever was left carefully, basically on my father's doctors and medications, and waited as patiently as she could for all of her children to grow up, so she could get more support, especially from me, since my graduation from college was not too far away.

This small windfall from my grandmother helped me feel a little more confident again and have faith that my father would be healed, once we had found a better doctor in the city who could cure my father's mystery headaches and other physical problems. I knew my father would be so happy and proud when he saw me graduate, build a real career, and earn a good salary to take home. I prayed that my father would at least remain as stable as he was until I had a job. My father counted down every weekend that was left before I graduated. Our celebration together of my biggest accomplishment yet I *knew* would help him feel relief and regain his old optimism.

We were running out of time, and we didn't even know it. In early June of 1987, when I was only six weeks away from taking my final exam, I was called out of class to go to the office. My father had been admitted to Trung Vuong Hospital, a very famous medical facility in the city. He was in very critical condition, the message had also said. The whole world spun and flipped upside down–again.

I flew to the hospital. My father was unconscious on his bed, surrounded by the doctor and nurses in the emergency room. My mother and oldest sister were crying at the door to his room.

My sister said, in a low whisper and trying not to cry, "He was feeling the same as he always does when he got up early in the morning today. Suddenly, he started vomiting and collapsed. We took him to the local hospital, and they transferred him here immediately because his condition was so serious. The local hospital doesn't have the medical equipment necessary to deal with this new problem." And she dissolved into tears again, and I held her for a while.

We waited for the results of whatever testing they had done from the doctor. We weren't allowed to go into my father's room, but they said we could wait at the door to his room. My heart stop beating whenever the nurses wheeled a gurney out of the Emergency Room and passed my father's door with a dead person on it, covered from head to toe with a white sheet. I felt sick to my stomach and shivered when I thought about how the next patient being wheeled on a gurney out of this room could be my father. He just *couldn't* leave without saying goodbye to me. I prayed desperately to God that he not take my father now. I had so many things still to tell him. He *had* to stay until I accomplished what I promised in the vow that I had made to him. My father's door got blurrier and blurrier. Our solitude and helplessness cut my heart.

Finally, the doctor finally told my mother that my father was temporarily being transferred to the Intensive Care Unit, while they waited for the results of more tests they had just done. They couldn't tell yet what had caused this complication, except that his blood pressure was extremely high again.

We followed the nurse who was pushing my father on a gurney to the Intensive Care Unit. My father was still alive, but he was as pale as a dead body, a cold stone. His eyes were closed, and he did not respond to our calls to him. His chest expanded when he breathed, but the rest of his whole body had shut down. He would wake up in a few hours, the nurse said, because the doctor had just given him a shot to help him relax and to lower his blood pressure, and she said the shot would put him to sleep for awhile.

The Intensive Care Unit felt like a morgue. It was silent. The white walls and white sheets all around reminded me of my uncle's dead body, which I will always remember having seen when I was only four years old. Why did my father belong here? Eight other patients lay in that room with my father, all in critical condition. Some were ready to move back to the regular patients' area to begin to recover, but some were waiting to leave forever.

No MRIs had been done, no x-rays taken, no scans made. The skills of the medical staff were very obviously poor. We were helplessly being led by the helpless.

My mother and I sat next to my father's bed, waiting. Every tick of the clock's hands struck a gong in my head. It had grown dark outside, but we stayed with my father all day; neither my mother nor I had had anything to eat or drink.

Nighttime at the hospital was silent and eerie, especially in the Intensive Care Unit: I could almost feel death floating in the air around our heads, waiting for the right time to lead the next one away. My mother panicked when the patient next to my father died quite suddenly. He had been talking and laughing just minutes before with his family, and then, he was silent. His family sobbed in a ring around his bed.

My father was still asleep, his beautiful face so pale, his eyebrows and forehead wrinkled, his slack skin seeming to fall off his bones. He looked ancient. Whatever disease he had was slowly destroying his body and suffocating the life within him. He was breathing rapidly, which showed that his body was experiencing severe pain. I kept rubbing my father's arms and legs with ointment to try to warm him up. I massaged his head and shoulders so he wouldn't get too stiff from having lain in bed too long. I stuck more pillows under his legs and dropped a couple drops of water on his lips in case he was thirsty and so they didn't get dry. I tried to fan away the famished flies and mosquitoes that almost seemed to be drooling around his head. I felt his pulse frequently and his nose to make sure he was still breathing.

My father finally woke up again very early in the morning, just as I had begun to fall asleep.

"Will you get me water, Loan? Where am I, Loan?" he asked quietly, but his voice was strong!

I was shocked to hear his voice, and I almost screamed out loud with joy at the sound of it.

"I am cold, Loan. Is there a blanket?" he asked.

My mother and I lifted him up so he could have a drink of water. Then we laid him back down again, since the doctor had ordered that he not get up.

"How long have I been here? Where are the others?" he asked, looking confused and a bit afraid. He didn't know that he wasn't at the local hospital, as he had been asleep for a whole day.

"They will all be here to see you soon, including my mother, dear," she said as soothingly as she could.

I covered him with more of the blanket over his chest and arms to keep them warm. He was breathing more slowly now, and his face looked more relaxed, his skin color regaining its normal, rosey hue.

The doctor came to see him at about seven o'clock in the morning, and my father woke right up. The doctor gave me a prescription but warned me that the medication was very, very scarce and that most hospitals never carried it! It would be difficult and even possibly dangerous for me to look for it.

But I was determined to find some, and I spent half the day searching the entire city, everywhere, every pharmacy, hospital, dry goods store. No luck. And then, after introducing myself to a long string of complete strangers, who had passed me from one to another and then yet another stranger, I found myself facing a lady of about forty years who eagerly showed me all kinds of drugs. Drug smuggling was a very illegal, risky business for which smugglers were sent to jail for a very long time, if caught.

I gave the old lady the doctor's prescription and was shocked when she told me how much it would cost. All the money I had would only allow me to buy a little shot of the medicine. The liquid in a clear tube had no label or packaging. I guessed that I was probably paying too much money for this drug and wondered if it was even real. I didn't trust anything about the whole situation, but it all boiled down to one thing: I had to save my father's life. I handed the lady all of my money, she handed me the little tube as if it were a hot coal, and then she disappeared into thin air around a corner!

The doctor immediately gave my father a shot of the liquid in the tube. He said that the shot could prolong and maintain my father's consciousness, even though his condition would remain very critical.

On the third day after his shot, although my father didn't get up, he stayed awake longer and talked to us for a few minutes. Something serious must have been wrong, something that they didn't want to tell us about. Other patients had been informed of their diagnoses or had been moved from this Intensive Care unit to different units for treatment. We knew nothing.

One minute seemed longer than an hour. My mother and I tensed up every time the doctor came in to visit my father, but he always left, saying nothing, leaving us with no new information, no hope.

All of my brothers and sisters took turns going to see my father at the hospital and then returned home. Every morning I cooked some fresh food at home and brought it to the hospital for my parents before I headed to school. Then, after school, I returned to the hospital to stay with my parents until my brother arrived.

Every moment of all of this was hell for me. I had to prepare for my final examinations, and I had to tend to my father. They were equally important to me, to my pride in my accomplishments so far, to my dreams, and to my future, and I knew they were very important to my father.

"He looks happier and seems to feel more confident when you are here," my mother told me quietly one morning. "He watches the clock for the time he knows you leave school and will return to him."

One more, long week went by. He started complaining and asking the doctor to let him go home because he felt homesick at the hospital. The doctor promised to let him go home at the end of the next week, if he felt better. This excited him, and he began to talk more than he had been and stopped complaining about his discomfort.

Often he turned to me, looking hopeful, and asked, "Do you think someone could cure me by reading my palm?"

I used to read all kind of books about psychics and palm reading, which I borrowed from my grandma. I had learned to look for a lot of signs about a person's destiny, but not my father's.

"I think you will be healthy again, since your palms are warm, and the color in your face is good, Dad. You must think positively because I believe that can make a big difference.

"Your ears are big and beautiful like the Buddha's ears, Father. You will live for at least one hundred years, according to what I have learned, and your good fortune is right around the corner, since the worst three years of your life have past," I told him, trying to sound as excited as possible, hoping with everything in my heart that my white lies would help boost his spirits. "And don't forget that, when you have recovered, you are taking us to China to see your family! Your fondest wish! What a miracle that will be for each one of us!"

He listened to me with a big smile and big tears in his eyes. He probably knew more than any of us that he didn't have much time left with us.

He had frightful nightmares that night. All night long, he mumbled, fought, and yelled in his sleep. He lost his voice. He began to choke and woke up in the middle of one night, scared and panicked. My superstitious mother believed that the spirits of people who had died in this hospital had returned to the Intensive Care Unit to hAuntie him. The doctor gave him sleeping pills but still wouldn't offer us any explanation as to his symptoms. Nothing. Always nothing.

"Am I going to die, Loan?" he asked me every day. "They won't tell me anything! And I don't know!"

I had no idea what to say to that awful question, as I was as in the dark about it as he was.

So, once again, I renewed my search throughout the city for a specialist and a better hospital to no avail. We *still* had not received the results of the doctor's tests. I guessed that they had probably given up on the first day my father was admitted to the hospital; but instead of telling us the truth, I think they preferred that we know nothing and wait for his time to come.

None of us would have guessed that June 5, 1987 would be the last night of his life because my father suddenly became happy and excited—as if by magic!

He sat straight up and exclaimed, "We are going very soon to China to visit my relatives, all of us, together!

"And," he turned to my mother and said with a very serious look, "Never doubt Loan: our family's safety and welfare lie in her hands. She is the one to bring happiness and glory to our family—to every one of us."

I sat down and pulled a chair up next to his bed, took both of his both hands, held them very tightly, and said, "Please do not worry, father. I will do everything I can think of to help our family rise up again, whatever it might be, and to make your dreams come true in a very short time.

"I promise to make you happy and proud of me, just as you think I will do."

My heart was as heavy as a stone after speaking those words: my words went deep in his heart, too.

He talked and laughed a lot that night. "Loan, please do not forget to cook me some bean soup. That might help improve my bowel movements!" and he giggled.

Then my father reached up and put his fragile fingers, which looked like tiny bird bones now, on each of my cheeks and pulled my face gently down closer to his.

"Daughter, I need you to make me a promise. Will you do that for me?" he asked, his voice suddenly beginning to weaken. He must have been tired from all the fun he'd been having, and he was beginning to go. I just sensed it.

I said, "Yes, father. I promise. Yes."

"Good," he replied, his voice fading, as if he were beginning to walk away while talking to me over his shoulder. "Someday, when you can, I want you to go find my family in China and tell them I am gone and that I send them my love. Look into their eyes when you tell them. Will you do that?" His sad eyes blurred with tears that stopped at the rims of his eyelids like water brimming at the very edge of a deep well.

I could only nod 'yes.' I could hardly breathe from trying to keep my grief deep inside and invisible from him. So I nodded and nodded and nodded to make sure he understood I fully meant what I vowed and would fulfill this promise I had made to him. And I knew I would never forget that promise.

"Thank you. You have been such a good daughter. I am so proud and grateful." And he closed his eyes for the last time, tears trickling down his handsome face from the far corners of each eye, but I have believed every day of my life since then that they were contented tears.

The paperwork to make my father's death official was completed. The doctor apologized to my mother for not having saved my father's life. I saw the nurses pushing him on a gurney toward the morgue. I ran beside him. I held his hands really tightly, so he wouldn't feel scared. I wanted no one to bother him before I left him. I even forgot my mother was still lying on the floor where she had dropped in a swoon when he died.

The nurses were trying to get her up when I returned from that long, final journey to the morgue. I collected my father's belongings and led my mother out of the hospital. My older sister had just walked through the hospital gates to visit my father, but she was too late, as was the rest of the family. I felt sorry for my father who was dying when seven of his children were somewhere else. I also felt sad for those of my brothers and sisters who didn't have a chance to say goodbye to their father and hear his last words.

The attendants loaded my father's body into an ambulance and helped my mother—who was about to collapse again at any second—into the ambulance. I climbed in behind her. As the ambulance sped along, I was so afraid that my father was hurt every time the vehicle drove over a bump or hit a pothole. It felt as if the whole city had turned its back and shut its doors on us when we went by.

Out the window, the blue sky turned a steely leaden color and covered the earth with the stench of death and grief. And it seemed to me that my hometown was dying, too, as we got closer to it, its colors and vibrancy fading away.

The ambulance finally arrived at the front door of our house. No sun shone on our backs as we got out of the ambulance, and tears dripped into our footfalls in the dusty path that led to our door.

All of our neighbors were waiting for us along our street at our house. They wanted to pay their respects to my father and welcome him home. I tried to rouse my father before the attendants took him into the house, forgetting, for a moment. I held his hands and walked alongside him on the gurney so that he didn't feel so alone, as the attendants pushed him into the house. Perhaps, I hoped, he even felt happy being home again, after such a long and horrifying journey. His eyes were closed, but his beautiful smile was still on his face: that very expression was forever etched into my heart at that moment.

Thousands of people came to my father's funeral. The townspeople loved him not only because he shared whatever he could share of his own with them and cared about each of them, but also because he was such a good advisor and faithful work partner. Most people in town had received assistance of some kind from my father during his life.

The funeral lasted for three days. The whole town had shut down for my father's farewell, and the traffic was halted for over ten miles. We screamed and cried out to him and went crazy when the elders lit incense for my father: we were furious with the elders for being granted the gift of more time alive than our father had been granted, and we didn't want any of them getting close to his coffin.

The time had come: we had to let him go. It was a very hot, sunny afternoon, and we all walked, numb, in our bare feet to the cemetery behind the coffin, a procession of thousands walking with us, except for my poor mother, who had had to be locked up in her room because her blood pressure had shot up so high from this huge loss. All of a sudden, an overwhelming, gray cloud slid itself across the wide sky and released a pounding, heavy rain that fell in sheets on all of us, just as the coffin was being lowered into the ground. I believe to this day that, at that moment, God was with us, sadly saying goodbye to the finest of fathers—mine.

I prayed the rain would wash off the misfortune and miseries that had hounded us all for so many years. I even wondered if my father tried to take our misery, pain, and heavy burdens with him so that we could have new, lighter lives. That would have been like him.

CHAPTER SEVEN

1987

We all collapsed at home after the funeral. My little sister Kim (?) and I were finally taken to the hospital after the funeral because we were exhausted and overstressed. Everyone in my family fell into horrible depressions. My mother cried every, single day and blamed herself for not taking better care of my father; she felt guilty for not finding the best doctors and a better hospital so that he could have had really good care and treatment. She felt sorry that my father was now so alone out there, wherever he was, when we were all together at home. Thousands of her memories made her cry, and her memories just added weight to our depression whenever she brought one up. Every night we sat together, sobbing and moaning, sorrow the single, common thread holding us all together. We never sat down together as a family at the dinner table the way we used to. Instead, each one of us found his or her own spot to hide, to be alone with our grief, and cry over the truth we could not escape: our beloved father had died.

Then, I became painfully aware of a possibly horrible consequence of our loss that had not even crossed my mind, even once before that moment: with my father gone, I could not bear to lose my mother, as well. She *had* to become strong again and stay healthy to live for and with us.

And so, as my father had prophesied, I was the one to step up, to push everybody forward, and to encourage them to walk ahead into whatever lay ahead in their lives. My father needed to be at peace and proud of us: that was the only way we could achieve that.

I began to try to reassure my mother, "Dad is in heaven with God and smiling down at us. Do not forget about the three years you cared for him when he became sick and how well and patiently you watched over him. That time was almost 1,000 days, nonstop, and yet, you never failed in your watch, sleep or no sleep. Be *happy*, mother, that he rests in peace, and his body is no longer consumed by pain. That is what *he* wants, I know."

Mother listened to me and slowly nodded her head, dried her eyes, and stared off into space. Very slowly, she became quiet and still, though I could tell she was not deeply at peace. But I could tell she was beginning to let my father go.

My final oral exams were scheduled for two weeks after my father's funeral. I had somehow taken all of the written tests a few weeks before my father passed away. Finishing my last three oral exams was critical to my being allowed to graduate and earn my Masters Degree. I had no choice: I simply had to stop mourning the loss of my father and fulfill my duties, as I had vowed I would do to my Dad. I had to let go and move on, as well.

And so I returned to school: skinny, pale, and looking devastated, my friends said. They all tried to encourage me just to concentrate on my oral exams; if I didn't pass them, I would have to spend another year in college.

I tried so hard to study for the exam, but my brain would not cooperate. Tired, confused, and depressed, my brain was useless to me all of a sudden. I felt as if I hadn't retained any knowledge since I began college four, long years ago.

My examination day came, and I entered the exam room with an empty and echoing mind.

Three professors called out my name.

I was so anxious that I called out to my father, silently in my heart, for help. It was the very first time I had called out to him as my angel, whom he had become. And from that moment on, I have called my angel, silently, wherever I go, whatever I do, and any time I am confronted with difficulties or dangers I sense are bigger than I.

I picked a topic question from a box on the table, as we were told to do, and waited for the professors to begin their questioning. I thought to myself, as I waited for them to begin, 'I should simply walk out of this room right now before they throw me out. This is hopeless, and I am useless.' The timing of this exam couldn't have been worse.

I looked at the professors, and they looked uncomfortably from one to the other and then at me. To my utter shock, instead of asking me to answer the exam question, they asked me about my family and expressed their great sympathy for us all. They told me just to tell them anything I knew, that they weren't going to ask me to answer the oral questions, as they were supposed to do. I saw very deep sincerity and concern in their eyes.

As if by magic or some kindness of God, my "exams" were over! I had graduated from college: my dream about earning that degree, despite living through a very sad and horrific situation right at the end, had come true! I burst into tears when the professors wished me luck at the end of our conversation.

Deep inside, I was mortified by and felt guilty about *truly* having passed my exams because I hadn't completed them as the "normal" students had: I had always expected myself to do exactly what was required, as I had been raised to do. However, to my great delight, I graduated from college and attained my long-anticipated goal at the end of July, 1987.

I went home after graduation to wait for a job assignment from the university, which was what normally happened for students after they had graduated. It was good to have some time again with my mother. She was still struggling to make her way through the most difficult time of her life. I spent whole days with her, trying to pull her spirits up; but, other than that, I could not do much for her and had simply to wait for news of my job assignment. My getting a job would most certainly give her some hope.

My career and future were completely in the government's control. I had enrolled in its training program; the university had fed us, and we had worked for the government. Therefore, my job assignment depended on the government's overall economic plans. Just like all university students, I had no choice whatsoever about the job to which I was assigned: I could be assigned to a job anywhere from North to South Vietnam, from the mountaintops to the ocean's shore.

I had slowly become wiser and more realistic about my personal reality and where I would eventually fit in this world, while I was at the university. My dream of getting a good job in the city was far too unrealistic a dream for someone like me: I had no money, no relatives, and no influential friends. I assumed I would be assigned a job somewhere far, far away, on a plantation, farm, or at a government-owned nursery. Even though I had studied every single one of the subjects the university offered, my major had been agricultural accounting; that single fact narrowed the range of job offers I would receive, as opposed to the choices "regular" (wealthy and well-connected) students were given. Even sadder was the fact that I knew it might be a year or even two before I heard anything, if I even heard anything, about a job from the university. That was the common experience of most college graduates. So I prepared myself to take the very first job offered to me by the government—wherever and whatever it was—because we needed the salary so desperately.

My family went even deeper into debt after my father's funeral. We had nothing left to sell: the last piece of gold my grandmother received from selling her house had gone toward paying for my father's hospital and funeral expenses, but it did not pay all of them. Hordes of people began to hound us for the money we owed them for food and other necessities we had had to charge for quite a while, plus the rest of the funeral services, the coffin, etc. These people were on our doorstep–right after the funeral! People began to laugh at us and thought my mother was irresponsible: no one truly believed that our poverty was very real and serious. The money my mother received from the government for her acts of heroism during the war actually turned out to be almost a joke and afforded us the ability to buy almost nothing.

It was in our mailbox one day: a letter for me, written longhand on a single sheet of paper by my professor who was head of the Accounting Program at the university. He wrote to tell me that there was a job opening at a big company located in the center of Saigon in the first district; my professor had been sending newly graduated students there every single year, and those students had always been hired at this company with his recommendation. Last, he gave me the company's name and address. His letter was merely handwriting on a single piece of paper, containing a referral to a company that was hiring and its address. But to me, it was an enormous door opening, and light *had* to be beyond that door so I could begin fulfilling my father's dying wishes and take care of my family.

Then my hopeful thoughts stopped dead: this *had* to be a mistake. It was *just impossible*, I thought. My professor had either sent the letter to the wrong student or was simply making a huge mistake by referring *me* for the job, an ordinary student who had almost failed her final exam! Why would such a big, successful company even *consider* hiring someone with no experience and whose only credential was a college diploma that she had almost not earned? Doubt and fear hounded me everywhere I went after receiving the letter. Should I contact the company or ignore it? Getting *any* job was of almost life and death importance to me and my family, but how on earth was an alley kitten to become a great tiger overnight?

That night, I couldn't sleep. I tossed and turned, trying to decide what to do, waiting for the daylight to come. The clock's ticking away every second was like a gong vibrating in my head– boom, boom, boom–and my mother's breathing rasped like a rough wind as she slept next to me. My heart beat like a hammer pounding on concrete, and my pulse ticked in my neck like an insect trying to break through my skin. Lizards scratched lizardy sounds on the ceiling, as they played chase, and the crickets cried somewhere underground.

But somehow, just as I had always somehow found the courage to jump on my bike and head into the highly dangerous jungle to find Batu, my angel, for instance, or comb Saigon for forbidden medicine for my father, I knew deep inside that again I had to summon my courage and take yet another huge risk.

I climbed up the steps of the very early morning bus to Saigon while the sun was still hiding behind the horizon. I had to get that job, no matter what. It is only right to honor one's promises.

Getting off the bus in Saigon, I had to walk for a long time through the city center to my brother's house to get my bike and then pedal quickly to the address my professor had sent to me. Eventually, I stood before a giant, many-storied building that was located in a very busy and prosperous commercial area: I felt like Dorothy, quaking before the Wizard of Oz's castle with hope and terror in her heart.

Before I entered the building, I wanted to find a mirror to see if I looked ready and capable of making this enormous jump in my life and meeting this company's demands or if I looked more like a poor, useless country mouse from Cu Chi. In a smudged glass storefront, I saw a very skinny, young girl peering back at me: she was not smiling. Dressed in an old white shirt; an old pair of slacks from college; and a pair of ancient, rubber tire slippers on her feet, I could see in her face and eyes that she felt alone, desperate, and she was certainly not attired in clothes suitable enough to meet and *impress* the people waiting to meet her inside that building.

I took a deep breath and said to the girl in the plate glass window, 'Well, maybe they will hire you to be a clown to entertain the employees or perhaps they will kick you right down all of those stairs and out the door! But you must try. Your family's survival rests on the boney shoulders inside the old white shirt you in the window are wearing."

I turned away from that shaking girl's blurry image, opened the creaky gate, and began to make my way up those stairs.

I met a guard standing right inside the entrance who asked if I needed help. So I stepped up to introduce myself to him and asked to be directed to the Accounting Department. The guard told me how to find Miss Giang, the Supervisor of the Financial and Accounting Department, which was located on the fourth floor. I took the elevator upstairs, and the doors opened right in front of her office. Somehow a sign? 'There is no turning around now,' I thought, as the elevator doors swished shut behind me.

Ms. Giang was talking to another woman in her office, and she signaled to me to enter her office and pointed at a chair, indicating that I should sit down, without saying one single word to me. She was very busy chatting with her partner who, from their conversation, was the Vice Supervisor of the Accounting Department, I decided.

They were so deep in conversation that they were oblivious to anyone or anything else, so I looked at Miss Giang. She was a middle-aged, North Vietnamese woman who wore very heavy layers of make-up, and her curly hair fell all around her shoulders. Her lips almost seemed to be on fire because of her vibrant, red lipstick. She had chosen to wear an obviously very expensive, peach-colored suit and luxurious, high-heeled shoes; those shoes must have suffered terribly under her heavy body, trying to contain such giant, bony feet. Her nails were manicured and polished with a shade of firey ripe, jalapeno pepper that matched her lipstick, and the reds she wore lit up her dark, dry, wrinkled skin. I guessed she was about my mother's age. Ms. Giang's hands were big and very worn, as if she'd once been a laborer who had worked very hard around a farm and farmhouse for many years.

I guessed that it probably took her at least an hour to apply all of the make-up she used to decorate her big, beautiful, brown eyes and heavy eyelashes. Ms. Giang appeared to be of mixed origins, perhaps East Indian, Vietnamese, or European, except that her skin was very dark: the many "coats" of white powder she had put on her face couldn't hide that fact. Compared to my mother, Ms. Giang appeared to be very healthy and strong.

When the two women finally stopped their endless conversation, none of which meant anything to me, the other woman left, and Ms. Giang looked at me with a start, as if she had completely forgotten I was even there, waiting to meet her. Finally, she asked who I was. I introduced myself, told her that I had come to look for a job at her company and that I had a letter of referral from my professor at the university.

She looked me up and down with undisguised disgust on her powdery face, as if I had just crawled out of an underground cave and was covered with dirt from head to toe or as if I were some sort of unearthly creature who had just flown down off a mountain peak with wings on my back. Her eyes seemed to say, 'Good luck, honey. You'll need it. And forget your dreams.' Her silent appraisal of me was so outright and insulting that it took every single ounce of resolve I had not to walk out of the office right then and there.

Ms. Giang didn't throw me out the office, though. She was not at all interested in my education or degree because I had majored in agriculture, and Ms. Giang's company was a trading company. But she *was very* interested in what my parents did for a living and asked if I had any relatives who worked for the government. When she found out that I had come from an exceptionally poor background, Ms. Giang was very disappointed. She didn't care at all about the fact that my professor had referred me: she was only concerned about my social class and decided I was beneath her in terms of style, wealth, fashion, and simply because of who I was and where and how I had grown up. I should instead be home, working the farm, rather than looking for work in the city.

She stopped my "job interview" very abruptly after she had learned what she really wanted to know and offered me a dismissive, very chilly, "Sorry," without giving me a reason, and waved me out of her office, as if I were a fly.

I certainly wasn't going to waste my time trying to win over someone like Ms. Giang. Instead, I rose from my chair; said, "Thank you;" and walked out of her office. I despised her for her filthy glares. She was like a stone, through and through.

I didn't want to show my face at home after an unsuccessful job interview. Instead, my incurable curiosity got the best of me, and I found myself walking around the fourth floor to see the Accounting and Financial Department before I was barred from that place forever.

In a small room in the very back of the department, some bookkeepers were working very hard, trying to clean up boxes and boxes of old files that had been sitting in the office for more than ten years. They looked exhausted, were covered with dust, but they were very friendly.

I offered to give them a hand. Not even waiting for their response, I rolled up my sleeves and dove right into the job of getting rid of the "garbage." I worked with them for many hours; we actually had great fun working together, and we all said goodbye to each other after we had finished the job.

They had liked me a lot! Maybe there *was* still a way for me to get hired. I smiled as I left and walked downstairs with a happy feeling. 'At least Ms. Giang hadn't kicked me down all these stairs, though she hadn't offered me a job that day, and at least I had met some nice people who worked for a big company exactly like one I had long dreamed would hire me.'

Heading down all of the stairs, singing my favorite song, I suddenly heard somebody calling my name from above.

She came down the stairs to meet me and thrust a piece of paper in my hand. "Go here," she said. "At this place, you might get help about a job there," she told me. Then she wished me luck in her soft, Northern Vietnamese accent with a very beautiful and honest smile, and said, "You are very intelligent and enthusiastic, and you deserve to be given a job anywhere you wish to work."

Her name was Phuong, a very sweet and good-looking woman of about thirty-five. I almost burst into tears and told her I was deeply grateful for her offer of help. I knew that being offered a job at that company was certainly impossible after my terrifying meeting with Miss Giang, who concerned me more than anything else. If I had to work with Ms. Giang, I knew right then and there that we would have an on-going, unsolvable conflict. My background and shoddy appearance clearly weren't good enough for her, and my expression probably didn't give her any indication that I would be an obedient employee, one she could order around the way she wanted liked, I was sure.

I sighed heavily and walked out of the building and away from my dream job.

I rode my bike around the dusty city streets for a while, weaving my way carefully through herds of people. I thought maybe I should simply go home, confess my defeat, and wait for another opportunity to show up in our mailbox at some unknown time in the future from some unexpected place or person. But images of my mother's face and those of the members of the rest of the family wheeled around in my head, all looking very sad and disappointed, as they welcomed a failure home. One hard fact loomed before me, and I was merely riding in circles around it: I had to get a job, no matter what, so I could help my family make it through their precarious lives.

My family…my father's expectations…I felt like Atlas holding the weight of the world on his shoulders… until all of a sudden, my fierce determination, the one I had discovered was within me during many other crises we had faced, flared up inside me again, stood me up straight, and propelled me into action. I would not accept defeat. I would follow Phuong's suggestion and look for the person who lived at the address she had written down for me. What did I have to lose?

I poured out all of the money I had in my pocket and stopped at the supermarket along the way to buy a box cake, a few packs of cigarettes, some fruit, and candy to take as gifts to offer the strangers I was about to meet.

And so it happened, on that very same evening of my disastrous interview, I met Mr. Phan, the Head Personnel Officer of Ms. Giang's company. Mr. Phan lived in a very expensive, secluded, and overwhelming house in a quiet area of the third district of Saigon. I parked my bike and stood before the imposing gates in front of Mr. Phan's "castle" for a few minutes, feeling once more like a country mouse with no business in the "palace." I paused and tried to organize my thoughts before I was ready to press the bell.

After a brief time, a young woman with two children came toward me to open the gate. I assumed that they were his wife and their children. I asked politely if I could see Mr. Phan.

The young woman led me inside the house, which had been professionally decorated, no doubt, and stunned me. Every single object and piece of furniture selected for the house was of rare quality, luxurious, and obviously extremely expensive. I peered around the "museum gallery" in which I was standing, my mouth gaping like a monkey until I caught myself. Suddenly, I thought of Batu, my angel Batu, and her slap-dash, broken-down hut in the jungle. What would she think of someone who could own such a house?

I handed the gift bag I had brought to the family to Mrs. Phan and took a seat on the couch in the living room. Mr. Phan entered, and I rose and introduced myself to him. He said he was very surprised that I even knew where he lived.

Mr. Phan was from North Vietnam and had moved south after the revolution of 1975. He was a nice and very open-minded person. He asked to see my referral from the school. (Finally!) I was embarrassed that my referral was just a simple, handwritten note from my professor, rather than an official document from school. I handed it to him, holding my breath.

My heart began to break, as I watched him reading the letter from my professor, his bushy eyebrows rose up and down dramatically on his forehead like two black caterpillars doing exercises. If he refused to hire me, all I hoped for was a reason for his refusal.

Mr. Phan looked up at me after reading the note and asked me about my family background. 'Oh, brother, here goes the job right out the floor-to-ceiling windows," I thought, depressed again immediately. But what did I have to lose at this point? So I told him that I was Chinese, that my father had gone from China to Vietnam a long time ago, and that he had just passed away. I told him about my family's difficult situation with complete honesty and in great detail, tears in my eyes. I prayed he wouldn't regard me with Miss Giang's dirty looks when he learned who I was and where I had come from.

I couldn't bear his pensive silence after I had finished telling him my story and was about to jump out of my seat, say, "Goodbye. Thank you for your time," and fly out the huge, ornate front doors. But I believe to this day he had read everything in my mind because with a big smile on his face, he told me come to his office at eight o'clock in the morning to sign a contract! Mr. Phan had hired me! I had a job! No more was I a failure!

I couldn't believe what I heard at all. He explained to me that my professor was very famous in the country, and Mr. Phan really respected him. He also told me his grandparents had come from China; so we were basically relatives, even though he couldn't speak any Chinese. He hoped that I would become successful, as he saw I was very determined to do, so I that I could help my family and my mother.

As I said goodbye to Mr. Phan and his family, in tears and with happiness surging through me in huge waves, I set out for home. Flying on my bicycle back to my oldest brother's house in the sixth district, I felt airborne by my great victory. I felt more blessed by God that day than anyone else on earth. And I could feel my father, somewhere out there, smiling down at me; so I looked up into the sky and smiled back, telling him not to worry: I would honor my promises. So far, so good!

Mr. Phan's words ran 'round and 'round in my head as my bicycle wheels rolled round and round. I thought that being honest about my Chinese background would make it easier for Mr. Phan to say no to me. The whole country was still boycotting the Chinese. Just as the snake is killed because its venom kills people, the negatives in my background *might* have made Mr. Phan want to kick me out of his house, as quickly as Ms. Giang had flicked me away.

Instead, my honesty had opened a door for me, as it usually had in the past.

One blindingly vivid, heavily made-up, big-footed hitch remained in the job I had just been given: Miss Giang. I knew an enormous challenge now lay ahead for me behind those hateful, heavily mascara-ringed eyes and firey lips. She was The Dragon Lady! But no jungle or crazy soldiers or poverty or loss of anchors in my life had stopped me yet: I would simply dig my rubber-tired heels in deeper and spread my roots in this new company, if she tried to take me on. High heels may raise you up, but they also put you in a precarious position.

I got hired on October 1st, 1987. Miss Giang was so angry, I could feel flames on my exposed skin when she found me back in the building and on her floor. Her well-drawn eyebrows shot straight up into her hairline when she saw Mr. Phan escorting me onto the floor.

She pointed her pointy, red fingers right in my face and screamed with her high-pitched, "How *dare* you to still be hanging around my office? I already told you that you are not qualified for any job I have!" She must have lost her voice every, single day if she talked that way often!

She then turned to Mr. Phan and yelled, as calmly as she could, "I already interviewed her! I don't have any place for her here, *anywhere!*" she squeaked out.

Mr. Phan, with a big, confident smile on his face turned to Ms. Giang and asked, calmly, "What makes her unqualified for the accounting job in your financial department?"

Ms. Giang cleared her mumbly, tired vocal chords. "She... she...is from Cu Chi, Mr. Phan, and she cannot know anything about accounting at all! How could she? Look at her, Mr. Phan!" she screamed like brakes on a truck, stopping quickly.

"Well, Ms. Giang, I beg to differ with you. She comes with high praise from her professor, and I have never, ever in my life been wrong to trust that man's recommendation when he refers a new graduate to me. So, thank you for accepting Ms. Ky as a new employee."

She opened her flamey lips to scream something new, but no sound came out, and her eyebrows were stuck in her hairline, in shock.

Then he turned and congratulated me. "You are in, kid," he said quietly and turned and left the floor without looking back.

It was too late for Ms. Giang, and this time, despite The Dragon Lady, with a little persistence and lots of resolve, I had won one more time: I signed my contract with the company and became a legal government employee.

Mr. Phan later took me aside, told me to be patient, warned me sternly *not* to fight with Ms. Giang, and promised he would always support me. In this big, crowded city, on another journey into uncertain – and terrifying–territory, I had found *another* angel, Mr. Phan, who had not only given me my dream job but had promised to watch over me and protect me.

Miss Giang lifted me up almost literally and dumped me in the back room with the other four bookkeepers and walked away, not even condescending to look over her shoulders and leave me with yet another one of her shriveling, dirty looks.

She had assigned me to do the fishing supply accounting, which meant that I had to keep track of the company's inventory of fishing supplies, such as nets, boat parts, and over a hundred thousand items. All of those products had been sitting in a company warehouse somewhere for over fifteen years without being used since 1975. They had once belonged to an import company, the owner of which had simply disappeared or had been arrested right after the revolution.

So, in reality, my first job was a simple, empty frame, compared to what my degree had given me the tools to accomplish. But, no problem: at least I *had* a frame to fill in–and a paycheck to go with it! I resolved to take no time off. In the back of my head, always, was the fear that I was dreaming and would wake up sitting in the streets of Saigon, penniless, filthy, and a failure.

On my first day on the job, the sky was very blue, and the sun shone vividly over Saigon. From the window of my office on the fourth floor, I could see the whole town sparkling beneath me. My view of the city was a lot more impressive than the only other one I had had of this company, standing on the ground in the heat and the rush of the city before its grand gates, a mere, timid, tire-shod mouse with only a dream. I could smell the fresh air blowing in from the Saigon River but not the fuel burning in and then being spit out of ancient engines. I could hear the sound of ships approaching the port of Saigon from all over the world but not the noise of one thousand vehicles chasing each other down the chaotic streets.

And I had become a permanent resident of the city, not a temporary student who spent a few years in town and disappeared after graduating. No more black-market smuggling of rice and groceries from my school or sneaking things from the government supermarket every day after school. This was my new and honest life.

A week went by, during which I tried not to breathe or talk too loudly. I shrank into the tiniest shell of a person possible, trying to keep out of everyone's sight, especially Miss Giang's. Every day I arrived at work, rode up in the elevator to my floor, and stopped right across from Ms. Giang's office. I quietly and quickly snuck by her office, trying not to annoy her with my presence. I was sure that she couldn't do anything to get rid of me, but I wasn't taking any chances. No more wars for me!

Miss Giang turned my college degree into her strongest weapon against me. However, I felt more confident after one week at my job because it was so much easier than I had expected it would be. In my very first week, I had finished the equivalent of a whole month's work *and* caught up on the work that had been left behind by the previous bookkeeper six months ago.

Even though I had greater abilities than those my current job required, I rather enjoyed what I was doing and the fact that I was getting paid so I could finally help my family, rather than worry about our precarious future. I spent most of my spare time reading the department's books and helping the other bookkeepers, if they needed me. After my first week on the job, I couldn't wait to see my family on the weekend so we could all celebrate my job together and the fact that I had passed my first week of being tested as an employee.

The trip home that weekend felt completely different from all of the ones I had taken over the four years I had been a poor college student. I used to ride in the very same, stuffy, crowded bus, but this time it seemed more spacious and comfortable. The passengers on the bus seemed friendlier and more polite than I remembered. My happiness and optimism probably were changing how I saw the rest of the world.

Next to me on my seat was a big basket of groceries and fruit like the ones my father used to ask me to bring him on the weekends I went home from school. This, however, was my very first gift to him from his employed daughter, and there would be more when I got paid at work.

For the very first time, my mother and all my brothers and sisters, instead of my father, were standing by the front door waiting for me. They were so excited to hear all of my news. They hugged me and jumped up and down and peeked into my mysterious bags from the big city.

Without saying a word, though, I went right into the house
and to my father's altar to put up some incense and asked him to
congratulate me on my new job. I wanted him to be the first one
to hear this good news from me—no one else. He smiled at me
from inside the picture of him on his altar.

My mother was watching me and couldn't say a word; she just
dropped into a chair like an empty apron and shook with silent
sobs that came from many different places in her heart, I'm sure.

That night was also the first night our family had been happy
together since my father had passed away. My stories about getting my job and about the job itself, all of which I told in great
detail, were so full of all of the feelings I had felt and fought that
they touched everyone else's heart.

Eventually I moved out of my oldest brother's house in the
sixth district and moved in with other relatives while I waited for
the company to find me my own housing. I gave my sister-in-law
some money from my first month's wages to help pay the hospital
bill for the birth of their second child, and I saved a small amount
of money for my mother.

To surprise my mother, I ordered a set of beautiful gravestones
that had been chiseled by the most gifted headstone carver in
Saigon. I had fought with my mother about buying the cheap
rock that she had bought and put on Father's grave, which she
insisted was all we could afford, since we needed every bit we
had, just to live. It wasn't easy convincing her to allow me to buy
these markers because we really *did* need money more for every-
day expenses than for a set of expensive headstones.

But my grandma always had a different way of looking at
things and of working things out. She was proud of me for what
I had accomplished so far in my life and trusted me to continue
to help my mother soon enough again. She told me she thought I
was the best child, a very thoughtful one, and she told me I had a
very special character. "Besides," she said, "these gifts are important to *you*, aren't they?" She knew.

She told my mother quietly that my mother should allow this, that the stones were my gifts to her, too. And thanks to my grandmother, today my father rests with dignity still under an intricately carved headstone and waits patiently for my mother.

My job was going very smoothly very quickly. The company had more than five hundred employees and over twenty branches all over southern Vietnam. Our business was based on the greatest potential of an unlimited resource of Mother Nature's along the shore: we fished, processed, packaged, and provided seafood and fish sauce, which comprised the basic dietary needs of people throughout the entire country. We were one of the government's most profitable companies and key to the growth of the national economy.

I worked at the company's headquarters in Saigon and soon was given the job of controlling a whole chain of mini-factories all over southern Vietnam. The main office of the chairman of the company was far away in North Vietnam. Our office was controlled from the main office, and we simply followed their policies and instructions. At least four times a year, they sent a group of inspectors to visit our company and investigate any loss or gain of profits.

My wages increased so quickly that they were suddenly four times larger than my oldest brother's wages, and he had worked for the biggest weaving factory in the country for over eight years. I made twenty times more money than my older sister did, and she was the schoolteacher in Cu Chi. In addition to all of that, I received many benefits, including retirement and big bonuses every quarter and at year's end.

One day, I happen to learn that I was the only one out of the thirteen bookkeepers in the accounting department who had a university degree, *including Miss Giang*! What a shock! I was one of the youngest employees and yet had had the most education. Once a month, when I turned in my activity report to the president of the company, it was "an excuse" for Miss Giang to became enraged and complain for days afterward that I was doing nothing but receiving benefits from the company.

Miss Giang was in the process of hiring three more accountants who had graduated from my university, as I knew the company had originally requested four graduates in all. And what a very warm welcome Ms. Giang gave to *them*! They all were assigned to very important positions, ones that meant working very closely with Miss Giang!

I was shocked by her welcoming treatment of them and the fact that she had discriminated against me, but I had to remind myself that at least I had a job, something that so many people desperately needed. Miss Giang loved to give the new hirees compliments and made a point of insulting me in front of everybody in the office. "This one, she is from the jungle. Can you believe that one?" she would snarl as she guided them past my desk.

She had tied my hands, so to speak, throwing me in a little corner without giving me any substantial work at first; my tiny office had nothing in it but a whole pile of ancient books that had been in a file cabinet for years. She relished defaming me, telling the new employees that I was helpless and always sitting around, just waiting to get paid. She told everyone my mother didn't have a job but stayed home and also did nothing. Poor Ms. Giang: on the outside, she appeared so selfish and jealous, yet she was only underestimating my abilities because of <u>her</u> own lack of knowledge and education.

I wanted to tell her that my mother was one hundred times smarter and one thousand times more successful than she would ever be; that before the revolution, my mother had owned and run a big department store and had had many people working for her who served her like a queen; and that though my mother didn't wear heavy make-up and expensive clothes, people bowed down to her anywhere she appeared.

But Ms. Giang's insults and put-downs weren't enough to diminish her rage, so she dragged Mr. Phan into her office to show him how bad my inventory was, just so he would fire me. Mr. Phan asked to see at *all* of the accountants' books before he would even say one word to Ms. Giang. Apparently, my inventory was a *lot* better that even the inventory of Ms. Giang's favorite accountant! Mr. Phan left her office without saying a word, a big, mysterious smile on his face.

Nobody in the office could figure out why she treated me–and no one else–so badly. The minute I accepted that job, Ms. Giang had openly declared war on me. I was just a little nobody from nowhere, a no one who wanted to work so I could earn some money to help my pathetic, little family. Not a single day at work went by without Ms. Giang's finding or creating some reason for yelling and screaming at me. Anytime I heard her high heels clacking like bullets firing against the floor, I prepared myself for the fight I knew was coming.

But because of the way I saw the world, I ignored her, didn't care what she might have to say, and simply continued my work. That enraged her even more.

I didn't complain to Mr. Phan or anybody else in the company about her terrible treatment of me. My co-workers thought I should look for another job, rather than suffer Miss Giang's wrath. They didn't know I had been born and had grown up on the bitter, harsh, barren ground of war where the local government had tried to crush our family to pieces. I was much stronger emotionally than they could ever have imagined. I was very aware that I was taking on this challenge with Miss Giang the minute I accepted the job, so I had simply made up my mind to stick it out until the very end.

As a result, Ms. Giang suffered around me more than I suffered around her. My calm in the face of her torrents drove her so crazy; she always looked like she was on the verge of exploding. No matter how hard Ms. Giang tried to make me quit, nothing worked. She couldn't persuade Mr. Phan to fire me, and so then she went straight to the top to try to get the company president's power behind her goal.

The president had been a South Vietnamese soldier who had gone north and lost one arm during the war. He then returned home after the revolution to take the president's chair in our company. His office was on the third floor, and he worked in a dark and quiet room, all by himself. He rarely came outside to communicate with any of the employees. I only saw him once a month for about ten seconds when I submitted my monthly report to him for his signature. He looked so serious and strict that I didn't dare to say a word to him, and I had never looked directly into his eyes or made a sound when I went to deliver my reports to his office.

However, Ms. Giang finally made me the president's business. One day, when I handed my documents to him, he suddenly looked up at me and asked me how Miss Giang treated me in the office. He wanted to know more about the negative information he heard about me from Miss Giang.

I wasn't surprised and had even prepared an answer, in case anyone ever asked me that question. But I had no idea which of us—Ms. Giang or me—he would support. It took a few seconds to remember the answer I had prepared. Finally, with a big smile on my face, I replied, "Well, sir, you know her better than anybody else in the company does."

The president laughed in a very loud and comfortable way when he heard my answer.

And after that one booming laugh of his, my life at the company changed suddenly and drastically. The president began to sneak upstairs into our department, and he caught Ms. Giang right in the middle of harassing me. Once, he was even standing right behind her when she started yelling at and scolding me!

I rolled my eyes, laughing silently to myself and thinking, 'What goes around, comes around!' Miss Giang just about passed out cold in front of everybody from embarrassment when she realized who was standing right behind her!

Soon, I became the president's favorite employee. Ms. Giang had a very difficult time trying to defend her behavior to her boss. I even felt brave enough to confront Miss Giang right in the office because I knew I had the protection of the president. The conflict between Ms. Giang and me died down temporarily because she had been reprimanded and told not to harass her employees, especially young women who had just graduated from college, as I had.

Fortune seemed to be pouring down upon me and somehow all at once: I was promoted when the government suddenly announced that it would begin to sell the fishing supplies that had sat in our warehouse for over almost twenty years to the public. Customers from all over Vietnam rushed to our store, trying to buy up the fishing gear.

I spent some time on my own, researching the free market and discovered that the government's current prices for these items were lower than their actual value by about twenty years, in fact. (Even when I was younger, I had a knack for selling and trading, as we all know.) I put together a new price list for most of the items we were selling that was based on their real, black market values in Saigon.

My efforts were highly appreciated by the company's heads, as my work and research helped them make a hundred times the profit on every single item sold than they would have, had they stuck to their old price list. I also received a lot of tips from our customers, since I also helped them locate some rare items they wanted (remind you of anyone else?), and I worked hard all on my own time to broaden our company's appeal to customers all over the country. I finally had found a safe place to show the real me and use my strongest talents to make active contributions to our company. Everyone in the office was so surprised to watch me come alive!

After one year on the job, I received an award of recognition from our company's headquarters, specifically citing my great contributions to the company's profits, and with it came a bonus check for two million Vietnamese dong! That check was equal to two years of work at my current salary!

One person in particular was furious that I had received this recognition and so much money: Ms. Giang, of course. The company had given Ms. Giang the award check to give to me, since she was the director of our department, and this was the straw that caused her to explode and go berserk. She pointed her flaming, pointy fingernail in my face, her long curls whirling around her head like Medusa's, and screamed, "Don't you even dare to think for one second that you will EVER get your hands on that money!" She had gone completely mad, having hysterics and announcing venomously to everyone within earshot that I, "*especially* that one," didn't deserved *anything* from the company.

She then went clomp-clomp-clomping immediately downstairs in her fancy high heels to the company's president's office and demanded that he change his mind about my receiving the prize money. But the president explained to her that he himself had not been responsible for making the decision to recognize me for my efforts or to give me a bonus; rather, the decision had been made at company headquarters in the north. He also warned her that she must never again interfere with the company's promotional policies.

She absolutely refused to listen to his orders and continued to insult me every, single time she saw me. My co-workers told me that she was also making up stories defaming me and defending her behavior. What a nightmare it was to be punished, every single day, for having done an excellent job!

I should have reported her to the president for harassment, but I wasn't brave enough to declare an outright war with Miss Giang. In truth, I felt sorry more for her than for myself. I could understand why she was miserable about my being recognized, simply because of the kind of person she was. I decided not to fight back and to forget about the reward money, whether my family needed it or not: if it were supposed to be mine, it would end up being mine.

All of my co-workers, who were supportive of me, were very worried that I would never receive my money. Miss Lan, the gen-

eral accountant, kept reminding me that my award amounted to
a *lot* of money, and that no matter how Miss Giang felt about me,
I should not take a chance and leave it in her hands.

Four weeks went by; then eight weeks passed. Miss Giang still
held my reward money and ignored me. Miss Lan once again
urged me to fight for that money.

I finally decided to tell Miss Giang to divide my reward money
among all of the employees in our department so that each one
would have some extra money for his or her family when it was
needed. She was more than happy to agree with this solution
because it meant she also received a big share of her own. It
would have felt demeaning to me to beg for something that was
rightfully mine; however, I was glad to give all my co-workers
gifts for which they were so grateful.

The president increasingly treated me as if I were his own
daughter. Whenever he saw me, he wanted to hear the latest Miss
Giang harassment story and always asked how my mother was
doing at home. Then he requested that the Human Resources
Department find me an apartment in the city from the company's housing listings so I could have my very own place to live.

My father, Batu, Mr. Phan, and now my company's president: I had four angels! How did I become so lucky? Safety and
protection did exist in the world, after all, despite how it might
seem at other times, and I had experienced both. 'Pink! Somehow
my lucky pink had to have played a part in this, too,' I laughed
to myself.

The company found me an apartment in the center of fifth
district, which was not too far away from my oldest brother's
place. My younger brother Tai and my younger sister Le came
to live with me while they were in college. That took some of the
burden off my mother's shoulders.

The apartment was in a big, three-story building that had been
a warehouse for a Chinese business. But the owners disappeared
after 1975, and the government had taken it over.

Each floor was divided into five units for each employee and his or her family, but each "apartment" was too small for even *one* person to live in! Each room was about fifteen by twenty square feet; none had windows for ventilation and fresh air, and the children had no yard or play space outside. Crowded, dark, lacking in privacy, and filthy, each 'apartment's' walls had been built merely of a single wooden board, so we could hear every move our neighbors made. At night, sometimes a wife and husband chased each other in the hallway, screaming and fighting with each other. Drunk people created a nightmare of noises when they came weaving home: they swore, screamed, broke windows, and kicked in doors. Sometimes a newborn baby cried loudly all night long, sometimes someone just sneezed on the other side of our wall, and all of this human commotion kept all of us in the entire building awake all night.

Children who had been born and had grown up there only knew 'home' meant a tiny, little place like a pig pen. They had slept together with their parents on the floor all their lives. I (and my sister and brother, when they stayed with me) only slept there at night and spent as little time in that poor excuse for a home as possible. Every weekend, we all went home to Cuchi and returned to the city on Monday morning. I felt sorry for the other families who had no other place to go; they *were* living in the big city, the setting for lots of peoples' dream, but they could only shove their entire lives and family into their small spaces and hope that life would bless them somehow soon so that they could move into a bigger place.

I lived very simply and moderately in my new home so as to keep my promise to my father, even though I had a lot more money than I had ever had before and was more successful than ever before. I had to keep a small portion for my own food and personal necessities. I also paid to take English classes at night that would enable me to win jobs that might open up an even better future for me at some point. But the biggest portion of my wages went straight home to my family.

Although my "tiny, wooden box" wasn't a decent place to live, I was at least proud of having my *own* place. My apartment was also useful whenever my mother had to come to see a doctor in the city. And although I was bitterly disappointed with the quality of housing the company made possible for me, it enabled me to make the very first move in my longed-for escape from Cu Chi and to prepare for the next step in my life.

At work, I became quickly well known as the company's best singer; I loved to sing at all of the company's social functions, and once I won a trip to Da Nang to sing at a corporate function. I was amazed that many of the employees in the company seemed to admire me: a young girl with a hard-won master's degree who had risen out of nowhere (the jungle and nowhere are synonymous) and flown into her dream.

Once in a while, I was chosen to go on a trip with Miss Lan and a small group of bookkeepers to the company's branch in southwest Vietnam to take a financial inventory of its activities. I loved those trips. We were always warmly welcomed and treated like the big bosses of the company. We stayed in the most expensive hotel in the town and ate at the best restaurants in the province. And always, at the goodbye parties they threw for us, they sent us off with lots of gifts.

My female co-workers started suggesting that I would an ideal catch for any one of the single, young men in the company, and they teased me by telling me that many young men came to visit our office just to have a chance to meet me. They said I brought the company alive and made the place much more interesting.

Miss Giang encouraged me–all the time–just to pick *any* guy in the company and get married <u>soon</u> because she assumed that that was one sure way to get me out the door for good. But, she also told me, in her next breath, "In reality, those young men are all too good for a country girl who just squeezed herself out of the Cu Chi tunnel."

Though my fortunes had changed incredibly, underneath it all, I *was* still that lowly earthworm of a country girl who rode her old bicycle to work every morning, and I knew, deep down, that I lacked fashion sense and had no desire–like most of the other young people in the city–to try to keep up with the latest fashion trends. To me, there were far more important purchases to make in this life.

The more I thought about my career, however, the more aware I became of an uneasy, undefined fear in my heart. I was living in my dream city, working for one of the biggest companies in the whole country, and had achieved more success than many others; but for some reason, I did not see my job as a permanent career nor did I find that it fulfilled me, after all. The money I earned was just a temporary source of relief for my family and me: I had a sense it would not last forever, either. I felt uneasy, as if I had begun to float in the mid-air of my life with nowhere to land where I truly belonged or wanted to belong.

In the early 1990's, the national economy faced a crisis. Private companies were growing and becoming more prosperous, which threatened businesses the government owned, such as ours. My company began to face serious financial problems. Our usual customers stopped ordering our products and slowly disappeared.

The president finally decided to cut down the size of our company's labor force by shutting down all units that had not been profitable for several years. We all prepared to be laid off, sooner or later, and many had already started looking for new jobs.

The president's budget cuts really challenged the unit managers to maintain their business activities. They visited our accounting department daily to beg for more funds, for any financial relief they could obtain. So Miss Giang ran in and out of banks all day, every day, trying to get a hot loan for as much money as they would give her and at as high an interest rate as possible. Of course, Miss Giang and the bank managers also received huge commissions from the government's budget for their covert exchanges.

The company was suddenly falling down a hole as if it were sure to crash as rapidly and freely as a meteor might plummet into the earth. But our department received more tips than it ever had when the branch managers received their free money from the government. Everyone was trying to get his cut of the action before it dried up completely.

Naturally, these leaks of liquid cash accomplished nothing more than to push our company further into debt. Miss Giang finally hit a brick wall in her borrowing 'business' because our company now owed the banks too much from her previous, still unpaid, hot loans. Some managers had even been arrested and gone to jail for overusing government money for their own purposes. Although Miss Giang had no degree in accounting or financial skills, helping the managers steal from the company was her expertise. Ms. Giang and the department managers had committed fraud by using local businesses to claim the cash withdrawal from corporate. They lived very extravagantly and very generously, not only for themselves, but also for their business partners at the corporate level.

To rescue the company from bankruptcy, the president set a new goal. He demanded that all employees seek out new customers, instead of waiting for the company to implode. Our wages had been delayed for a while because the bank was now denying our loan requests, and the bank didn't trust Miss Giang anymore because the company no longer had a business plan to submit to the bank to demonstrate that it that could eventually cover its outstanding loans. Our accounting department had become useless.

However, as had happened to me many times before in my life, this crisis delivered a new kind of fortune to me. I became known in our company as "Our Queen of Fish Sauce." On the very first day of the president's new plan, I took a sample of the company's fish sauce out to potential customers: I sold several thousand gallons of fish sauce, just in my hometown alone! Without any investment, I took advantage of the company's credit and paid later. I actually made tons and tons of money very easily, a hundred times more than my monthly wage had been. My brother-in-law helped me by using our pick-up truck to load the products at my company and drop them off at my customers' stores. When I went home every weekend to collect the money from my customers, I also took their new orders. I gave all the profit I saw to my mother and left it up to her as to how she spent it. I only kept enough to pay for my costs, which I owed my company.

My business grew rapidly every day. From Cu Chi, I started selling fish sauce to towns and cities in other provinces, and my job became so easy that I really didn't need to spend too much time in the office at all.

Miss Giang was upset about my blooming business, but there was no way she could stop me because it had been sanctioned by the president. Miss Giang was really beginning to see how badly she had underestimated my abilities and education as a college graduate accountant.

My success with this venture made me proud, but it shocked my co-workers. They admired me, but I began to sense that they had become a little jealous of me. They watched me do my business, their mouths watering. I was young, single, and still lived a very simple life; had I not lived quite so simply, perhaps I would even have been considered rich. Though they were very curious about what I did do with my earnings, they never found out about the huge group of relatives completely dependent on me for their mere survival.

Luck always seemed to walk with me now, regardless of what I did or where I was. I felt as if I could probably pluck stars from the night sky very easily, if I could reach that high. Elsewhere—and sometimes only one door away or somewhere across an entire province—people were hanging on by mere threads, when there was I, reaping tons of money like a wizard. Many of the risks and steps I had taken throughout my life seemed touched by luck, if not at first, then eventually. I couldn't ask for anymore than I had and should have been the happiest person on earth.

Instead, I had no peace of mind. My responsibilities constantly weighed heavily on my shoulders, as if an elephant were draped across them. No one would have believed so many people depended on me. And I also had to put enough aside to be prepared for the worst-case scenario.

All of the country's businesses suffered from the drastic plummeting of the economy. My mother began to complain again frequently about her finances because, once again, the family truck sat at home most of the time, rather than fly around Cu Chi and beyond with magic fish sauce. It was a sore reminder to her of her situation. The family made only a little bit of money from selling fertilizer to farmers. The kids were growing, and the family's expenses were increasing. The farm hadn't made any profit from its crops that year, and my brothers' and sisters' school fees went up every day, it seemed. My mother still supported my oldest brother and my older sister's family, and that cost us even more.

Every weekend now, it seemed I could only find enough money to pay for the goods that I owed to the company, which left me with nothing for the family. My mother had been borrowing from my customers for a while before I got home. Essentially, I had no regular wages because the company had begun to deduct debts that I owed my department from my checks.

Then, my mother began to send my older sister to hunt me down at work to ask me for emergency advances from my check. No matter how much money I had made, it never seemed to be enough for my big family.

My mother got furious any time I complained about the burden I suffered because of my responsibilities to the family. I used to look forward to going home on the weekend; increasingly, it made me crazy to see them living in such punishing conditions that only grew worse and worse every day. My older sister's two kids and her husband drove our truck, delivering goods around the city. My older sister was a schoolteacher, and her salary wasn't even enough to pay for her work dresses, make-up, and hair care. Her children were growing, and they needed more and more food and clothes. My grandma needed medications: my family's list of needs grew and grew.

Once again, my mother began to talk about selling our house – our last and only possession of value–or of looking for a job as a cook or a housekeeper for someone in town.

I began to feel as if I had never done anything substantial to lighten my mother's burden. I would tell myself, 'The money from my salary and my business profits together *SHOULD* cover the family's expenses.' However, that was just an illusion. I was actually sitting in the same boat as my family, despite my job and earnings. I couldn't take it anymore. I had to get off my sinking boat to save us all.

My company was wobbling from its footings up to its roof. I didn't want a new job because no matter how hard I worked or how much money I might make, it would never, ever be enough. I heard people in town telling stories about picking money off the trees in some country on the other side of the ocean. My family ate shrimp tails and stale vegetables.

I needed to escape. I had given up.

My dreams had turned into a painful, disappointing reality. If I could have turned the house upside down and shake it or crack it open like a piggy bank, I would never have found gold enough inside it for a trip I had suddenly decided I had to take. I needed three pieces of gold or about fifteen hundred dollars for this trip, as a friend told me. I had made so much more than over three years of working, but I had kept just dimes for myself. No relatives or friends had any money to lend me. And half of my grandma's house had already been sold, that profit money long gone.

The most disastrous part of it all was that our family's pride and reputation, which my father had worked so hard all his life to build for all of us, would soon disappear like smoke into the night. We would be invisible–or worse–in town.

I decided, for the very first time in my life, I had to take care of myself first and not worry as much about the rest of the family. I knew I could easily find a good man in the city, get married, and forget about my brothers and sisters at home. Was it my responsibility to help them *forever?* They were supposed to stand on *their* own two feet as they grew and became more independent. I needed a break from the promises that I had made to my father before he passed away, telling myself I wasn't as smart or capable as he had thought I was. My father probably forgave me for underestimating what his wishes would require of me. With all the money I had made over the years, I could have bought myself a house in the city, but I had nothing left after three years of work. I had not wanted to get married because then I would be unable to share my income with my family, even though it seemed my sacrifices had never amounted to anything, in the first place.

My company was a giant, dead body, soulless. Half of the employees had left over several months: from the custodian to the planning department and from the personnel department to employees in the company's various branches. The big building was silent and empty: no talking, laughing, or arguing about the business. Our accounting department was extremely dead, except that someone had to do the monthly reports. Miss Giang was gone; she had been promoted: HA! The company had always wanted to get rid of her so they could hire a more skilled financial specialist than she had been, and since she was "fat" with all the fraudulent money she had taken, she was ready to leave the financial department.

Finally! I felt less pressured and less threatened in her absence so that I could put those monthly reports together.

Some of the other bookkeepers had quit and found themselves better jobs around Saigon. But I didn't want to look for another job; I waited until the company's last day before I made a simple move just to keep my small business alive. I told myself I had to stop worrying about anything but my own life. I needed to be happier, more relaxed, and more sane without heavy worries on my back: I needed to be free of my family. If I didn't take myself out of my family's future, everyone was going to drag me down with them for the rest of my life.

I started crying and talking to my father. I blamed him for his last blessing that our family's fortune would depend on me. He was responsible for what he had asked of me. I talked to him in my sleep; I talked to him, as I stared at my thin, plywood walls; I talked to him at work—no matter where I was. 'Why *me*, father? Why *me*?' I asked him out loud, over and over and over. After all, what good had I really done in the end? And what about all of the pain I had suffered trying to meet his expectations?

However, in my heart—right where my father was, as well—I knew very well that I couldn't run away from reality or my origins: destiny had brought me to my own family. I would never have peace if I knew my family was in trouble. I was who I had become, a pink rose that had grown and bloomed on steel ground: I could either move forward into the terrifyingly uncertain future with my family or disappear forever inside my own hometown.

I truly had no choice: I had to remain a part of my family's reality, regardless of how hard and painful it might be. My father smiled warmly in my heart when I finally allowed that decision to rest.

CHAPTER EIGHT

JUNE, 2009

Through a very dense haze of sleep (through which Rick said I had been mumbling something about "impossible" and "tragedy" and "I QUIT!"), I also heard the stewardess announce our being only hours away from our final destination.

I opened my eyes, and Rick was smiling at me.

"We *really* are getting there now, Julie! By the way, with whom were *you* fighting with in *that* dream? Man, it was as though you were fighting for the heavy-weight crown of the century! I was just relieved you didn't punch *me!*" He laughed, and the corners of his eyes crinkled up into little nests of fine lines, just like the ones around his mouth. Always made me smile.

"Aren't you hungry *yet*, Julie? We've been up here for hours and hours, you know, and all you've done is toss and turn and fall back to sleep, drink water, and repeat, which I guess is good," he said and held out to me the box in which my "snack" had been wrapped in layers of crinkly, clear cellophane. Plastic cheese, plastic crackers, a plastic knife, and napkin: what I would give for even a tiny bowl of my father's once-famous pho!

I peered underneath the cellophane and scowled disdainfully. "Are you kidding me? That's not food! That's plastic. I'd rather eat shrimp tail crumbs, as we did in the old days, than that stuff. I will have some water, if you have any," I replied.

Rick handed me the bottle and said, "You have almost reached your destiny, Julie. It's truly amazing. Aren't you *proud?* Aren't you excited?"

I had no words for the emotions coursing through me as we neared the place I had dreamed about visiting for so long. It almost wasn't real. Sometimes when I looked at Rick, my good and perfect match of a mate, I thought, 'How is it he happened to me?' I put my hand on his cheek, smiled, and said, "Wait 'til it's over, ok? Then I will tell you how I feel about all of this. I'm too jumbled up inside right now about it all, as it is."

"Ok: deal," he said and smiled.

'What a good guy,' I sighed to myself happily, flipped my limbs around several times and drifted away again, quickly and down into another dream.

1991

Once again, I had to devise a new approach to my family's financial problems. Finally, I came up with one, as I always had, and started working on it. I knew some customers who lived on the shore of Southwest Vietnam. I thought that they would help me escape Vietnam by sea in order to get to America and that they could then collect the money I borrowed from them for my trip from my mother after I had left the country. Even if my grandma had to sell her house as a result of my new idea, I would make myself find a way not to care.

I left Saigon and went home to Cu Chi the following weekend and packed up all of the personal belongings I thought I would need for this trip.

When I told her about my newest scheme, my mother was absolutely terrified. She kept crying hysterically, "You are going to die at sea, in the middle of the ocean, so far away from home and your destination. I just know it! You cannot do this!" Just like she had known that I would never make it in Saigon! "And remember that all of the islanders refuse to allow refugees or boat people from Vietnam to live on their land anymore!" She threatened to call the police, if I tried to escape from our house.

The fighting in my family over my newest scheme suddenly became fierce. Our fights were so loud that we attracted our neighbor's attention. When my neighbor learned about my scheme, she suggested I marry a young Amerasian who was eligible to enter America legally and offered to introduce me to one such young man, if I were interested.

This was an enormous gamble, perhaps the biggest one I could take, the stakes being my life and freedom. But there was no turning around: I decided to throw my whole life, career, and pride into a fifty percent chance to win. I didn't even care at this point: if there had been only a one percent chance, I still would have taken the risk. I knew all about risk, and it was time for me to go.

My mother relaxed about the whole idea because she could temporarily forget about me dying in the middle of the ocean.

My older sister Ngoc was really upset, though, and said, "You are *really* crazy, Loan. This is a truly dumb thing to do!!"

I didn't respond. I thought to myself, 'She would understand if *I* had once hunted *her* down at *her* office to beg for an emergency advance from *her* salary! Or if *I* had taken money from *her* business before *she* had even had a chance to see it!

'She would do exactly what I am about to do. *And* if she could only take care of *herself* without leaning on my mother, I would never even *have* to do this thing she thinks is so dumb!'

But I also understood: how could *anyone*, looking at me from the outside, understand the complex and tangled build-up of anger and frustration I felt from trying to uphold sole responsibility for my entire family's well being?

Our neighbor's friend had an Amerasian son whose his name was Ngan. Ngan's mother had worked at the military base during the war when the U.S. Army came to Vietnam, fell in love with an American soldier, and gave birth to their son in 1969 before he returned to America, leaving the mother and son without support and to face shame and discrimination from their neighbors.

Ngan was one of more than one hundred thousand Amerasian children whose fathers had left them behind in Vietnam after 1975. The mothers received no assistance whatsoever from the government in Vietnam. Without the education necessary to enable them to have a career, they worked as farmhands or servants for rich families. The Amerasian children were illiterate, too, as they had hardly ever been to school. They faced empty futures. Half of those children became orphans after their mothers had died in the war, became ill, or gave their children up and disappeared forever.

Ngan was one of these unlucky children, growing up without love or support from the people in the small community around them. Therefore, most of them were angry, and they grew into very stubborn and uncontrollable young men who poured their frustration out wherever they lived, caused fights, or became drug addicts and alcoholics. I remembered him from school when we were much younger. He was a trouble-maker then. As they grew, they destroyed their lives because they had only broken hearts and emptiness; underneath it all, they were torturing themselves for feeling so hopeless. No one trusted them or would listen to their life stories. Ngan's mother loved him very much, but she was overwhelmed by caring for all of her other children, as well as Ngan; by their poverty; and by trying to keep their heads above water. Ngan was also the favorite of his grandparents, so he loved living with them and was not as unhappy as some young Amerasians.

Their relatives looked down on them for being mixed-blood children, avoided seeing them, or stayed away from them because of their mothers' stigma. Those poor children weren't regarded as fit to live in this country. Their skin color was different from that of the rest of the nation, and this caused them to be excluded by other children from all activities. Those who were about my age had to work hard wherever they could get hired to survive, while we got to go to school. Those who could at least live with their mothers were luckier, but then sometimes stepfathers and half-brothers and step-sisters would abuse them and treat them as a burden to the family. Very few of these young people lived in a happy family or even received support from their relatives.

Before 1975, my hometown of Cu Chi had one of the biggest U.S. Army bases. Therefore, the number of Amerasian children in my town was higher than anywhere else in Vietnam. We had witnessed the tragedy these children, young people, and their mothers faced every single day since I was little.

After the revolution, the U.S. government had sponsored the Amerasian children and their mothers so that they could come to America to find better lives. This sponsorship had opened a big door for those unlucky children, changing their lives incredibly, almost overnight, from being homelessness to being given a chance to walk into the 'promised land,' the United States. Everyone in Vietnam dreamed of going to the United States where they believed they would find many opportunities they could not find in Vietnam. The Amerasian children suddenly became the most valuable and beloved children in Cu Chi.

This miraculous new U.S. program unfortunately created a very tragic situation: the Amerasians became victims of Vietnamese people who sold them on the black market. People combed every corner of Vietnam for Amerasian children. They seduced them with money, gold, drugs—whatever worked to gain their confidence, filed for their visas, and then sold the children to a new owner for a large sum. Lots of Amerasians had been sold two and three times. Some had applied for visas at least three times using three different names. One Amerasian was permitted to file for papers with over ten people listed on his application as his relatives who were actually all strangers. From rich to poor, from teachers to businessmen, from the elders to the young, everyone tried to take advantage of this generous program in order to realize their own American dreams.

In my town alone, the Amerasian program made tons and tons of money for some of our people who simply used those children. This program had also impoverished many families because they had cheated and lost everything, trying to realize their American dream; but they weren't afraid then to file a lawsuit in hopes of being allowed to try again. Some families failed the interview held by the U.S. immigration office, so they filed again, using a different child's name. In some cases in which white-skinned kids had filed applications, black kids showed up at the interview. After applying for their visas, some escaped from their owners to get married and have their own family in their own country.

This situation became so serious that the U.S. Immigration Service became very strict about applications and made the interviews they conducted even tougher.

The Amerasians became trapped in the chaotic and poor society to which they were vulnerable and from which they seemed unable to escape. They were told what to do and obeyed their owners until they had passed the interview. If they passed, all of a sudden they were treated like kings and queens. Rich people gave them whatever they demanded. They weren't worried anymore about starving or sleeping on the street or being harassed as they had been for so long. Their owners decorated those Amerasian's bodies with layers and layers of real gold jewelry to keep them excited about the process and gave them very expensive motorcycles to ride around town with their boyfriends or girlfriends until they received their U.S. visas.

Quite simply, those Amerasians had become very handy tools for Vietnamese people to use to step into *their* dream of heaven on earth; at least the Amerasians were also able to escape their ugly, rotten, and terrible hell. They were given a way–if a difficult and immoral one–to walk into what they dreamed was a luxurious new life while they waited for their visas to arrive, allowing them into their fathers' homeland.

So, this was the basis for my newest scheme: to become one of those people looking desperately for a change in their lives, for the door to America to open to them, using the Amerasian program as the key.

After more than one hour of walking on the thread of a slippery and dangerous deer trail, my neighbor and I finally found Ngan's family's house in the middle of nowhere on a water field. As we approached the house, my neighbor pointed out a tall, young man playing soccer with whole bunch of kids on the field. That tall, young man was Ngan.

Finally, we stood in front of a tiny house with a coconut leaf roof and bamboo walls, which indicated that they were very poor. Ngan's mother opened the door and invited us inside. A very old couple, whom I guessed were Ngan's grandparents, were also sitting in the room, splitting bamboo to make baskets to sell at the market.

My neighbor introduced me to the family and told them my story. They were all very nice and felt sorry for me and my family's bad fortune. Ngan's mother called him in from the field and told me to walk out to meet him. She said many, many people had come to find Ngan, but he refused to see them because he was terrified of strangers trying to use him.

I was so nervous, walking out to the field to meet him. A lot of Amerasian kids used to stand outside the gates of our school and scream and yell, just to annoy kids who were luckier than they were. What if Ngan had continued to grow into one of those angry people?

Then I noticed that Ngan left the crowd in the field and ran really fast on the rice field bank toward me and his house. Ngan was half Vietnamese and half black American. His skin wasn't completely black but very dark brown, and he had beautiful curly hair. He was very tall, compared to all the other young men in the village. Ngan looked like an athlete, someone who played sports every day and was very healthy and very quick.

His mother had told me he was really very shy and timid. He had rarely met anyone new. But I saw his face lighten up with a big smile, showing his beautiful white teeth from even far away. I guessed my luck was still with me, as he did not seem to be the wild kind of young man I thought he might be.

We said very little on our way to the house. We entered, and he sat at the end of the table and listened to the rest of the story my neighbor was telling his family about my family and me. He didn't say a word to anyone.

I asked him if he had a girlfriend; his mother laughed and told us he was far too timid to have a girlfriend.

At the end of that day, Ngan told his mother he would do whatever she wanted him to do.

His mother finally asked Ngan if he would marry me, and he said he would do whatever she wished him to do. I almost bowed down at his feet to thank him for the enormous fortune he was granting me. I wanted to cry but didn't dare. Ngan was my next angel to give me some hope, something to hold onto.

Ngan said to me, "This is the destiny," and smiled.

That was when I burst into tears in front of his whole family, who were then completely silent. We all said farewell at the end of my visit, wearing happiness across our faces. I could not wait to get home to tell my Mom.

My mother was way beyond happy and was so grateful to Ngan for saving my life, instead of her crazy daughter, heading out by herself to get killed on the ocean. Everyone in my family loved Ngan, all except for my older sister Ngoc. From the beginning, she was already against me about the whole idea, but now she was even angrier. She thought I was stupid to bury my life in our little village. She said I was throwing away my master's degree to marry someone who couldn't even spell his own name. She was ashamed of her intelligent sister who had done such a dumb thing, in her eyes. And, the worst part of all was that from that moment on, my income was to be split between both families.

From the bottom of my heart, I felt very guilty for having done such a weird thing. I thought of my father out there somewhere who was probably not happy at all, watching me throw my whole life and reputation away on a fifty-fifty chance to win a very risky game. But I also thought that this was, in a way, part of my father's doing because he knew I would never give up, even if it meant risking my life. I called out to him again and again before I made my final decision to leave the country.

Our wedding was held at our house because Ngan and his mother lived at his grandparents' house. This place was just big enough for them to put a few boards down so they could sleep at night. The front room was separated from the bedroom by a very thin fabric. All of Ngan's relatives came to our wedding reception, which was just a bog, warm, fun, family party at which my oldest sister, despite her disgust, and my younger brother cooked.

Ngan gave me a tiny, little ring that his grandparents had given to him as a gift; they had bought it with the money they had earned all of their lives making baskets. His mother was so sad that she had nothing to give because she had only been able to get them by, to survive.

I was still working in the city and went home every weekend to see my family. I also brought home all kinds of food, clothes, and some money for Ngan's mother and grandparents. When I was working, Ngan visited my family and picked berries in my mother's backyard. I had bought him a bicycle so he could ride back and forth to Cu Chi. I could only offer to buy him some cheap clothes, a pair of shoes, and a tiny ring from the small amount of money I was then earning.

We filled out our visa applications at the U.S. Immigration Office and waited to be assigned a date for our interview. Ngan's mother was so happy that he finally wanted to go to America. As she said, they were so poor, and it was far too difficult for them to make enough money to live every day. They couldn't afford to pay for him to file for his visa by himself but decided instead to trust me, who was, in reality, using him for my own purposes. But I did try to help them, too, as much as I could.

Now I had truly risked my life, my future, and sixteen years of working as hard as I could in school to apply for a visa to go to America, as the potential of our failing the interview was enormous. I worried constantly about the odds against my reaching this new goal.

The difference between our two backgrounds was like night and day. Ngan had never been school and didn't know how to read or write anything but his name. He had been born and grew up on a little island in the middle of nowhere; his life had been very simple, and they lived completely out of contact with civilized life in the towns and cities. He had never even left his grandparents' home or lived away from his little village for a single day. I, on the other hand, had already traveled to many different places in the country, looking for all kinds of opportunities, trying to survive and to earn enough to support my family all by myself. Ngan had never earned a penny in his life, and I had already made millions of Vietnamese dong. He hid behind his grandparents and his mother anytime he felt unsafe, while I had had to stand up alone and look many enemies in the eye. People all over the country knew my name: from the officials at the local county office in Cu Chi to all of the people I had met through my job in Saigon and those I met when I traveled for my job. Ngan had been playing ball on the field with children somewhere in a lost corner of the countryside, while I was growing up, hard and fast.

I was finally fired from the company three months after we had filed our application at Immigration. I had been prepared for this the second after I made up my mind to go ahead with my plan. It was bound to happen because of government policy: I could not be a government employee because I was betraying my government.

I didn't care anymore. I craved escape desperately, and the only way I could see to escape was taking this route. I didn't care about Ngan at all: I had only my own dreams and my family's future in my thoughts.

My older sister Ngoc started complaining about my craziness again. She did not understand how I could be desperate enough to risk my future on a wild chance without thinking twice about it. She was furious when I shared my income with Ngan and his family, and she went absolutely berserk when I lost my job.

I didn't care and still felt very confident. I saw only one way to live or die trying. Nothing else mattered. Ngan and his mother felt sorry for me, and they, in turn, didn't know what they would have done if I had not fallen into their lives.

It often took Immigration as long as a few years to process applications. Waiting for their call for an interview would drive me insane, so I had to do something else while I waited. I found another job as a bookkeeper for a private company. My wages weren't as high as my salary at my previous job, but I felt comfortable there, and the work was a lot easier.

My boss was a very kind and generous Chinese businessman. He owned a huge factory in which they produced cardboard cartons for businesses throughout the entire city. He treated me like a family member. He was really rich and famous in Saigon. I got along very well with my boss's wife and four children, all of whom were so kind, from the first day I worked at his office. Eventually, I grew quite close to my boss's family, and they adopted me very quickly, too.

I felt no pressure at work, as I had at my previous job. My boss even offered me one of his houses, if I wanted to stay there. He valued my abilities and wanted to keep me there forever. This would have been an ideal solution for a lot of people who had lived a simple life, but not for me. Unfortunately, my time with my boss and his family was to be transitional only.

I quit my job after eight months because one of my relatives asked me to work for him as a tour guide for a Taiwanese company. My boss had been so pleased with my work for him that he hired my younger sister Le to take over my old job. My mother was so happy that she finally could get a little more help because my younger sister Le started making money and became independent.

My new job was a huge opportunity, bigger than I had anticipated it to be. My salary was higher than I had ever dared dream of being paid. In addition to my wages, I had received a lot of tips and bonuses from the tourists I guided, most of whom had come from Taiwan. I left Saigon often to guide a tour, which usually lasted one week, and I did this twice a month.

In my spare time in between tours, I worked in the office to prepare for the next group: filing visas for the visitors, making hotel restaurant reservations, and planning sightseeing areas spots all over southern Vietnam. I set up the whole package for each group that could both minimize the expense and make my boss really happy. I basically handled the budget and assisted the tourists with everything they needed during the time they were in Vietnam.

I was an expert at planning trips. I loved this job at first because I was able to travel around Vietnam to places I had only dreamed of visiting. However, the job wasn't as easy as I had thought it would be: I had to work so very hard and constantly on every trip, not just planning it, but actually guiding the group on our tour. I had to get up very early in the morning to take the tourists out for breakfast and usually had to stay up until midnight, waiting for tourists in my group who were still at a bar or nightclub to return to the hotel. Checks and credit cards were not accepted in Vietnam; my country was still only set up to make cash transactions. Therefore, I had to carry a giant bag of money and the passports of my group on my shoulder everywhere we went. Although we stayed at the best hotels in every town we visited and ate at the best restaurants, I didn't enjoy it as much as I thought I might because I was worried all the time.

I was nervous when the tourists didn't like the food at restaurants or when they complained about a hotel's condition. We had to spend a lot of time driving around the city we were visiting, even as late as midnight, looking for a hotel better than the one I had booked for us. It made me crazy and angry when my group complained that the hotel wasn't clean enough or the beds weren't comfortable. Why were they all so ungrateful and picky?

My heart broke when some tourists in a group wanted to go right back to Saigon because they didn't like my tour. In addition to all of this, I worried all the time about the safety of my group, about our being robbed in the hotels. Security in the entire country was so bad that I could have been beaten up and robbed of all the valuable items I had to carry along with me each day, especially in the quiet highlands or mountain areas. From the minute I got on the bus to leave Saigon to the day we returned to Saigon, I carried full responsibility for my group. It felt so familiar, so heavy, and I hated it.

I was almost robbed once on the Dalat plateau by a whole group of gangsters when I took the tourists shopping in a city nearby. This incident scared all my tourists, and they swore they would never return to the plateau country ever again. I myself swore to God, every single time anyone complained, that I wouldn't continue doing this job for another day, if I could find a better job.

However, my hard, horrible work paid off at the end of every week, when I returned home to my family: my big suitcase was stuffed full of money I had received as tips from the hotels, the restaurants, the resort centers, and the shops. I had made more money in a short period than I would have earned in one year, which was enough for me to help my mother and Ngan's family.

This job was another temporary one. I had taken it only to fill up my time and earn enough money to pay for the fees and paperwork required by the U.S. Immigration Service. Then tourists decided it wasn't worth it for them to explore Vietnam or invest in our country, and it began to look as if the tourism business itself was phasing out. Most of the tourists who did come to Saigon were businessmen who had a small business in Taiwan, and they were looking for a cheap market in Vietnam. They were so disappointed about what they found Vietnam to be after their tour that they never came back.

The government eventually learned that prostitutes followed the business tours all over the country, and so the police began to keep a very close watch on all travel agents. They stopped our tour buses on the highway to inspect them and my clients any time and anywhere they wanted to stop us. The tourists felt threatened by and uncomfortable with the police scrutiny. Recreation centers were falling into ruin rapidly, as they had not been upgraded in a long time. The National Resort Center had simply been taken over by the government and local residents. We eventually lost most of our Taiwanese business.

As a tour guide, I had to lie to my clients about our tours. I was mortified about lying to the tourists about the beauty they were going to find in our country right from the moment they arrived at the airport when, in fact, they quickly realized Vietnam was not even close to what most had expected it would be. Some of my clients were very angry and felt taken advantage of; others felt some sympathy for our land and people, all of which had been destroyed by bombs and gunfire for over thirty years. Most tourists found sightseeing too boring, the museums had been robbed of all of their valuable items, the market was unstable, and security forces were everywhere and obviously on high alert. The inner city was jam-packed with traffic, twenty-four hours a day, nonstop. Pollution, crime, and the constant police scrutiny scared all of my tourists on their first night in what I had told them was the "big and beautiful" city of Saigon.

Our trips to the ocean didn't give them any better an impression of Vietnam, either. The shore was filthy with litter and defecation left there by the locals. Tourists did like to shop for antique items; but they soon realized that the "antiques" for sale were all fakes. They also learned quickly that they had been cheated by local vendors for objects for which they had paid a couple hundred dollars that were actually worth only a couple of dollars.

But prostitution was the biggest problem for me in my career in travel. The young and beautiful prostitutes saw my tourists as delicious bait. From the very beginning of a tour, when I had just picked up my new clients at the airport, these young women were right there, waiting for them. Someone had picked up very accurate information about our entire trip from the travel agencies and passed it on to the prostitutes. Hordes of hookers followed our bus to our various destinations: hotels, restaurants, museums—anywhere we had planned to go. They befriended some of the tourists who got drunk at the nightclubs, and the prostitutes got the money they were after from the foreigners by the end of the evening.

I was responsible for my clients' safety, and I told all members of every tour in no uncertain words that my company did not tolerate prostitution and that our clients could not charge my company or me personally with negligence if anyone in our group were to be robbed by a prostitute. So I simply had to ignore what might happen after a party we had planned to attend, for instance, but that was not easy for me.

This job had turned out to be far more complicated, stressful, and dangerous than I had anticipated. I wrestled every single day with whether I needed money or peace of mind more. I had learned a lot about the tragedies that also were involved in my uncle's tourism business after less than one year. I needed a new job quickly so that I could stay sane.

Someone was watching over me, for suddenly—exactly when I needed it—I received the schedule for our interview with the US-INS in the middle of 1992. I was shocked because they had processed our application faster than I had ever expected they would. I was a nervous wreck and thrilled more than I had ever been thrilled before: my future depended solely on our final play in this game. I was either about to win a ticket to go to America and gain my freedom or lose access to that life I had dreamed about since I was a little girl. I would be forever stuck back in poor and miserable conditions, forever responsible for supporting everyone around me 'til I simply lost my mind.

Ngan, on the other hand, clearly from lack of experience, didn't worry at all. But his mother was worried: she didn't want to see him ruin the rest of his life, getting stuck, penniless and without any opportunities, on a little island in the middle of nowhere.

We asked Ngan's mother to come with us. At first, she didn't want to go with us, but then she changed her mind. She asked Ngan to add her name to the list of those being interviewed so she could take care of him in America. She taught him how to answer the questions that she had learned we would be asked from some of her friends who had been through it all. Ngan was stubborn and confident about the interview; his mother was petrified. Mother and son warred with each other every single day over the interview.

I was working on trying to stay calm. I tried to look forward to the day without getting too emotional: if I invested too many feelings in this one interview, I would be completely sunk if we did not pass. Even if storms were in my way, I had learned to keep moving forward. That was my father inside me. I tried to appear calm, while my imagination gradually spun out of control, and my blood began to feel like it was on a slow boil. I tried not to miss any work, even though I felt like passing out in the office, as I waited for the big day.

My entire destiny depended on Ngan and his mother. I prayed the caseworker wouldn't ask them too many personal questions because Ngan had a hard time remembering anything, even his own birthday! He got mad when his mother reminded him, over and over, about all the dates that he should remember or the family's daily activities. She kept repeating the colors of all the objects in the house and the colors of the clothes that we wore at home. She had tried to prepare Ngan and herself for any of the questions that our caseworker might ask. He went crazy over what he called his mother's 'overreacting.' That terrified me. And there was nothing I could do. He wouldn't listen to anyone.

The interview day arrived. The three of us took the bus to the Immigration Office in Saigon early in the morning. On the bus, not one of us said a word to the others. Ngan looked really happy and full of confidence; his mother was exhausted from her anxious worrying and tutoring; and I, too, felt exhausted after what had been such a long, difficult, weighty, and hurdle-filled journey to take this very bus ride. If Ngan made even a tiny mistake during the interview, I would lose everything that I had worked so hard for and earned, including my reputation.

I suddenly felt sick and developed a bad headache from thinking too much and riding on a crowded bus far too early in the morning. I pinched my forehead to relieve my headache, as I used to do at home anytime I had a headache; this created a big red mark on my forehead. Ngan and his mother worried that we wouldn't it make into the interview because I looked sick and wondered if we should turn around and reschedule our interview. I told them not to do that: we had gotten this close, and I wouldn't be able to wait a second longer.

Our bus finally arrived in Saigon and stopped right in front of the Immigration Office. Ngan and his mother held me up on either side so I could make it into the building. Inside, we found ourselves in a very spacious room filled with hundreds of people, all waiting for their interviews. The room was almost silent; the air was tense, close, and stuffy; and everyone's faces were tight with stress and anxiety, hoping to earn their tickets to America.

Families who had failed their interviews had gathered by the front door, crying out for help. Others had brought fraudulent paperwork, had been caught, and denied their visas. They had gathered together in a different area of the enormous room together to discuss their problem and trying to learn what to do next by listening to the experiences of others who had failed.

We took our seats at the far end of the building. We were told our estimated wait time for an interview could be up to five hours. A few American caseworkers circled around the room, collecting paperwork with the help of Vietnamese interpreters.

I suddenly felt very nauseous and exhausted, both made worse by the heat and humidity in the building. I closed my eyes, leaned back against my seat, and listened to the American and Vietnamese voices of the caseworkers, calling out names.

Suddenly, one of the Vietnamese interpreters crossed the room right toward Ngan and told him to follow the caseworker and bring his family with him for his interview. I thought there had to be a mistake because our case number was so far behind the others on the waiting list, and we had arrived just a short while ago.

As we followed the caseworker into an interview room, people in the crowd behind us in the great waiting room began to fight and yell because their families' interviews had been pushed further down on the list because we had been taken before them. The interpreter tried to calm the crowd and then turned and followed us.

Ngan got very excited, and a big smile spread across his face. His mother burst into tears from nerves. I said nothing and simply followed everyone. I bit my lip and tried not to show my panic, even though my heart was beating like the drum in the dragon dance at a Chinese New Year celebration. I felt like crawling across the floor because I was so weak with so many emotions. My hands were shaking, and my eyes blurred. I thought I was about to collapse from my fever and headache. A thousand stars seemed to sparkle over my head, and a stream of hot air blew into my face as soon as our caseworker shut the door behind us.

Two American officers and one Vietnamese interpreter were already seated in the room, waiting to interview us. We sat on the chairs that were positioned to face the interviewers directly. We all held our breath when the caseworker asked us to take an oath before the interview.

What happened in the next few minutes I knew would stamp and shape me, once and for all of the time I had left on earth. I was finally unable to hide my sheer terror any longer; we waited for the interviewers to speak or offer us a decision, which would feel more like a prison sentence, if we were denied.

Ngan, on the other hand, looked so comfortable, as if he were at a party. It had seemed to me all along that Ngan saw going to America as more of a burden than an opportunity. I guessed that in his heart he probably would be happier to fail the interview so that he could return to his small village life with his grandparents and play ball with the other kids on the field. I doubted that he had ever once thought about the concept of "future," that it had no meaning to him. I felt sure I would hang myself if we failed, while Ngan looked as confident as a rock. Ngan even exclaimed out loud that his mother was exaggerating when she said she would die if Ngan weren't given a chance to go to America. I was so afraid that there would be a big fight between Ngan and his mother, if we were all denied. I afraid to look up and see Ngan smiling at the caseworker. His mother, just like I was, shivered with horror, watching the way Ngan was behaving. She was afraid the caseworker would be disgusted with us because Ngan wasn't behaving respectfully.

I closed my eyes and started praying quietly. I had asked for help from all of the spirits who had died in my family, from my grandpa, my father, my uncle, my parents' unborn baby that my mother had miscarried when I was little. I prayed to everyone I could remember. I absolutely had to go to America. Otherwise, I would suffer, living in 'exhaustion hell' in Cu Chi for the rest of my life. I would probably lose everything that I owned, including my confidence. I didn't want to go home to spend the rest of my life without its having had some real meaning. My mother would be so sorry that my dream hadn't come true, but I imagined my older sister would be even angrier about my stupidity than before.

The silence in the room grew louder and louder, second by second, while the caseworker went through our documents. The pages turning sounded as loud as cymbals being rubbed together.

The caseworker finally looked up, ready to begin the interview: it was time to confront the reality of our situation.

Time went dead.

The caseworker looked directly at me and asked me a question in fluent Vietnamese, "Are you sick?"

I thought I had misunderstood him at first, for some reason; then I realized what he had asked me. I did not answer for a few seconds and then said, "Yes, I am sick."

The caseworker then turned to Ngan, "Do you have any questions?"

I almost died from the tension of Ngan's long silence before replying to the caseworker's question. *When* would Ngan begin to ask questions or even speak?

Ngan still wore his big smile, and finally he said, "I want to add my mother to our group so that she can go to America with us; she didn't file an application when we did." And he smiled that wide smile again.

"Of course," said the caseworker and nodded 'yes.' "This interview is concluded. Congratulations and good luck!"

No personal questions about either one of us or about our marriage or Ngan's mother!?! No tricky inquiry or more thorough information requested about our family of three, as we had heard people had had to deal with before!?! It had been too easy! I had almost cried when the caseworker had asked me about my health, as they seemed more concerned about us personally than interested in investigating us in depth the way police might interrogate prisoners. They had probably also been watching our behavior since we had first walked in the building and had noticed that I wasn't feeling well. That was probably why our family was called in for an interview before we would have been, if we had had to wait to be called according to the order of the application numbers.

I wanted so badly to express in English my appreciation for their thoughtfulness and for being so kind to us. "Thank you very, very much, sir," we each said, in turn, and Ngan's mother said it twice. Each of us shook the hand of the caseworker who had handed us the decision, bowed to him, and then filed quietly out of the room.

Once safely outside the interview room, immediately I collapsed in the hallway onto my knees, screaming and crying out in joy, thanking the Lord for His goodness and generosity, for giving us this seemingly impossible gift.

As we walked (I wobbled) out of the Immigration Office building, I looked up to the sky, thanking God again and again for accepting my prayers, even though I felt that all of the thanks I could ever give would never be enough for His act of merciful love.

My fever and my headache had disappeared as soon as the caseworker had announced we had passed the visa interview, and I felt a heavy weight lift from my shoulders. I felt good, and my strength had suddenly returned. I felt full of energy and refreshed, as if I were a brand, new person. My day was full of light, unlike the darkness that had seemed to hang over us all the way to Saigon.

We took the bus back home in the very beautiful, late afternoon. Although the sun had almost set behind the horizon, it still had a chance to shine up the world to celebrate our victory.

Riding on the bus, I drew in my mind images of my mother's and everyone in my family's great joy at our news. I imagined a perfect picture of my family in the very near future. I used the brightest colors to paint out all the darkness and miseries that had trapped and held all of us down for so many years. The shower of money I would soon send them washed off our shame and poverty. In that beautiful image, my mother wore a big smile for the first time in a long time, and her pocket was full of U.S. hundred dollar bills that had been sent to her from her daughter in America. My family sat down at a table laden with fresh meat and fishes, all to help my grandma and all the kids grow healthier. In one little corner of that picture, I saw a line of people, those who used to harass and look down on my mother, now bowing down in front of her, asking for help. The picture was so complete and real and very soon *would* be a reality. I smiled to myself as I painted away in my mind and listened to my heartbeats of happiness.

My grandma was right at the front door of our house with my mother and siblings when we returned to Cu Chi. I will never forget the tension on everyone's faces; they looked from Ngan's to his mother's to my face, trying to read what had happened to us at the visa interview. No one asked a single question.

But no one had to wait very long, as Ngan's mother finally cried out, "We are going to America! We passed!"

No one said a word for a moment. My grandma congratulated us, as my mother walked away with tears in her eyes. She was happy that my dream had finally begun to come true but felt very sad because I would leave her to go to America.

"You are going to leave us? Is that true?" my oldest sister Chau asked with tears running down her cheeks. She decided to try to break the sadness by telling us all that the dinner she had cooked for us while she was waiting for our return was ready.

'Yes,' I thought to myself. 'Yes, I am going to America. Yes!'

It took a few months from the day of the interview for us to be able to leave Vietnam. I decided not to quit my job because we were going to need a lot of money to make our journey. I quietly prepared for my enormous leap across the ocean without telling anyone around me. I dared not to make a noise or walk too fast. I tried not to get people's attention. I quit taking the tourists on trips and worked in the office, in case procedures or paperwork that the Immigration Office required us to complete arose.

My mother wanted me to stay home and spend more time with her before it happened that we wouldn't see each other for a long time. I refused to do so because I didn't want my presence at home to bring her more memories to remind her that I had left. I promised her that I would stay home with her for a whole week as the date approached. I pretended to stay calm, but inside me, huge waves were rising and falling up and down in the turbulent ocean inside me.

My time in Cu Chi grew shorter and shorter. Every night, I hurried to finish the last pages of a journal I was writing to give my mother and family when I left the country. The journal was full of my tears, hopes, emotions, and happiness. I had prayed for this event for long time; however, though I worked hard on it 'til it was time to go, I still ran out of time to express all of the things I wanted to tell my mother and my siblings, things I needed to keep secret until I was really gone. My thoughts poured out of me onto the pages, together with tears that flooded my heart. Word after word in the journal conveyed the pride, joy, and deep cuts in my heart that no one would understand. I had been a big tree for my family to lean on, and I also had been the only safe haven for them when brutal storms tried, over and over, to sweep us away.

I stood in front of my father's picture on the altar for hours; I cried and sobbed, telling him silently how scared I really was. The time had ended for me to be able to look at and feel all the objects in the house where I was born and had grown up. I tried to pick out certain special belongings of mine to give to each my relatives as mementos before I left.

My poor grandma suffered the most over my departure. She was shocked and in pain as soon as she knew that I would leaving our home very soon. She tried to convince me not to go. She saw me as a lost, little bird that had been separated from its flock and had to look for nourishment on its own. I knew I would probably never return home. My promised land was thousands of miles away across the Pacific Ocean. I wanted badly to ask her if she saw another option for me; very suddenly, seeing her suffer, I would rather stay with the family than to be lonely and launched into the great, infinite world. My grandma was too old and too fragile for this terrible separation. She choked up, and her voice died and shook anytime she tried to talk to me about my leaving. I tried to stay away from her and my mother, for I knew their tears would soften my weakened heart and weigh down my enthusiasm for what I was about to face. Instead, I made myself wear a big smile on my face at all times to comfort *them* and convince *them* that I would be successful and safe. Maybe I was trying to convince myself a little, as well. I only hoped my father in heaven would forgive me for making this decision because he had never let any of us out of his sight when he was alive.

My last week with my family was far too long and miserable. My older sister was right: the longer I stayed home, the more pain and heartbreak I was causing everyone. At breakfast, lunch, and dinner, we cried together more than enjoying each other's company.

My oldest brother took a week off from work and brought his family home to spend some time with me before I left. All the poor grandkids saw the adults suffering. They were so innocent and too young to understand. My oldest sister Chau tried to cook me some of my favorite foods, but I couldn't taste them anymore. My grandma tried to feed me all kind of fruits that I had liked as a child. My older sister Ngoc bought me whole bunch of clothes for summer and winter, just in case I couldn't find them anywhere "out there." She was the expert in this department, of course. My little brother gave me a lot of the treats that we used to share when we were younger, and my two younger sisters cried more than they talked.

My last surprise gift for my mother and her dearest wish was that my younger sister Le became engaged to Kiet, my boss's son. I had introduced my younger sister Le to Kiet on the first day she replaced me at my job, as his mother had asked me to do. Kiet was the gifted child in his family. Responsible, kind, and generous, Kiet also helped his father run the business. He would be a wonderful husband to Le, I knew.

As I had planned, my good-bye party was held on September 2, 1992, two days before we were to leave. I wanted to combine my party with my younger sister Le's engagement celebration. My mother was so happy and proud of me for arranging everything. As she said, I had given her the most valuable present she could hope for. I hoped Kiet would replace me in the family and fill the hole in my mother's heart after I was gone.

CHAPTER NINE

1992

Ngan, his mother, and I arrived at Tan San Nhat airport early in the morning on a very sad, wet, and dreary day. It hadn't stopped raining since the night before. I tried to memorize my last views of Vietnam on the way to the airport.

I felt tired and had a headache because I had stayed up all night the night before to talk and cry and to say my last words to my grandma and the rest of my family.

Suddenly, that next morning, I felt extremely nervous and worried. We had absolutely nothing in our hands–no papers whatsoever–except the ID cards that we had received from the Immigration Office. Would we be rejected at the airport because someone had made a mistake while processing our visas?

At the entrance to the airport building, standing in front of the glass door, I held my breath and hurriedly ran to check in without saying a word of goodbye to anybody. I was so scared to think about the possibility of having to go back home with my family, if our trip to America was cancelled for some reason.

Ngan and his mother quietly followed me, passing through the glass door at the gate without saying goodbye to their family, either, because I had told them all we would be back to say good-bye. However, we were pushed quickly through the customs process, step by step, right up until it was time for us to board the airplane. I felt so awful about our families who were waiting to say good-bye to us outside the glass door. Now we had no time or way to return to them.

That was the first time I had ever entered an airport. I was shocked. The atmosphere was very intense and busy and loud. It was so clean, luxurious, and comfortable—and air-conditioned! It was a completely different world from the one on the other side of the glass doors where heat, noise, and filthy air blanketed the crowd. I wondered how much difference there would be between Vietnam and the country I was headed for.

No one was there to give us instructions or guide us. I had to complete many pages of paperwork by myself, which I eventually finished after hours of struggling through it. Leaving the country was so complicated, especially to someone who had never left the country before. We had had to answer so many questions for which we were not prepared at the airport's Immigration Office, but our paperwork had to be completed before we could receive our airplane tickets.

I took a deep breath to celebrate completing the first step in moving towards my biggest dream.

Our last step in getting on the airplane was a very difficult one for us to complete: a horrible exam at Customs. I felt like having a heart attack when the custom officers went through our files. We would be thrown out of the airport if they found that some of our information was incorrect, even if they noticed a little spelling mistake. Police were everywhere. They were watching all the passengers with eagle eyes. I felt chills running up and down my back and my neck when we passed by a policeman. They gave us degrading looks, as if we had been convicted for a terrible crime and were waiting for our sentence.

But we finished, and I was about to throw up from relief when I realized someone was walking behind me. I also almost jumped out of my skin when the Customs Officer called me back to get the receipt that I had left on the counter for some fee or other I had paid. I did not look back. I was betraying my country. I avoided looking straight into the Customs Officer's eyes. They all seemed to be laughing at me, as though I were a loser, running away from my own country so fast that I had left behind the receipt. Or all of those kinds of thought could have been a figment of my imagination. I didn't want anything to go wrong, after coming so far and being so close. I was prepared for the worst.

Sitting back in the waiting room, I relaxed a bit and then realized that my relatives were still waiting for us to come back out through the big, glass doors. Now we were separated only by those almost invisible, floor-to-ceiling sheets of glass, and Ngan, his mother, and I had entered an entirely different world the very minute Customs stamped the last endorsement on our passports: we could no longer turn back. I waved to my mother, but she could not see me. I wanted her arms tight around my shoulders once last time and to hug everyone who had driven to the airport with us. At this very last minute, our hearts were the most wounded.

Vietnam Airlines' giant metal bird sat out on the tarmac, waiting for its passengers to board and ride inside it across the ocean. I hadn't seen such an enormous airplane up close before; it was mysterious and almost impossible, a hundred times bigger than the ones that had soared over my head during the war. I never, ever dreamed or wished one day to actually sit inside one and fly away!

But now, I couldn't wait to fly up through the sky toward the sun and ride above the clouds. And I couldn't wait to see what the ground the giant bird would place us upon would be like. I imagined heading toward a heaven.

The flight attendant announced over a speaker that our flight was to begin boarding. I looked back at the glass entrance one more time and waved to anybody who might see me, though I knew no one would. At least I knew I had done all I could.

I called out silently, 'Goodbye, Vietnam, my home of many beautiful and painful memories. Goodbye, everyone who had shared parts of my life full of tragedy, much pride, closeness, and many tears. Goodbye to all the darkness at my father's life's end because we were too poor to find a better doctor and a better hospital to cure his illnesses.' I put my hand on my heart and called out again, silently, 'Father, come with me on this trip. Your spirit is the strongest support I have ever had and will need when I am on the other side of the ocean. I give you my promise again, father: your wishes will come true in a very short time.' I didn't realize my face was wet with tears until Ngan's mother offered me a cloth.

We climbed up the metal stairs, up, up, up into the side of the giant bird. The airport building then looked tiny when I turned around at the top of those stairs one last time to see my homeland.

From my window, as the plane roared and pulled us up, up with all its might away from Saigon, the city's shiny skyscrapers and busy streets gradually vanished, and my window was veiled by puffy white clouds. I was in the middle of the sky, alone really, for the very first time in my next, new, adult life.

It took a lifetime, it seemed, to get from Vietnam to the Philippines. Most of the other passengers had fallen asleep, including Ngan and his mother, after our long day of struggles at the airport. As I peered around at the other passengers, I realized I was the only one still wide awake. I was too excited to sleep and miss a single moment of my whole trip. Plus the many different sounds the airplane made during flight and the possibility of bad weather all made me too nervous and scared to sleep.

The flight attendants woke everyone up and served us dinner before we landed at Manila Airport. It was the best dinner I had ever had, and my first American meal was so delicious: a piece of beef, salad, some fruits, and a roll with butter. I also drank my first glass of fresh milk and juice, the best beverages I had ever tasted—so far. The whole trip away from my country was full of hope and happiness and good food!

Our plane landed at Manila Airport late in the afternoon. We had been told in Vietnam that we would be staying in the

Philippines for six months to go through an orientation before going on to America. Manila was much bigger and so much more beautiful than Saigon. A bus picked us up, together with many other families who were to go to a transit station for one night.

It started pouring just outside Manila. The rain suddenly called up memories of my family, whom I had almost forgotten since I had first flown away into the clouds, and I burst out in tears. Then all night, I thought about my family and the tears I had felt in my heart just that morning, letting go of them. It seemed as if I were a million miles away from home now, as if I had fallen down to the bottom of the earth and was hoping to be reborn again in a new life and a new place. But where would that be? I didn't really even know where I actually was. I sat in a dark corner at the transit, crying by myself.

But then, I spoke silently and clearly to myself, 'You cannot let yourself feel so desperately broken down at the very beginning of your new journey! You've made a choice, and compared to your miserable past, where you are heading has to be better. Just keep moving on, and don't look back. That is what Father would say; you know that.'

That night, we were instructed to prepare for a long trip of almost six hours to the refugee camp in Bataan. The next leg of my journey was about to begin.

Early in the morning, we got on a big bus and traveled across Manila through beautiful mountain ranges, along rivers, and lush forests to get to our destination. The road was in awful condition, full of ruts and sinkholes and washboards, and it got even worse as we approached Bataan, where our refugee camp was: in the middle of nowhere, surrounded by mountains and cliffs. The mountain ranges were green and very mysterious, but Bataan was too far away from any city for me, almost completely isolated from the rest of world. As beautiful as our surroundings were, I panicked at the thought of spending the next six months of my life in this very still and uncivilized mountain valley.

The only thing that I had heard about our camp was that many Vietnamese boat people lived at the camp, as well, and they were still waiting–some for as long as ten years–to get to their next destination. Panic again. I had never once considered the fact that I might <u>never</u> get to America or reunite with my family!

We finally entered the refugee camp in Bataan on a sunny day with a brilliant, blue sky overhead. From far away, I could see hundreds of people waiting at the gate to welcome us–and some of them I recognized from Cu Chi! Their families probably had let them know we were on our way to the camp. Everyone was so very excited to see us. They must have grown lonely and were dying to have some friends or relatives with them after all the time they had spent there. They cried a lot when they saw my little family, as if they were seeing their own blood relatives for the first time in a decade.

The view from the refugee camp, which had been built on the side of a mountain, was breath-taking. Looking down into the valley, we could see the entire refugee camp, vivid green mountains, mysterious cliffs, and the romantic, pale, lapping ocean. My tour guide self thought it would be an ideal place for tourists to visit or for artists seeking inspiration from the gifts of Mother Nature. The beauty of this natural world seemed almost too extravagant for all of us who had come to the camp, were living on charity from the US government, and waiting for help, I thought, terrified, to myself.

But our orientation wasn't as boring as I had thought it would be. For six months, our lives were filled with activities. Every day, we went to school to learn English and receive a cultural orientation to help us adjust to American life. We were examined over and over for medical issues to make sure we were healthy and free from any contagious diseases before we were allowed to emigrate to America. We were given job-hunting and interviewing skills. In addition to our schooling, we did some voluntary work for the community at the camp, such as picking up garbage, gardening, etc.

Since I was one of the most educated people in the camp and had also learned some English years ago in Vietnam, people began to know and respect me. I quickly became an assistant teacher and interpreter for the United Nations Office and the Immigration Office at camp. People also began to ask me for help with anything from health problems to paperwork they were struggling to complete. Rich Vietnamese refugees who wanted to learn a little more English asked me to tutor them in the evening. I made really good money from teaching this special English class, and that was a big help to us while we lived in the camp. Fortune was still watching over me in the form of a surprising source of income, which enabled me to buy extra food and household supplies for our family.

The housing structures in the refugee camp were wooden with metal roofs and concrete floors. Five units per building were separated by wooden walls for five families to share. We had no beds but were given floor mats to sleep on the floor.

We had absolutely no privacy. At night, our next-door neighbors would cough, talk, or fight, keeping us awake for hours. We were also fed poorly in the camp. Each week, we received some eggs, a chunk of fatty pork, a quarter of a chicken leg, and some kind of fish to which we developed allergies. We received plenty of rice, which was mixed with grass seed and rocks, so we had to clean the rice carefully before cooking it. It didn't matter to me; I was positive that this would be our last challenge before we stepped into heaven in America. I kept thanking God that we only had to live for six months in the camp. I could live in slum-like conditions: it was no big deal when I thought about what I had already survived and about the reward for surviving those challenges.

Every single night, after my English classes, I lay down on my floor mat and cried. I missed my grandma, my mother, and the rest of my family. I still regretted not being able to say those last few words I had wanted to say at the airport before I left forever.

I cried every time I opened my luggage and saw the gifts my sisters and brothers had packed in it: dried food, soaps, shampoo, an umbrella, my favorite snacks, and my little brother Tai's special notes. I loved them and was so grateful to each of them for these gifts and felt so guilty because they probably needed the things they gave me more than I did.

Sometimes, when I opened my luggage, I hoped to find something I hadn't discovered yet: a fingerprint of my mother's on my belongings, notes from my other brothers, or even a receipt. I held the object that each of them snuck into my luggage and held as if I were holding that person's hands. When rain plunked down on the metal roof and crickets cried somewhere out in the wet darkness, those sounds took me right back home.

Ngan's mother hid in a dark corner of our house unit, moaning and sobbing all night long. She had lost so much weight from being homesick and missing her parents and her children. Her eyes were red and swollen; she was silent all day long. She didn't want to eat.

Ngan was the only one of us who was very happy and comfortable. He was having so much fun with his new friends in the camp; he played ball with the neighbors and chatted with his classmates after school. He seemed to be doing very well in this new environment. He probably missed his grandparents, who had always spoiled him, and the kids who used to play with him all day long on the field. He loved getting free clothes at the office and dressing up like a fashionable guy. He had an eye exam at the doctor's office and asked for a brand new pair of eyeglasses, even though his vision was completely normal. He was also happy to be able to go to school for the first time in his life. Everything had changed for him since he had left Vietnam. Life at camp had introduced him to the material world, a new way of living that he was very attracted to.

Crimes were committed almost every day at camp. The boat people who had escaped from Vietnam had been denied immigration to the U.S. That denial trapped them in this camp forever. They were furious, as they had lost everything, had no family at camp, were ostracized by others in the camp community, and had no future. They eventually became violent criminals.

They began their violent attacks by killing each other for personal reasons. Thousands of boat people who'd been killed by their own had been buried in a huge cemetery down in the valley. Thousands more boat people who had died at sea on their trip toward freedom were also buried there.

Life might have seemed really peaceful during the day, unless you knew better: after dark, it became terrifying and stressful. We were such a small community, but the jail was always full of thieves, troublemakers, alcoholics, drug-addicts, and crooks who cheated people and gambled.

The policies at the refugee camp were very strict. Even though we were legal immigrants, we still underwent a few more interviews by the U.S. immigration office before we were released to go to America. If one person were found to have committed a crime, his whole family would be retained at camp forever. Many people had been retained for years and years without so much as a second thought by the Immigration Office. I was so worried that Ngan might allow himself to be seduced by the gangsters in the camp and would use alcohol and drugs. I refused to take any money from relatives who sent it to me from America. I would rather have stayed poor and "invisible" at camp until the day we were to leave for the Philippines than to attract gangsters and thieves with the smell of U.S. money. I didn't want to lose the future I was so close to actually living for any reason: I had to get out of that terrible place as soon as I could.

My co-workers suffered many tragedies. Those in our small assistant teaching group had complicated and very frightening relationships with their families. One lady and her husband had sold their house, their property, and saved everything they had earned during entire lives to buy an Amerasian child in order to bring their own children to America to have a better life. She was constantly worried that their Amerasian kid would turn them in to Immigration before they could make it out of camp. Her husband had heart disease, and it had worsened since they had arrived at camp because their Amerasian kid had become stubborn and uncontrollable.

Some college students had pushed their parents to sell the last piece of property they owned in order to pay part of ownership of an Amerasian kid to look for a new life. Arriving at the refugee camps, those students were miserable because their host families harassed them and made them pay more money to live with them. These Amerasians were only children, brothers and sisters, or they were the Aunties and uncles of the Ameriasians. They all lived as a huge family, but in this huge family, not a single person was related to any of the others. None of them lived in peace as they went through the process of realizing their American dreams. One family had fought from their first day at camp, which made the possibility of their being caught by the Immigration Office obvious.

Another Vietnamese friend of mine in the camp suffered in a different way. He had purchased the file of a black Amerasian for thousands of dollars to go to America. Then he had paid more money to pass through Customs and Immigration at the airport to get to the Philippines. He didn't realize that he would be interviewed again at camp. He became very depressed and cried every day. His life was over, if caught. It was obvious that his face didn't match the photograph of the guy whose file he had bought. He prayed to go back to Vietnam or for a miracle. He could either have a bright future in America or become a criminal and spend the rest of his life on this awful island. He was afraid his mother back in Vietnam would die alone because he was her only son. He had lost over thirty pounds in a couple months from his depression and feeling of hopeless. He looked like a corpse walking around the camp, crying like a little kid anytime he talked to anyone.

Hung was a third-year engineering student in Vietnam. The doctor at the camp diagnosed him with tuberculosis, and he was very poor and lonely with his host family. The doctor also told him he had to be retained at the camp for treatment until he had recovered his health, and none of us knew how much longer he would have to stay at camp.

Though we all struggled with our rotten life at camp, we at least saw a bright light at the end of the seemingly endless tunnel to America. The price of surviving to reach our promised land was very high and much more difficult and scary than we could ever have imagined. And anyone could suddenly become a threat to anyone else—someone who was angry that he or she failed his re-interview, for instance—and it could happen—day or night, rain or shine.

The Buddhist temple was the most crowded place in the camp. Everybody went to the temple, crying for help, begging for a blessing from God. They wished Buddha could share their problems and give them another chance, if they had failed the exam or come by boat. Some wished that they had been denied by the U.S. Immigration Office and stayed in Vietnam than to have to endure this camp. Camp was worse than prison; it was completely surrounded by fences, and no one could get in or out without permission and inspection by the authorities.

I spent most of my spare time at the temple, too, praying for myself. The Buddha statue at the front of the temple was the most beautiful object in the camp. He looked so gentle and relaxed. His eyes were closed, but there was a smile on his face, and he always comforted my heart. His smile was my greatest inspiration: that smile kept me going through everything I had to face, just as my father's would have.

The very rich families in camp suffered immensely. It was too late for them to return home. They had sold their houses and businesses in Vietnam. They were so frustrated and miserable at having to live such degrading lives on this camp's dead terrain. Eating terrible food, as if they were homeless people, and having to sleep on concrete floors, instead of their soft beds at home, made them feel that their lives had been turned completely upside down. They took the bus to go to school with the rest of us and cooked their own dinners themselves in the afternoon after school. They had to learn how to live without servants to help them. They realized they had paid far too much for their American dreams, and they would still have to pay more if their gold mine–their Amerasian child–turned them in to the Immigration Office. Having no knowledge of the English language, they had to start over in that respect, as well, and they must have wondered if their new American lives might wind up being even *more* difficult.

In contrast, the poor people in camp became more confident and received many more benefits than did the rich ones. The poor had left their homes with nothing in their luggage but burdens of poverty and a few pairs of old clothes and personal items. But, once at camp, they didn't have to worry anymore about their basic daily needs, as they had in Vietnam. They were given everything: housing, food, clothing, dental care, healthcare, etc. They had never seen a doctor or a dentist before, and they were so grateful to be given whatever care they needed. The food at camp wasn't great, but it was still a lot better than they had *ever* had in all of their lives. The housing wasn't great either; but at camp, they were given places for all members of their families to live together. This was the first time they'd been treated with generosity and kindness. Their lives at camp were more meaningful and colorful than they had ever been, and they knew their children would have an even better life in the United States.

Over the course of my life, I had experienced both–the best and the worst in life, having been born and growing up in a prosperous family and then quickly plummeting down to the bottom of society. We once had servants; then we went bankrupt and had to live through the pain of losing my father. I understood well and could empathize with both the happiness of the poor people and the misery of the rich.

Suddenly, the six-months long training course at the refugee camp was finally over, and we received our tickets to America. We had passed all the health exams and were legally allowed to leave after going through a few re-interviews with Immigration. We all felt such conflicting emotions at the goodbye party held for us with the teachers and the staff in the camp. For the first time in my life, I danced like crazy with everyone in the community to celebrate. I had simply packed all of my important personal belongings, pictures, and some books for my luggage. The rest, I gave to our neighbors, who had to remain there for more orientation. I gave all the money I had earned from teaching my English classes to some poor families I had come to know so they could buy a few extra things for their children. I didn't forget to give Hung, my classmate, some money for his time recuperating.

On a very beautiful day in March, 1993, we boarded the bus going back to the Manila Airport. The road didn't seem to be nearly as rough as it had when we had first ridden to camp; it seemed seamless instead, even though nothing along the way had changed in the past six months. Trees along the road were a more vibrant green; spring flowers were blooming everywhere and painting the mountainside and the cliffs with the entire palette of colors that reflected my joy. 'Goodbye, Bataan! Goodbye, refugee camp, where I learned so much more than I had known about life before.

'And hello again, Manila!' We were to spend the night in Manila, as we were scheduled for an early flight the next day to go to America. Unlike six months ago, Manila looked beautiful and peaceful to me now. The sky was prickly bright with stars. Even sleeping in the same crowded place, in the same little tiny room, and in the same bed in which I'd slept six months ago, I felt as if I were staying in the most luxurious hotel on earth.

That night, I prepared carefully for my long trip in the morning. I carefully unwrapped and hung up my very special blue suit that I had kept safe and pressed over the six months we had spent at camp; it had been made by a famous tailor in Saigon for my trip to my new world. As I fell asleep, I wove lovely images of the new world on the other side of the ocean: it was waiting for me.

CHAPTER TEN

JUNE, 2009

Still deep in dreams (the *only* way to fly, I believe), suddenly I *thought* I heard Rick's voice calling my name, over and over, "*Julie! Julie!*" But Rick had had nothing to do with my first steps on American soil; so I turned over and fell back deep down into my dream again. Sometimes dreams can trick you.

MARCH 18, 1993

We boarded our plane at the United Airlines terminal early in the morning and traveled across the Pacific Ocean—almost ten thousand miles—to freedom and San Francisco. I couldn't wait to see San Francisco, as I had heard and read so much about this magical place. Looking down through my oval eye-window, the brilliant California sun highlighted the city's majestic architecture, which made the city and the ocean all around it sparkle like a carpet of giant gems below us.

The plane landed with a long shudder, shaking everybody, especially all of us sitting in the back of the plane. Our group of fifty had to wait to get out of the airplane until all the "regular" passengers had gone, as the flight attendants had instructed us.

Crawling meekly out of the airplane at last, wearing huge, IOM name badges on our shirts and carrying IOM bag in our hands, I'm sure we stood out in the crowd as "foreigners" among the thousands of Americans in the airport. They knew where they were going, but our faces alone gave us away: our eyes showed our confusion, vulnerability, sense of being lost, terrified, exhausted, and beaten down; we were as skinny as nails and filthy as earthworms that had crawled out from under the ground. We were uncertain and wobbly, like toddlers just learning how to walk.

We were told to stand in a line along a wall outside the terminal to wait for help. People passing by stared at us as if we were aliens from outer space and not even human beings.

San Francisco was just the first stop in my particular journey, a social worker told me after we had passed through Customs Administration. We three were taken from the rest of the group after saying goodbye to everyone else and told to get on the next flight before it was too late. We then learned we had to face <u>two</u> more flights to reach our final destination: Fargo, North Dakota. I had wanted the location of my new home in the U.S. to remain a surprise, and our social worker ruined the surprise—twice! He told us our destination, and it turned out that I had never heard of this place that our social worker told us was "somewhere in the middle of North America."

A Lutheran church in North Dakota had offered to sponsor our family. We had no relatives in America who had offered to sponsor us; some distant family members had made it to America before us, but they had not offered to sponsor us at any point along our way, whereas most of the other refugees had been sponsored by their American relatives. We were wholly dependant on the charity of volunteer agencies in America for our new lives in the U.S.

Even though the social worker had spilled the beans, in my imagination, I just knew Fargo would be a wonderland: thousands of acres of land covered by lush, vivid green grass and bright, cheerful flowers, Fargo was sure to be peaceful and prosperous, more so than anywhere else on earth. It would be a place to run around freely on sunny days and pick plump berries that grew along the street. The neighborhood market would be overflowing with fresh produce and foods, and I imagined myself walking to the marketplace every day, my eyes shining at the bounty I found there, my arms full of stalks of flowers of every hue.

The perfect, bright day we had awakened to that morning in San Francisco was a sign to me that fortune was indeed waiting for me in Fargo. I closed my eyes and fell asleep as our final plane pulled us up into the wide sky toward our final destination.

Fargo was up to its waist in snow the night we arrived, and the black night sky was almost grey because it was so thick with heavy, white snow that it looked like curtains of whipped cream were falling from the sky. Ice was also now glazing the snow that had fallen earlier. What a shock. The city looked swollen, its buildings now shaped like tall, looming creatures or cakes, and everything continued to grow and swell so quickly, second by second! I *had* been so excited about seeing snow–but not *this* much!! The cold air stung us, and the falling snowflakes made everything seem mysterious.

Our sponsors met us right at the arrival gate. All of the stocking caps, gloves, and extra coats and jackets they had brought for us weren't even enough to keep out the cold. We followed them very gingerly across the ice-slick parking lot. My brain was numb as we drove away from the airport. I could see nothing but snow and black sky, and I could only feel the icy fingers of air, wrapping themselves tightly around me.

Only twenty-four hours had passed since I had left Asia, and this new, frozen earth on which we rode was terrifying. The extreme and sudden change in the climate scared me to death. It was even worse when we had to crawl between the towering, icy walls of a snow tunnel to get into our apartment in the middle of the silent night.

'Welcome to America, Loan! Welcome to Wonderland!' I said to myself, sarcastically. My lungs ached and my icy, frozen nose hairs tickled inside my nose when I inhaled. We followed our American sponsors silently through snow tunnels, and finally they stopped in front of an old apartment building in a very dark neighborhood.

It was two o'clock in the morning when our sponsors opened the door and invited us to enter our new apartment home.

"The temperature in the apartment has been set at seventy-five degrees!" one of the sponsors informed us, with a big smile on his face. "Will that be warm enough for your family?"

My English wasn't good enough to suggest that it would be better if were turned up more, so I just nodded that it was fine because I did not want to bother them. I would figure it all out after they left.

I didn't even look at anything around me for one second: all I needed to find was a thick, heavy blanket and a bed. After forty-eight hours on the road to America, I needed a long rest to prepare myself to make the most of my new life, despite how frightening and unexpected the situation appeared to be so far.

My intense fear kept me wide awake in bed, absolutely scared stiff of all of the snow and frozen air outside. How did people survive in such a treacherous climate? How were we even able to walk through the air, if it so cold? The snow I had seen in pictures or in movies was so different from the reality of Fargo's snow. It was mystifying to watch but not to feel on my body, any part of it.

When I finally dragged myself out from under the heavy blanket of sleep I finally had dropped into, I noticed that day was dawning on my first day in America, and I heard birds fighting outside the window. When I could open my eyes fully, I found myself in a very old apartment. The ancient carpet smelled like cigarette smoke, which I later learned was because smokers lived downstairs. The electric heater didn't seem to work at all. The air in the rooms had felt as cold as the air outside all night. I crept out of bed, my blanket wrapped tightly around me, and cranked up the heat to eighty degrees. But that didn't result in nearly enough heat. So I turned the thermostat up as high as it would go. The old heater clicked and cranked and complained from being over-worked, but the room finally warmed up. It was probably ninety degrees in that apartment, but I could finally smile.

Ngan and his mother were sound asleep, so I sat on the couch in the front room, taking a good look around the apartment for the first time and relishing the quiet and being all by myself. As I looked at each piece of furniture and the objects they had placed around the apartment for us, to my surprise the apartment was perfect! The sponsors had obviously been very thoughtful; from kitchen to bedroom to living room, everything they had put in the place was of nice quality, and the apartment was clean and neat. The refrigerator was packed full of fresh food–exactly what I had dreamed of having my entire life. Thanking God, I *had* landed in heaven after all!

I did fall asleep again on the couch for a few hours before the daylight fully paled the strong, blue sky. When I looked out the window, shock: the whole town was buried up to its neck in sparkling snow. Though the sun was out, its power was as weak as our apartment's heater: too weak to melt *anything*. 'The sun's rays must freeze as soon as they reach halfway down through the atmosphere and never reach the snow,' I thought to myself.

Outside, this world was eerie: all I could hear was an echoey, endless silence and then suddenly the fighting of black crows outside on dead, stiff tree branches. I had never seen that many crows before in my life. Their fighting was fierce, awful, and rau-cous, loud enough to crack the frozen air, as sound can break glass. From the ground to the rooftops of the houses, layers upon layers upon layers of ice covered everything, glittery icing on the snow beneath it. A few squirrels were scrambling back and forth for food on the icy ground. The trees seemed dead tired; they had been completely denuded after the long winter. What hell it would be to stand outside while snow fell in torrents upon your naked limbs! I pulled my blanket closer.

Not a single human being was outside anywhere as far as I could see.

Snow and ice had barricaded me in, and I suddenly did not know how dreams of any kind had space to grow in this barren Fargo. It had no lush, green grass; flowers; or berries that I had looked forward to picking from bushes along the road. And even worse, last night on our way to the apartment, our sponsors had told us that the closest store was miles away from our apartment. Inside, I suddenly felt my heart tighten and begin to bang against my ribs. I was imprisoned in a completely alien land where I supposed to find freedom!

I had been born into and grew up in a tiny town at the very edges of the deep, dangerous, and hot jungle. After that, I had lived in a metropolitan city during college: neither one bore any similarity whatsoever to Fargo. Small and secluded from any civilization, if there even *was* any civilization nearby, Fargo bore no resemblance to San Francisco, which had led me to believe that American cities were going to be fantastic and beautiful. Fargo was simply alone, sticking out in the air in the middle of nowhere that I knew and sinking under the white, weighty burdens of its long and frozen winter. Even the sun in Fargo was different from the sun in Cu Chi's sky, which pushed its hot hands heavily down upon my shoulders and the top of my head. Here, though the sun was trying as hard as it could to share some of its warmth with earth, it never arrived.

Except for our doctor's office and the Department of Social Services and Health, to which places our sponsors drove us, we had nowhere to go, except school. It felt as if we were walking all the way to Cu Chi, just to get to school. Every morning, we hurried between and through towering walls of snow on very treacherous, icy roads to get to school, which was six blocks away, our breaths making eerie, white shapes that hung in the cold air.

One day, I noticed that Ngan's mother was bruised all over her body from having fallen down in the icy streets. For some strange reason, though, her bruises didn't bother her at all. She was so happy and excited about being able to go to school, learn English, and find some Vietnamese people in Fargo. Every single day, no matter how bad the weather was, she got up at four o'clock in the morning to walk to Goodwill or was taken there later by church members. She picked up used clothes and sheets that people had put in the donation bins. She made over thirty pairs of pajamas for herself from old, donated bed sheets and then used all of the laundry detergent we had to wash them. She hung her pajama creations up in the bathroom around the bathtub to dry and accidentally turned our bathroom into a garden: giant mushrooms–bigger than Pho bowls–began to grow like crazy in our "bathroom garden" because water dripped from her drying pajamas onto the carpet. The social worker was shocked when Ngan's mother asked him if she could eat the mushrooms she was growing in the bathroom!

Then, in the afternoon, she loved going to the church to pick up free food. She walked from the apartment in the cold weather and almost died right on the street one day of hypothermia. I had no idea how far away the Goodwill store was, but any distance in that cold air was too much for an old woman like Ngan's mother. She considered the free food a great blessing from God. Food and clothes were the two things she had had to struggle so hard to acquire all her life for her children. Many times, she came home from the church in joyous tears, proud to show us all the free things that people had given her. She was so grateful for these gifts; but she also felt guilty about the rest of her children who had remained in Vietnam and were still living in poverty. She wished she could somehow share her bounty with her children far away, bursting into tears every time she told me of her wish.

Ngan's mother loved going to the grocery stores anytime the sponsors offered us a ride, just to see what she could find. But she had difficulty converting U.S. dollars into Vietnamese dong; she also thought American products were far too expensive and preferred to pick up free food and clothing at the churches than to pay for them from her own pocket.

She was told by Vietnamese neighbors about a tiny Japanese store in town run by an old Japanese couple, but she didn't go there often.

Overall, Fargo was Ngan's mother wonderland, ice and snow and cold and bruises and mushrooms and all. In Fargo, she had discovered a bounty she had longed for.

Ngan, too, was content with his new life in America. He liked chatting and smoking with his new Vietnamese friends who lived in the apartment downstairs. He could survive without food but not without cigarettes, he declared. Ngan and our downstairs neighbors got together every day early in the morning and talked and smoked until midnight. In the refugee camp, he had constantly complained about not having enough cigarettes; one his dreams about living in America was having as many cigarettes as he could smoke, always.

Ngan didn't care much about learning English or about having a career, and he usually forgot everything he had learned in school that day, as soon as he had walked out of its doors at day's end.

But he was very proud of the victory he had won as an Amerasian man. In the small Vietnamese community in Fargo, Ngan made more friends, sometimes staying at these friends' houses in town for days on end before returning to us again. He was very popular, and he loved driving from town to town, sightseeing with his new friends, even though there was really nothing to see but snow, as far as I was concerned.

"We just came back from Minnesota!" he told us excitedly once, after he returned home, having disappeared for several days and never having let us know where he was or when he would return.

Ngan bloomed in his new life in the U.S. He dressed like a 'real, young, American man' in the used clothes that the sponsors had bought for him at Goodwill. He proudly told us people always thought he was a good-looking, American guy until they got up close enough to see and talk to him. He paid socially for not understanding English, but that didn't make him want to study any more than he did.

All of the young American girls in town began to pay lots of attention to him, and they began coming right to the apartment, looking for him. Only then was Ngan embarrassed because he couldn't talk to them. We tried to convince him to learn some English, but he still didn't think he needed to learn how to speak it, even though his friends who had come to America a long time ago had learned how to speak it and were doing pretty well. Nobody could change his mind about not knowing English. He said he refused to suffer any more because now he lived in heaven, he told his mother. He insisted on enjoying his life before our eight months of welfare ended, and that was what his friends encouraged him to do.

Watching Ngan and his mother celebrating their lives in America, I felt incredibly jealous and depressed. I wanted to enjoy freedom as easily as they seemed able to do. Instead, I felt I needed to hurry all the time and work as much and as hard as possible; I was stressed out and burdened with thoughts of my mother and everyone else in the family in Vietnam, all of whom were waiting for my help to arrive and save them. Every day, sitting behind our living room window, watching the snow fall down and down and down, I began to feel as if I was going crazy. My time was too valuable, and I couldn't waste it any more. I had already wasted six months in the refugee camp, unable to accomplish anything I needed to do, and I didn't want to waste any more time now. But I was held captive in this white wasteland.

I was well prepared for my American journey the minute the airplane landed in the U.S., and I was eager to get a job to begin to make money to send home, instead of simply sitting back and enjoying my sole victory in reaching America, as Ngan and his mother did.

And the snow kept falling, falling, falling down, locking me in.

Finally, green spikes of grass started to poke up through the disappearing white that had begun to melt into the ground: winter was almost over! The sparrows followed signs of spring to Fargo, and here and there, birds began to thrive again on the branches on which buds had begun to sprout. I could feel the sunshine, reaching all the way down through the atmosphere easily to warm my face. The roads were slushy and wet for a while.

Daylight stayed with us longer, too. It was soon hard to remember that only several weeks ago, Fargo–and all of us–had been hibernating, deeply asleep–or numb–like a bear inside a giant snow cave. My mood lightened. I could walk down the street and looked forward to learning my way around my neighborhood, instead of hiding inside the apartment after school just to stay warm. I could walk outside in the sun and shop for food at the tiny Japanese grocery store in the neighborhood. My winter nightmare was finally completely over when I could feel the sun massaging my bare toes in my bedroom each morning.

Our social worker started pushing us to go out and hunt for jobs. My English wasn't good enough to get a good job, except as a chambermaid at a small hotel or as a fast food worker at the food chain restaurants in town. Fargo was a little town with few businesses, but it had churches everywhere–north, south, east, and west. The residents in Fargo gathered together on the weekends in the churches, which were the only places they could be together. But none of them were looking for career opportunities.

My sponsors offered to drive me around town to look for a job, but I had no luck. The Masters Degree I had worked so hard to earn in Vietnam was considered useless in America. I started worrying seriously about my future now and my plans and wondered how we would ever survive after our welfare program ended, which would be soon. I would have to start all over from the beginning, learn even more English, and earn another degree to ensure that I would eventually be able to get hired for a good job. However, nobody in the community offered any support or instruction. I was on the verge of giving up—completely.

Only a few hundred Vietnamese lived in Fargo. Most of them had come to the United States from the countryside in Vietnam. These Vietnamese had had no education, no job or career, but they were very willing to take any job offered to them, just to survive and remain in America. I tried to lower my expectations, as they had, and to take any job that was available in town. But no one would hire me for a job anywhere. After reading my resume, none of the employers who interviewed me were interested because I didn't have any specific experience for the particular job I had applied for, even if it was a room service job!

I wanted badly to go back to school to learn what I needed to know to succeed, but then who would help support me when Ngan and his mother couldn't begin to support themselves? Opportunities I was sure I would find everywhere and open to all in America were completely out of my reach. Life in my new home wasn't anywhere as easy as I had thought it would be. My mother and my big family in Vietnam were all still waiting for my help, and their continued suffering haunted me. I felt like a worthless failure, even though I had tried everything I could do to get a job.

Slowly, but suddenly very obviously, Vietnamese families began to leave Fargo to move to other states. I panicked: was this a sign? I could not bear another severe winter in North Dakota, and it was right then I decided to move to Washington State. I hoped I might get help from my mother's cousins who lived in Seattle, even though they had never offered to sponsor me when the learned I had made it to the Philippines and still had not contacted me once I arrived in the United States. I had only seen them maybe once before in my whole life, and I figured that the government was the one to place me somewhere. Besides, I didn't think they would want to be bothered by me.

Ngan and his mother refused to come with me because they loved their lives in Fargo, and they did not want to depend on my mother's cousins. I, however, had never let go of my dreams and never would. I had been walking, step by step, forever it seemed, to find the one place where I would accomplish my goals and fulfill my dreams. Fargo was *not* that place, *my* promised land, after all.

CHAPTER ELEVEN

JUNE, 2009

Panic woke me: "Michael? Where's Michael?" I cried out loud, turning to Rick, my eyes wild and wide as plates, my husband said. "It's ok, Julie," Rick said. "Shhhh! He's sitting right behind you."

And suddenly Michael appeared, crouching down in the aisle next to our seats, his beautiful face smiling. Michael said, "Mom! You're going to scare the whole crew and all the passengers! What's wrong? I am right here, and we are on our most special mission of all time, and every one of us is here, together, *remember*? And Dad's right here, and everything's fine! The stewardess just announced that we have only two more hours until we arrive at the airport! Isn't that great?!...Mom...are you *ok*, Mom?" he asked, a little hesitantly.

I looked back and forth from one very special, puzzled face to the other, just to double-check that Michael *was* safe, that we were all safe, and then I knew my dream was real: we were all together on the flight of our lives, and we were all fine.

Rick offered me some orange juice and a dry, hard pastry with shiny, white icing latticed sloppily across the top. I was starving, so I wolfed them down and turned to Rick and smiled. "Imagine that! They have figured out how to make almost edible food in America out of cardboard! Except I am not even going to try to guess what they made the icing out of! Definitely *not* any form of paper!"

We all laughed. I smiled into each of the two sets of eyes that were smiling back at me, and I then let myself sink back deeply into my seat again to digest my "food," and my seat responded to my weight with that leathery, whooshing noise again. So many long, long, *long* trips in my life, always, *always* heading toward a dream...

"Julie, what the heck were you dreaming about, anyway? You and your dreams..." Rick shook his head and smiled. "You're such a wild sleeper and an even wilder dreamer! Do you remember what made you wake up, so worried about Michael?"

"No idea," I said, truthfully. I did not remember. Two more hours. Not bad. This trip, which had been only a dream for years and years, was a reality, after all. Everything *was* going to be all right, as my father had always assured me.

A heavy, dark curtain of relief slid down over my eyelids, and I was asleep again before I even knew it.

June, 1993

One more terrible fight with Ngan and his mother was the last straw for me, as far as staying in Fargo went. We had fought a lot, actually. Ngan's mother was always furious with Ngan about going out into town with his friends because she was scared he'd be attacked by gangsters or drive around drunk and get into big trouble or, even worse, be killed on the Fargo's winter roads.

Ngan and I fought about a lot, too: his smoking was number one because I had an allergy to it, and he was a heavy smoker. He also claimed he didn't need anything in the world but cigarettes and food, and the money we received from the government wasn't enough to buy both. On top of that, he now refused to go to school at all or to look for a job. We never ate together as a "family" because Ngan was never home.

The night before I left Fargo, he refused—and his mother refused, to my surprise—to go with me to Seattle. He would not leave his friends and start over, when I had no friends and was terribly isolated. I had to get out of Fargo right then and there and get far away from them: winter would be bearing down on us all too soon again.

Knowing I would never go back to Fargo, I made sure I thanked anyone who had tried so hard to help me during my very first days in the U.S. I *had* seen my first snow there: actually, it had prepared for our arrival with a big bang of a snowy celebration, right as we had gotten off the plane that first night. Seeing snow was *one* of my wishes finally granted; I had hoped to see it since I had learned about it as a child. But now, after having lived in Fargo, I knew snow was two-faced, gorgeous and literally a dangerous menace, even a killer, and I never wanted to have to skate gingerly along icy roads to get to school and back every day. I *had* come to love the peace and quiet I found in North Dakota, but I was also scared of the dead quiet winter trap.

And so, I traveled on. A bus whisked me away from Fargo on a beautiful day in June 1993, two months after I had taken my first step onto U.S. soil. I crossed the thousand miles from North Dakota to Seattle: vivid, green grass spread like a rich man's carpet on either side of the road and as far as I could see. Yellow buttercups, golden dandelions, and red, blue, pink, and white wildflowers decorated the carpet. Far away in the distance, it seemed as if the farms and nursery sites were chasing each other, one after another after another, all the way to the horizon. Bounty was everywhere I looked: my dreamland and my blessing from God existed after all! The air had been nourished by thousand of acres of wheat and corn and other healthy produce, and I breathed deeply of it, feeling newly clean, clear, and alive inside.

Mountains, rivers, lakes, forests, and hundreds of cities sped by as we drove through Montana, Minnesota, and Idaho. The presidents on Mount Rushmore peered down at tiny me peering back at the American giants from my little window of the bus.

Washington State: I felt I had found home as soon as we had crossed its border. The environment reminded me of the evergreen province of Dalat, my favorite place in Vietnam, as it was full of mystery, romance, and legends. Located in the beautiful highlands of Southern Vietnam, the French had chosen not to destroy Dalat when they first invaded Vietnam in the eighteenth century so they could use it one day as a vacation site. In Dalat, flowers of all kinds–roses, dahlias, cherry blossoms, lilies, and tulips all bloomed the entire year around. The province was sur-rounded at its edges by majestic pine trees, which gave the valley a "separate and mysterious" feeling. Lovers, poets, painters, musi-cians, and many others had gone to Dalat for the inspiration they found there, and many legends have been passed down and are known by all Vietnamese about Dalat: "Doi Thong Hai Mo" (The Twice Grave Pine Hill) and "Thung Lung Tinh Yeu" (The Love Valley). Everyone who visited Dalat–lovers, the simply curious, and those drawn by its beauty–wanted to solve the mysteries behind Dalat's legends.

As we drove along, our bus was sometimes swallowed entirely by a giant mouth of monstrous fog, and then suddenly, towering bodies of pine trees, cedar trees, and fir stepped out of the fog, close enough to us that we could almost reach out and touch their needles.

Compared to the boring flat land of North Dakota, Washington State contained quiet foothills, proud passes, and angry, bustling waters in the harbors. As the bus approached Seattle, the city seemed to be standing halfway on a hillside and the order half sweeping down toward the water. My heart was full: I had found my dreamland.

As soon as I stepped off the bus into the boarding area in Seattle, it all descended on me, once again: I was *not* in Seattle on vacation. I had lost precious time in Fargo City, time that I was supposed to be getting some important things underway as quickly as I could. But I knew Seattle was full of Vietnamese people, and I prayed silently that they would help me and give me advice.

My distant relatives were waiting to pick me up. My mother's cousins lived somewhere in the country in Vietnam, had come to the United States somehow, and I had not seen them in a very long time—some I had never seen. Our meeting on the day they picked me up at the bus was a little awkward for me, at least, as I wasn't sure at all how they really felt about having me stay with them, even though they had said it was all right when I had called them from Fargo.

And to my great surprise, my Auntie had big tears of happiness in her eyes, and she gave me a big hug and told me she had not been able to sleep the three nights before I arrived. My uncle seemed even more excited about the whole thing than my Auntie had: he stroked my head, as if I were his daughter. And my cousins Long and Annie were there, too. I was so happy to meet two relatives I had never known. They had each brought me flowers, and they told me not to be scared anymore. I burst out in tears, being with real relatives for the very first time since I had left home.

They took me on a little tour of Seattle and, of course, Chinatown on the way home: they knew I was starving for these things. The bought all kinds of foods at the market that had been imported from Asia because, again, they were trying to make me feel at home.

Their house turned out to be part of a housing development for low-income people and the elderly that was located about 30 minutes from Seattle. Their house was brand new and spacious, and my uncle had a beautiful garden full of colorful flowers, and I felt right at home the minute I walked in their door. At least I had finally arrived in Seattle, had a roof over my head, could get on with my future, and I was so grateful to them for taking me in. And I needed time away from Ngan and his mother to get my own bearings for now. My mother's cousins had made all of this possible for me.

I attended a Vietnamese church with my relatives and met many people. We went out for picnics and celebrated holidays with friends in the community. Chinatown was such a fantastic shock and discovery: I could find any Vietnamese food I could dream of eating in Chinatown–and inexpensive Vietnamese food, at that!

Seattle's vibrant energy was exciting. It wasn't a crowded city, but a beautiful one that felt full of opportunities. I could get a job and work for any Asian restaurant in town without a problem–talk about having had plenty of specific job experience in the restaurant business! And there were so many things for young people to do for fun! Seattle was an enormous door that opened to the promising future I had been dreaming of–all around me.

I rushed out to look for work as soon as I could. I worked two jobs: as a bookkeeper for a couple that owned several restaurants in the city and as an aide at a local nursing home. To improve my English, in the evenings, I went to school full-time. I felt brightness all around me (and I wasn't seeing stars from being so exhausted!): I had absolutely no doubts whatsoever about having chosen to come to Seattle.

And my heart laughed with pleasure when I imagined my mother receiving that first, huge chunk of money her daughter had sent to her all the way from America: in my head, I saw her sitting on piles and piles of my money, all of which probably would make everyone else in Cu Chi jealous! What a delicious image!

I had come to believe that it was now a very crucial part of my job to help every member of my family in Vietnam learn to stand on his or her own two feet. So, I began with my oldest sister's family. I bought them a house so they could have their own place to live, instead of having to live, crammed together, in my mother's house. I wanted them to have a better life and to recoup some of the losses my family had suffered since my parents had gone bankrupt.

Thousands and thousands of dollars of my wages flew like green, paper birds across the wide ocean to Vietnam. I did save just enough of my earnings to pay for my own tuition, shelter, and food, and I was even able to buy a little, old, 1981, blue Toyota Tercel from my cousin for very little money, so it made it easier for me to get to my jobs, school, and then home again every day— sometimes. That little blue horse of mine made lots of people laugh because it was *so* ancient, its blue roof had turned white from sitting for so many years in the sun. I began to be recognized by people in town when I rode by! Sometimes, that blue horse didn't want to go where I needed to go; its windshield wipers fought with each other when it rained, and I had to wait in the car in the pouring rain until I didn't need the wipers anymore! But, for me, it was pure luxury! And since it had been a gift, I had some money to pay my cousin back for fixing it.

What an amazing place this America was turning out to be! I hadn't yet seen money growing on trees, as someone back home had said he had heard, but I had already had lots of opportunities fly close enough for me to reach out and grab them.

Even when I was sick, I did not to go see the doctor, as I didn't want to use a single penny: I believed my family in Vietnam needed each penny more than I did. I only shopped at Goodwill: not a stitch of *my* clothing came from the mall! People in the community laughed at me for being so raggedy and so cheap, but it didn't matter to me. I was upholding the responsibility my father had given me so that my family could become more prosperous again and bit my tongue.

I worked relentlessly, like a machine, and only slept for four hours a day. I had started going to night school, hoping to become a nurse. My days were completely filled, even holidays. I was struggling to live and work on my future at the same time. My bank account was always empty, even though I worked hard. It didn't even cross my mind to buy a more reliable car, even though my little, old Tercel was constantly giving up on me. I just ignored the inconvenience; my cousin fixed it for me and charged me very little money for repairing it. I had lived through so many incredibly more difficult situations in my life that the sacrifices I was making in Seattle didn't bother me at all. I simply counted the days until my family's misfortunes were over with my help, and then I would be free.

Time flew with my dollars flapping themselves in huge flocks overseas. I had lived in Seattle for over one year. One day, I called Ngan and asked him if he and his mother wanted to move to Seattle yet. I thought perhaps they had finally gotten tired of their lives in the Ice Cube City, Fargo. I had spoken with them several times over the year since I had been in Seattle, just to check in and see if they were ready to move to Seattle. I had felt very guilty sometimes about leaving them behind in Fargo, especially when I had gone on to find and actually live a much better life in Seattle.

But Ngan refused to go anywhere. He was still happy in Fargo. But his mother had not been. She complained all the time to Ngan about her job and the severe weather in Fargo. Walking to work one day, she fell on the slippery road and broke her arm. Then Ngan had gotten into a fight with a co-worker and was hurt so badly, he had had to stay home for almost three months. Ngan's mother begged Ngan constantly to move to Seattle with me. I felt sorry for her, but there was nothing more that I could do. I called her almost every week for a while after that to see if she had changed her mind about coming to Seattle, but then I stopped calling for a long time. Nothing had really changed in their lives from the time I had lived there with them.

Then one day, I just decided to give them just one more call. It had been quite a while. They reported that they each had a job: what was a shock! And Ngan had a girlfriend, a black American soldier, which fact made his mother crazy. He also told me he wanted to file for divorce. In one phone call, our marriage was over. I didn't mind at all: I was now freer to focus on my family in Vietnam.

Ngan and his mother eventually moved to a town somewhere in Minnesota, and I never heard from them again.

By the end of that first year in Seattle, I had begun to suspect or feel deep in my bones that something was not right back in Cu Chi. I could sense it inside. Increasingly, I could hear an underlying but unspoken—at first—message in their calls and letters that I *never sent enough* money. Apparently, my grandma had been sick and in and out of the hospital many times. My mother was sick all year round, had been all of her life, and she constantly needed medication. The family's rice crops weren't producing much, and the cost of the children's educations kept rising. The enormous sums of money that I had been sending home began to feel more like pinches of salt thrown into the ocean that was quickly indistinguishable from the salt already there, and they disappeared before they ever reached the distant shore.

I hadn't changed my family's financial condition at all! *Why had it taken me so long to see the truth of the situation?* All of the money I had been sending home was being misused because no one in the family was using the money to try to change his or her life so as to stand on his own feet: they simply waited for their "monthly pay" from Seattle and had continued to live as they had been living all along, poor and lazy. My mother got *very* upset any time I tried to ask her about money, so I simply stopped asking. I didn't want to upset her about what I was doing for them: I had, after all, made a solemn vow to help them all—*without any restrictions.*

Then my mother began to ask for even *more* money! This was *very* troubling and mysterious, and I thought to myself, 'With all the help I've given her, she ought to be able to live very comfortably for a few years!' Instead, she said she was suffering. She broke down and cried every time we talked on the phone.

Suddenly, one night, I wondered whether my mother was telling me the truth or not! *Was anyone in the family being honest with me? It was suddenly scary to be so far away from home, to feel even more detached because you guessed you were being lied to, and not to see for myself what was actually going on.*

I had no choice: once again, I had to practice being patient and wait for my mother's instructions, instead of making any decisions on my own, as I had been doing over the past year. She complained and demanded and complained and demanded even more. As I had lived by her rules my entire life, I sighed heavily and decided that a few more years wouldn't make much of a difference in terms of my future. My fondest and only hope was to hear her laugh and know she was truly happy. I reminded her that her youngest children were almost grown up, would soon be able to stand on their own two feet, and she would soon be free of *their* care. That did not seem to register with or make a difference to her.

As much as I longed to know my mother was finally, for the very first time in her life, truly happy, a knot-like, painful truth opened inside of my heart like a bud blooming: *my family saw me simply as their very own, deep gold mine, whose endless bounty they simply waited to receive.* I had never <u>once</u> suspected that my help was *not* being used by each family member to advance him or herself so that eventually my promise would be fulfilled. *What an idiot I had been, dreaming pipe dreams and holding such high and impossible expectations of them all–and of myself!*

And yet, *were* they pipe dreams? Where was the rule that stated that my family could *not* use my help as something other than a welfare payment?

I was about to collapse, face first, on the American soil I had been tilling so hard and for so long–even before I reached America–all for each and every one of *them*! I *had* promised to help my family, and I *had* made a sacred promise to my father that I would take care of them, and I promised to uphold it until I died. But I had never <u>once</u> given a thought as to what this promise might cost me: exhaustion in every bone and blood vessel, trying to keep myself simply walking, one foot after the other, ahead through each day. I never had time to go out and make new friends or participate in any activities in the community. I quit going to church because I needed that time to earn more money to send home instead. My relatives started telling me I was "crazy" to keep my family "on my payroll." And I began to *feel* crazy from trying to handle all of the pressure I was constantly facing. My classes were getting harder, and my health naturally plummeted dramatically: I had horrible headaches, allergies, and grew weaker from a lack of sleep and proper nutrition. Plus, I couldn't eat anything after seeing the bodies of sick and dying patients in the clinic where I was working. Then confusion and forgetfulness set in, and I couldn't finish my homework at night because I was too tired.

I was truly terrified. But, as I always had in the past, I finally rallied and figured out ways of fixing my own problems. I realized that I *couldn't* handle as much as I always thought I could at once and that I needed to spend some time making friends and relaxing, instead of working all of my waking time and burning myself out to make more and more money for my family.

I decided to quit school for a while to get my body back to normal. The nursing program, on top of everything else, was draining me in every way possible. I had even begun to have horrible nightmares about the needles I used and blood I drew at the hospital where I was practicing my nursing skills every day. I had not had any time to make friends who might at least support me and sympathize with me about my situation. I was completely alone, and not one of my relatives was very helpful or sympathetic.

I decided to take the U.S. Postal test in my spare time, just for the heck of it. I also applied for a job at Boeing. At that point, I would have taken any job, as long as it held a promise of my earning more money. What did I have to lose? Besides, one truth had been burned into my mind over the course of my life: *one never knows what might happen next.*

I cried to my father for help every night in bed. I hoped that, somewhere out there in heaven, he was listening to my prayers. I didn't know whom to blame for my misery; I simply thought the way my life had unfolded was just my destiny–meant to be. I couldn't figure out why it had all had to be so complicated and that I never seemed able to find a way too simplify it.

All my new friends seemed so lucky, as *their* families supported *them*. They spent money freely and did not have to worry about shelter or food, as I did. At the very least, they didn't have to support anybody else. I walked far behind my relatives to church, feeling even worse about myself because everyone looked so fashionable and luxurious. It felt to me that they were showing off their stylish clothes and expensive cars, and I certainly didn't belong in their presence, the only one in the crowd wearing a cheap get-up from Goodwill.

My appearance and material possessions certainly were never the things I had ever cared deeply about. But something troubling was rubbing a spot deep inside me raw, even though I couldn't identify it. It seemed that the harder I tried to concentrate on finding and building a career, the more depressed I became; the more I tried to think about my future in general, the more sharply I saw the horrible truth of the reality in which I was caught.

I began to pale and then disappear into my own shadow: quiet, empty, and withdrawn. How was I to escape now? A husband? My first marriage had not been good, but it hadn't been a real marriage, after all. And, if I couldn't even take care of myself now, how would I be able to work with someone else so that we took good care of each other in a real marriage? And who in all of America would want to marry a poor woman with nothing to her name but a rust-bucket of a cantankerous, old blue Toyota and a huge, helpless, and needy family in Vietnam? The family riding on my back was a heavy burden that would never go away, I believed, for the rest of my life. What in the world would make them give up the certain treasure I had been providing them all this time?

Who was I, anyway, to think that I could appeal to a man? I lived with relatives in low-income housing in a city slum. They basically relied on welfare and food banks for their survival, which was looked down upon by most of the people I had begun to meet. I couldn't step up a social level to be equal to my new friends, so I was forced to remain down at my relatives' lower class level. I wanted to escape from the low-income housing and have my own home, but I didn't have enough money to do that. Again (and again and again), I had no choice but to be patient and wait until I graduated from nursing school; then I could have a real career that paid me well. In the meantime, nothing was going to help me right away.

When the sun was shining, I would disappear into the shadow of myself. I felt as if I were fading away until one day, I would be invisible.

CHAPTER TWELVE

1996

Sometimes, God works silently among us and *for* us in *really* strange and completely unexpected ways. When we're about to give up because we've looked *everywhere* we can think of for help and can't find a door out of our misery, something amazing can happen: God puts the very thing we need in a neat package of some shape or other with an invisible bow on top–right at our feet!

Reading the paper early on a Sunday morning, a personal ad written by a white man looking for an Asian girlfriend caught my eye. Just on a sheer whim, I decided to answer the ad. I wasn't interested *at all* in a serious relationship, but I was very curious to know why he was looking for an Asian woman.

After talking to each other for a while on the phone, I thought this Rick guy sounded very nice and was very easy to talk to. Soon we both felt comfortable enough to make a plan to meet. We agreed just to be friends; I only wanted to learn and practice my English, and he wanted to learn about the Oriental culture and business, as well, which I did know a lot about, after all. Getting to know each other sounded like a perfect solution to two friends' needs, and I really began to look forward to making a new friend, exactly the kind of person I needed so badly in my life and hoped he would turn out to be.

Our first meeting was even better than I would have dared dream it could be. We decided to meet at Wendy's, and I drove up in my cranky, funky, ancient, blue horse. Rick, a general contractor then, drove a pick-up with his company's logo on the side. He told me that he had a few employees, and they mostly worked on renovating houses and shops. We talked the whole evening about everything under the sun–food, my schooling, my job–he was really good at making me laugh. He also told me that he had an invention that he needed help with: he wanted a connection in Asia where he might find a factory to make his invention and fulfill his dream. Thus, the Asian woman he was looking for. Now, *here* was someone who spoke my language!

After that first date, we began to see each other as often as we could for two straight weeks. And then, just as easy as it is to turn a page in a book, Rick and I fell in love.

Rick was tall, dark, and handsome (an American dreamboat!), and he was just as easy to talk to in person as he had been during our first conversation on the phone and on our first date. We discovered very quickly that we were both very stubborn and strong-willed when it came to our own beliefs; but we also learned that we could easily get ourselves out of a tangle or fight of any kind we might be having and end up laughing (my gift from my father).

Only one thing bothered me enormously about the whole situation: I was suspicious that Rick might be married because I had heard so many stories about situations like that happening to Asian women (and American women, too) who answered personal ads, and I did not want another, even potentially dangerous, mess in my life: I had had more than enough of those! So Rick took me to the courthouse to prove he was single: he paid $80 for a marriage license, and he then had to make a solemn vow that he was single, which was witnessed by the secretary who had issued the license *and* me. I was so relieved and ecstatic.

Two weeks later, Rick called me one night to tell me that our marriage license was going to expire in ninety days. By that time, it simply seemed natural to us to get married, and, as easy as turning another page in our book, we were married in November 1996 before the license expired. Two months had passed since we had first met!

My getting married shocked absolutely *everyone*. My bosses, Mr. and Mrs. Sun, were very worried about me and what seemed to them to be my "crazy decision;" they thought that I was "nuts" to have risked my life to get to America and freedom, only to turn around and marry a man whom I had only known for a couple weeks. My co-workers were worried, too, and thought the whole thing was even dangerous. They wondered among themselves if the wedding would even really happen or if it was just another one of my jokes–for which I had become famous at work now, too.

My news completely stunned everyone in my family, too. They were, unfortunately, the last ones to know about my wedding because their invitation didn't arrive until after the ceremony. They simply couldn't believe that I was serious about getting married. When I told my mother on the phone, she said to me, "Oh, Loan! This is just one of your famous pranks! I know you and how you love to kid people!"

And what people were saying about our marriage *was* true: I actually didn't know who Rick was and or even where he lived! From his ad, I did know that he had a small business, lived somewhere in Seattle, and whenever he came to see me, he drove his pick-up truck with the construction logon painted on the side of it. But the truth was that I simply didn't care about where or how he lived, and I didn't care if he was rich or poor. I loved his great sense of humor, and to me, he was the most handsome man that I had seen in the U.S.! We loved being together; we argued and laughed like two little kids every single time we saw each other. We have actually never agreed with each other about much since that first meeting, and we probably never will. But that makes it interesting, especially if you can laugh about big disagreements eventually. I was an Asian woman, he was a white man, and I loved him. That's simply how we saw it. It was all the result of an impulsive call on my part, and I had no idea that *anything* would come of it!

I was calm, content, and had always believed in destiny. What did I have to lose but my dignity? I really couldn't distinguish between a good person or a bad one. Who really could? I had learned not to question or suspect anyone, if he hadn't bothered me. I had been taught not to cheat anyone; therefore, I believed there was no reason for anyone to cheat me. I was so grateful to my bosses, all my co-workers, and my relatives for their concern, but I wanted so badly to keep moving forward. I had shot the arrow and had confidently picked the target. Mr. and Mrs. Sun finally gave up trying to convince me not to go ahead with it.

And so we proudly mailed out to all of them the most beautiful invitations to our wedding reception.

Our wedding was more than I could have dreamed of. It was held in a chapel near Ricks' parents' home so that everyone in Rick's family could come, and Mr. and Mrs. Sun had agreed to stand in for my parents, as Mrs. Sun had adopted me! About sixty people witnessed our taking our vows.

My wedding gown was the most beautiful one I'd ever seen, and it had a very long train. Rick had picked it out for me at a shop in Seattle all by himself. We took our wedding vows at a chapel nearRick's parents' house so his family could be there, and an American pastor presided over our ceremony. We exchanged vows and rings; Rick had bought me a beautiful diamond ring, and I gave him his ring, as is American tradition.

Mr. and Mrs. Sun very graciously offered to hold our reception at one of the restaurants they owned in Seattle. My husband's whole family was there, as well as many special guests from both of sides of the Sun family. When we entered our reception room in the restaurant, we were shocked: the staff had decorated every inch of it for our party with enough flowers to fill an endless field and pretty handmade paper flowers, too; they decorated the walls with Chinese paintings and posters. It was gorgeous, and I felt right at home.

We all drank champagne, and we were all happy and laughing and singing and telling jokes and stories all night long. Mr. Sun had ordered for the entire party a twelve-course Chinese banquet: seafood, beef, chicken, Peking duck, barbecue, and on and on. It was delicious cuisine, the meal composed of traditional Chinese recipes, every single course of which had been prepared by the most famous chef in Seattle who also worked for Mr. Sun!

When it came time for our wedding cake, two waitresses slowly walked very carefully out of the kitchen and placed a stupendous creation on one of the serving tables. Rick had ordered an enormous, three-tiered wedding cake decorated exquisitely with pink roses–my favorites! My new husband has always been so sweet and thoughtful.

Though I was very sad no one from my family could be there, I felt the warmth of my father's hand on my shoulder several times during our celebration, and the best day of my life was everything I had dreamed it might be.

CHAPTER THIRTEEN

And just as quickly as Rick and I had fallen in love, our happy life as newlyweds was flipped upside down. Life proved—*once again*!—that we *never* can know what's around the corner. Very soon after we had been married, my husband and I found ourselves grappling with a horrible financial problem. My husband's business had had financial problems for a while, and, as a result, his business license had been suspended. Rick had also been forced to wait until a bank released a sum of money it was holding for one of Rick's clients; the client owed the money to Rick but wouldn't pay it to Rick because of a mistake in the client's contract.

What a depressing mess. I had no job, Rick fell into a depression and could only sit around all day. Because we couldn't afford to pay rent anywhere, we had to live in a fifth wheel container. The trailer was attached to a truck so Rick could pull the trailer anywhere he wanted to go, and our little home was parked on my cousin's property where Rick was finishing a remodeling job for my cousin.

Inside, the container was only big enough inside for our bed, a small kitchen, and a little tiny shower room. The roof leaked in the rain, so we all got soaking wet in the middle of the night. What a way to spend our romantic "honeymoon period."

That God! He is *full* of surprises! For no sooner than Rick's business gotten into a snarl and we had moved into our little love nest than we discovered that I was pregnant! Blessings and curses, sometimes fall upon you at the same time!

Throughout my pregnancy, I felt so deeply guilty about not yet having kept my promise to my father and also that now, with a baby, it was going to be even more difficult for me to work and support my family in Vietnam. I told my dad not to worry about our family and promised to hold my American son in my arms and work even faster and harder than I had before to honor my family's wishes and needs.

I stared into the darkness as I was falling asleep, and I thought I could see my father's big, gentle, Buddha's face smiling back at me: everything was going to be all right. Sometimes you simply have to trust and believe.

The night I went into labor, my obstetrician told my husband that I had no chance of successfully delivering my baby naturally because my body was far too small to manage the birth of a baby the size of mine. I made Rick promise me *over and over* not to let the doctor give me any kind of shot at all, even if it meant I might die during labor: I wanted to be awake, to be the first one to see my baby, if there was any way I could.

The doctor was furious with me and was very nasty and condescending toward us when I complained about the pain; she said that only medication or a C-section would relieve it and/or save my life. Of course, she had absolutely no idea what this particular pregnant woman was capable of enduring and surviving. Once she had resigned herself to the fact that I wasn't going to change my mind about her advice, she snapped the metal-covered chart she was holding shut with a loud slap, turned her back on me, and walked stiffly out of the room, leaving us with a nurse to monitor my labor.

Rick held my hands, and he prayed and prayed. He had learned already in our new marriage that I am *not* easy to persuade about *anything*, but he was also very worried that the doctor's predictions might be right. I made Rick promise, too, that he would not let me fall asleep or pass out during labor. He gave me his promise. His face was full of fear.

The pain was excruciating every, single second of my labor. I screamed and called out to my father for help during what were probably the most frightening moments of my life, and I had already had made it through so many! I lost my voice from crying and screaming so hard.

At one point, when I had finished screaming for maybe one minute, I overheard the labor nurse asking Rick, in a whisper, why I was calling to my father all the time. She didn't understand why I would call my father, of all people, when almost every other woman in labor called for her mother.

Michael was born two hours later! My doctor was severely shocked: she couldn't believe the baby had been born in such a *very* short time and *completely naturally*, instead of taking whole days and nights, medications, or surgery to bring him safely to us. There he was, my blessing from God.

And then, to top it off, I stunned her into utter silence: when the nurses lifted Michael up and started to take him away to be bathed, I leapt right out of bed and demanded that they bring my baby back to me right away. And from that moment on, Michael stayed in my arms. And no one dared to take him away.

His skin was just like so many other many American babies' complexions: soft as air and pure, textured like a white rose that glowed pink from the rosy, little fist of life beating away inside of him. He looked a lot like my husband, but his hair was brown, like mine. I examined every inch of him, over and over, from head to toe: his minute fingers that he wrapped around my baby finger when nursing; his pearly toes and tiny paddle-feet, which would bear him who-knew-where in this world; his red lips forming a bitty 'o' of what I was positive was a smile whenever I touched his cheeks. I put my ear on his tiny chest when he was sleeping so I could listen to that strong, insistent heartbeat: he was to be a survivor, my child. He was also blessed with a very peaceful soul.

So God had given Michael and me a huge obstacle to overcome *and* a blessing to accept with so much love, *all at the same time*! Sometimes, it was so cold in our little "love nest," fifthwheel container, we brought Michael into our bed to sleep with us so we could keep him warm. We both adored our son and spent many nights lying in bed, all together, Michael sleeping and Rick and I staring at his beautiful, brand new being.

But God wasn't done with surprises! On top of everything else, almost as soon as I had come home from the hospital with Michael, it began again: my brother began to call from Vietnam, asking me to send them some money! How on earth was *I* supposed to take care of anyone else? I ignored him and all of the others who kept calling and tried to concentrate on helping Rick solve *our* problems: we had no money and no real home, yet my family called–made *collect* calls–rang every night. I didn't want to contact or see anybody because I felt so ashamed and hurt. I never thought that there would ever be another time in my life when I would feel desperate again–and without a warning sign.

People in the Vietnamese community came to see me and told me to go to church because I might receive some help from them. I was miserable and bitter, having to bow down and accept people's charity and feel their pity for us. But we needed help.

I waited a little bit longer before trying to do anything else. 'The sun will shine after the rain,' I told myself, over and over, and I encouraged myself to be stronger and more positive, when I really felt so frustrated and completely hopeless. But I knew Michael needed us to be as strong and peaceful for him as we could be. Once he had fallen deeply asleep at night, I cried and prayed for yet another miracle; I begged my father's spirit to help us get out of this heartbreaking situation.

Once again, just as suddenly as our life had darkened, the black clouds and bad luck vanished. My husband was able to return to work after more than one year of struggling with the bank over completion of the paperwork that had caused our problem in the first place.

Rick always worked really hard for us. He fully supported my responsibility to help my family in Vietnam, as he had promised he would, sending money to feed them and to help with the costs of the children's schooling. He bought a house for us and helped my oldest sister and her husband open their own store.

And then, a few years later, Rick bought an old, small, two-story house in Everett, which was about thirty miles from Seattle. Rick completely remodeled the entire house so that it was essentially brand new. The house had two stories, five bedrooms, and three baths. We lived in very quiet neighborhood that was close to the hospital, Michael's school, and all the stores I needed to have close by. Another blessing!

My husband loved and took good care of Michael and me; he was very responsible and always positive, once that nightmare with his business had been resolved. We stood together, hand-in-hand and back-to-back, after having made it through such tough circumstances right at the very start of our lives together.

Not too long after Michael was born, I suddenly received letters from Boeing and the Post Office; I had applied for jobs at both companies before I had met Rick. They offered me an interview, and all of a sudden, I, too, had a job! I became so much more confident and felt so much better about the future. I was earning so much money at the Post Office that I could send my mother as much money as she demanded. My husband took two of his friends to Vietnam to marry my little sister and my niece so they could return to the States with their new husbands and have better lives in the U.S.

Then, I decided to sponsor my mother so she could to America to live with us. She left Vietnam in 2002, leaving behind the burdens she had borne for more than twenty years. She arrived, just as her kidneys were on the verge of failing unless she got medical treatment, which we could make sure she got in the United States. I did whatever I could do for my mother to make up for the loss of my father, who had passed away because we had been too poor to afford better doctors, a better hospital, and better medication.

God had given me an incredible power to change our entire family's destiny. I was able to keep the house that my father had owned and worked so hard to keep all his life, and I was finally able to help all my brothers and sisters as often as I could.

Our family's victories made everyone in Cu Chi jealous, especially the ones who used to spit on us when we were so poor, and my having achieved success in a way paid off the debt those people in Cu Chi owed us for ruining our family's reputation long ago when I was younger. I had become my family's pride and a role model for my brothers and sisters. People back in Vietnam who used to insult me in the market because my parents owed them money now came to see my family, wishing to become our friends. The power of U.S. money had not only healed our wounds of so many years, but it had washed away the dishonor our family felt when my father passed away because we didn't even have the money even to give him a proper grave.

My mother returned to visit Cu Chi in 2005 and was received with great honor. She felt once again the pride she had felt when, a long time ago, she and my father had still been some of the richest and honored people in town.

My family's successes became the dream of many people in town. Every time we went back to visit Cu Chi, a huge crowd of people came to our house with fistfuls of money to give us for their "ticket to America," begging us to help them. I was furious. We had achieved our success all by ourselves, and it had required making huge sacrifices; taking dangerous risks; suffering misery and starvation; so many tears; and having to bear years of shame caused by what our own people regarded as our failure. They probably thought their money could buy them success in America or that money really did grow on trees in the U.S.

I knew better and was grateful for having worked hard enough to earn the chance to find out.

CHAPTER FOURTEEN

JUNE, 2009

"Julie! Julie! WAKE UP! *WAKE UP!*" Rick was shaking me, hard, and really yelling in my ear.

How long had I been asleep, anyway? And did I have to go to the restroom! I smiled at Rick, rubbed my eyes, and stretched. We had been on this plane *FOREVER*, and I had been so deep in sleep and dreams. The only way to fly.

"Only an hour left, Julie! One hour! You'd better stay awake now. Want some juice?" Rick asked, holding out a little carton of apple juice.

Only one hour! An hour is a lifetime when you've been waiting for something practically your whole life. I peeked between the tall seatbacks at Michael and said, "Boo, you!! Are you awake?"

"Mom, you *know* I'm awake. Man, you can be so silly sometimes. Boo back!"

I laughed and stood up, stretched again, and then tried to move my limbs carefully past Rick's legs and those of the old man who was sitting in the aisle seat of our row.

"Sorry, sir," I said, as I worked my legs past his bony knees and feet. "I will be careful, I promise." All I needed now was to step on his old foot, for something to go wrong. So far, this dream had gone perfectly.

I wobbled down the aisle—having been asleep for so long, I really didn't have my land legs back yet—and walked toward the rest rooms. One was free. Once done, I walked back toward Rick and Michael. It felt really good to use my legs. I looked at all the faces I passed as I walked down the center aisle, wondering where they were all going, if they were on as life-changing an adventure as I was. Some smiled back when I smiled at them. One man was snoring his head off, sounded just like a chain saw.

When I got back to our row, I went very cautiously through the hassle of getting back into my seat, made it safely past the old man's feet and Rick's, and plopped down. The leather made its lovely whooshing sound as I settled in.

"Well, this is it," I said to Rick. "This is *really* it. I have never been as excited as I am right this minute."

"Not even at your own wedding?" Rick teased.

"*You* know what I mean! I never dreamed I would really be making this journey one day."

Rick pinched my arm. "There. You don't have to pinch yourself to see if you're really awake or dreaming! It's the real deal!"

I punched him lightly on his arm and said, "Now, neither do you!"

APRIL 2009

One piece of my promise to my father was still unfinished, and it bothered me, day and night, non-stop. Though I had tried and tried, I had been unsuccessful in finding my father's relatives in China, as he had asked me to do. I didn't think, back when I made my promise to him, that my father would die *before* he could tell me where in China they lived! During his illness, even at the very end, I had still held onto hope that he would pull through and would be able to take all of us to see them himself when he had recovered. My father didn't leave behind *any* information about his family, except the name of his hometown, which had been carved on his gravestone. He had lived somewhere in Guangdong, a province of Southern China. I had nothing else to go on—no address, no pictures, no letters, and not the name of a single relative. Not even my mother could help.

The war in Vietnam had separated my father completely from his relatives and home. He had left China with his oldest sister to escape the ruin that was being made of the country during the war. All communication between two countries had been strictly prohibited for over thirty years. My father had waited so long to see his family again that he finally died with what I was now afraid had been tears of regret. He would never have a chance to take all of us to his first home and to meet the other half of our family, and now it seemed that I wouldn't be able to help. His happiness in heaven—and mine—would never be complete, all because I wasn't smart enough to figure out how to find my ancestors in China.

My life had been so full and so busy that I had finally given up looking for his family, praying my father would forgive me for not trying harder to find them. Once in a while, though, the unsolved issue demanded my attention, reminding me about my Chinese heritage—and now Michael's, too—and my appreciation for my father, his great gifts to me, and his graceful ways of teaching how best to live my life. I always proudly introduced myself to people as a Chinese woman who had come to America from Vietnam. I always celebrated the Chinese New Year and all the festivals that my father had taught us about, as they were his family's traditions. I loved to tell people that my father always told me that I looked exactly like my Auntie in China. I also loved to impress people with stories about my father's many talents because he was one of the best fishermen in our village, was known for his excellent cuisine in our region, and had run two highly-respected businesses. I could tell people my father's hometown was on the ocean somewhere in Southern China. However, I had absolutely no other details about where he was born and had grown up.

My husband felt awful that I felt guilty about and burdened with the one promise I had not kept, so he had never stopped encouraging me to look for my family in China. Unlike me, he was very positive, and he never gave up searching on the internet for my family in China. However, he couldn't even find even a twig from our family tree because I didn't know my grandparents' names or my father's date of birth. He had emigrated to Vietnam without a single documents to serve as his identification. He couldn't speak any Vietnamese, so he gave the authorities his Chinese name–Zhi–when he arrived; I had almost never met anyone with our last name, Zhi, in Vietnam or in America. The Immigration Service didn't exist in Vietnam 60 years ago, so he could file his own immigration papers the way he wished. Generally, he was a Chinese man without any proof of his existence! I did look through old records and paperwork my father *had* brought to Vietnam, thinking I might find some identifying information in there somewhere, but nothing was hidden there.

In addition, I realized all my father's friends were most likely very old now, and most of them had probably even passed away. I sadly gave up and tried not to think about looking for my relatives anymore.

You know what? *NEVER* give up! I had already been taught and tried to live according to that rule, but I guess I still had to keep being reminded of its value!

In April, 2009, I told my husband that earlier in the year, I had signed up at the Post Office to take a few weeks' vacation in June. Rick himself had already planned to go to China on a business trip at about the same time. I had planned to pick up my oldest brother and my oldest sister in Vietnam and to take them on a trip with us to visit the Great Wall and Beijing, a city I had always admired.

But Rick thought that was the wrong way for me to spend *any* time in China: he believed I should hunt for my relatives, not go sightseeing! He suggested that we go to Guangdong and look for anyone who had the same last name as my father's. But that idea seemed useless to me because it was highly unlikely that millions of people in Guangdong still shared my father's last name, and I didn't know any other names that members of our family might have since acquired through marriage, etc.

But that Rick: he kept pushing me and pushing me to call every single person my father had ever known because *someone* might have known about or even lived in the town when my father had lived there. So we decided to narrow our search and try once again to find relatives on Guangdong.

This was a huge project for us. My husband first suggested that I call the woman in California whom I called "Auntie" because her husband had been my father's best friend; I used to call him "Uncle." He and my father had escaped from China together and traveled to Vietnam in the same boat with my father's sister and her family. They had become god brothers and had depended on each other in order to survive the trip. Uncle's family had lived and had had a business somewhere in central Vietnam before 1975. Uncle had come to visit us once in a while in Cu Chi when my father was still alive, and he had helped our family deal with my father's funeral.

However, I knew Uncle had died fifteen years ago in California, and so I didn't think calling Auntie would do any good now. But I called her anyway, and to my complete shock, right away Auntie gave me the phone number of her husband's nephew in Guangdong; she was afraid it wouldn't help because I couldn't communicate with him in Chinese, and that was all he could speak. I had learned some Chinese when I was very little, but I really hadn't had many opportunities to practice speaking it.

I was so uncomfortable about calling Auntie's nephew because of the language barrier, but Rick pushed me to call him, confident that I could do it. I finally gathered up all of my courage, took some of Rick's, and made the call.

The phone rang for a bit, and then I heard a man's voice on the other end of the phone. My heart just about stopped beating the second he answered. It turned out that he *was* my Uncle's nephew, and his name was Song Hui. As soon as I mentioned my father's name to him and told him I was looking for my relatives in China, he told me to call back the next day at just about the same time. He did not say why, and, for some reason, I did not ask.

The next day, I was nervous all day long the next day, thinking, 'What I should ask and where I should I start? My father has been gone for such a long time, so why would they even want to talk to my father's daughter who lives so far away on the other side of the ocean? Would they even believe I really am my father's daughter or think I am just some stranger?'

Without much time to learn more Chinese, I still pulled out all the Chinese books that I had brought from Vietnam fifteen years ago. I stayed up all night long, trying to practice my father's language.

Once again Rick, who was so excited, sat with me when I made the phone call to China the next day. The phone rang; Song Hui answered again and said that all my relatives were right there with him, waiting for my call!

I was so shocked that I burst into tears. It seemed impossible! After so many, many years, I had found my real relatives after making one phone call, and they were all 'right there' together on the other end of a telephone line somewhere in China. My cousin Zhi Zung Hao, my Uncle's youngest son, told me *his* family had been looking for *our* family everywhere for over twenty years, too! Zhi Zung Hao had even gone to Vietnam several times to find us, but he could not find anyone who knew where we were.

My cousin told me many things he had heard from his parents about my father, some details my father had told us when I was very young. Such great memories of my father when he was still alive welled up inside me. From my cousin, I learned that my real uncle—my father's brother—had passed away five years ago and that he, too, had wanted for so long to see my father, his youngest brother, once more. This had been his dying wish, just like my Dad's.

We were all crying and talking at the same time. It was truly stunning and amazing to have found them. I told them we would fly to China in June to meet them.

Thank God! Still another miracle had been granted to me, and this miracle meant I would finally be able to fulfill my promise to my father, something I had almost given up on. God bless Rick for pushing me just a little more, as always. A wild wave of happiness and gratitude rolled through my heart when I found out our family wasn't alone in this world.

I wished with all my heart to be able to see my father's eyes when I told him his children were finally going to be with the rest of his family in China, just as he had desired. He would have been so happy and gratified to know that his family had never stopped looking forward to the day he would return home to China after over 60 years! He would have cried with joy. Although we had never, ever seen each other, we shared an invisible bond that would never die, whether we were in the same room or an ocean apart from each other. That one phone conversation had pulled us all tightly back together and made everyone so eager to be a family after all this time.

I told my cousin that my father, too, had spent his whole life, anticipating the day he would be able to see his little brother back home and that he always said he couldn't wait for the war to end quickly just so he could go home to see his family and brother. The two brothers' spirits were so close.

On the phone, I had a hard time talking because I couldn't stop crying, so I just listened as they told stories to me. I promised to bring all my memories about my father to China in a very short time and share those memories with them all. A new promise!

We were scheduled to leave for China in eight weeks. Now, that was *far* too long a time for me to wait. I wanted to fly to China right then and there to see everyone. So did my husband! He had been hoping for this huge event to happen from the first day I met him.

Neither one of us could sleep that night after our astounding phone conversation with my relatives. I was overwhelmed by our victory and grateful to Rick for giving me that push I needed to move ahead. It seemed impossible that we had found them with our very first call to China! I even wondered if they were really my relatives because the whole thing seemed so unreal, once we had hung up the phone.

My mother was elated because she finally was going to have a chance to know more about who my father was from his relatives. We even packed our luggage right away, even though our trip was weeks away! I called my brothers and sisters to let them know we were on our way to Vietnam to pick them up and take them with us on an amazing, family reunion in China: we were going to be able to celebrate our father's fondest and last wish.

CHAPTER FIFTEEN

JUNE 11, 2009

We were soon to land, and my brother and sister had slept the entire trip, Michael told me, just as I had, and they were still asleep. I guess we were all still making up, once in a while, for all of the sleep we had missed as children.

Then, the flight attendant snapped us awake to reality by announcing on the raspy, loud intercom that the plane was going to land in Guangzhou airport in ten minutes. I watched out my window; from the sky, the majesty of China was breathtaking: its mountains, rivers, and endless, green farmland spread along Southern China pleased me for my father. I wanted to yell out loud into the air to make sure my father knew where we were, his reward that I had earned for my hard work for over fifteen years in America.

After a terrible shudder and shake, the airplane landed on the ground of Guangzhou airport at about noon on June 11, 2009. The weather was beautiful, warm—about eighty degrees Fahrenheit—and sun-shiny. Out the window, I happened to notice a huge medical team rushing out of the airport across the tarmac toward our plane. I wondered what on earth they were doing.

I turned around, kneeling in my seat, and looked at my brother and sister over the back of my seat to the row behind me, where they were *still* sleeping next to Michael.

Michael had held my oldest sister's hands when the plane was taking off from Tan Son Nhat Airport in Vietnam and told her quietly, "Don't be scared," because she had never been on a flight before in her life. Then she had proceeded to sleep the whole way! My brother had smiled broadly as soon as we had boarded the airplane but had not said a word, which he never did, anyway.

Looking at them, peacefully in dreamland, I shouted, in my loudest, most demanding voice, "Hey! You guys are going to miss this whole thing if you don't wake up *RIGHT NOW*!!! We are landing, for Pete's sakes! Get that sleep out of your eyes and look out the window!"

That did it, that highly effective, attention-getting voice I had perfected during my street-selling days.

They came to, rubbed their eyes, stretched and stretched hard, and smiled at me. "Hi, Loan. Where are we?"

"We're THERE! We're HERE, I'm telling you! Look out the window! LOOK! *HERE*!" I pointed out the window. "We are so close to Father's home! Yay! We did it!" And we all cheered and clapped together. Everyone else on the plane probably thought we were nuts, but we didn't care. We were right at that moment so very close to our other home, one we had never seen.

I knew it would take us forever to get off the plane and pass through Customs. We gathered all of our bags and sat patiently, waiting for our row's turn to walk down the aisle and exit the plane. I had tons of packages: I had brought lots of chocolates from America as a treat to give everyone, especially my Auntie, who was the only elder in the family still alive. All four of my father's other brothers and sisters had passed away.

As I thought about my father's family, I imagined that their living conditions would be bad. I imagined they lived in a really poor, small village, just as my father had once described it, in a tiny, old shack somewhere along on the shore of the South China Sea. They probably only had a big pan of sweet potato rice soup to share among them for every meal. I hoped they had enough clothes and shoes for the winter, instead of suffering through the deadly cold, as my father had described having to do 60 years ago.

I imagined that my Auntie, who my father had said was just like me, probably hadn't slept since we had talked on the phone because I sure hadn't! More than anybody else, we were so important to her because *her* husband's, my uncle's, last wish had been the same as my father's! In my mind's eye, my Auntie was probably a tiny and frail, old woman who had struggled and survived tropical storms on the shore, protecting and caring for her family all by herself since her husband's death. I was so happy to be able to see her before it was too late.

My husband and I had brought some U.S. money so we could build my Auntie a nice place to live for the rest of her life. We also wanted to help with whatever my cousins needed. We planned to buy a lot of food to give as a gift to the poor people in their village, too: a gift from my father's long-lost relatives, finally returning home.

We were all silent, deep in our own thoughts, wearing big smiles on our faces and happy tears pooling in our eyes. We were all sharing a moment of silent ceremony. I think my husband felt it, too, as he had such a loving and pleased expression on his face.

Suddenly, the big medical team I had seen on the runway was right beneath our airplane. The swine flu epidemic that had spread around the world had caused many problems for travelers who came to China, especially from America. My cousin had warned me so many times about this before we left Vietnam.

They boarded the plan and first cleaned the air inside the plane with an enormous suction pipe. Then they started walking up and down the aisle to take the body temperature of every single passenger. Michael was very worried and kept asking me if we were in trouble. I felt really confident telling him we were fine. We were all healthy.

But I got caught because my body temperature was 0.3 degree above normal. For God's sake! I was furious at having to be quarantined in the airport for what sure seemed to me to be no reason at all!

I tried to explain to the nurse that the weather there was so much warmer than our weather in North America, the clothing I had chosen to wear was too heavy for Asia's heat, and I probably was also feeling nervous about meeting my relatives.

However, they ignored my protests and threw me onto a separate bus, which took me to the Medical Examination Office. Over thirty people had appeared to have what the medical team suspected were swine flu symptoms, and all of us had even been on different flights! We were all crowded into a tiny, little room, waiting for the doctor's diagnosis. My family had passed through Customs easily with the rest of the "healthy" passengers, and they were waiting for me to be released.

I felt so scared and tense. I refused to have to turn around and go back home when we had made it so far on this trip! I *had* to meet my relatives, who I'm sure were waiting for us, just outside the airport. There was no reason for the medical team to hold me hostage in the airport because I was completely healthy. So I quickly swallowed two Tylenol that my sister had secretly snuck into my hand before we were split up. I drank a lot of cold water, ate tons of ice chips, and washed my face with cold water, trying to cool my body temperature down. I would do whatever it took: I would not fail now!!!

One of the other "detainees" lost his patience at being delayed this way at the airport because he was now too late to make his next flight connection, and he began to fight with another passenger. People were screaming and yelling at the medical assistants, who were trying to do their job. A crisis suddenly exploded in the medical exam office.

'This is so ridiculous,' I thought to myself. The Chinese government had annoyed and inconvenienced travelers, just to be extremely cautious. The swine flu wasn't a big threat to all of us, but it was China's custom to handle it this way.

We "swine flu victims" had been completely isolated in an area where no one could come close to us at all. I was so afraid that my relatives, who were supposed to pick us up, had already left the airport by now because I had been detained for so long. I borrowed a cell phone to make a quick call to my cousin.

He said, "Don't worry! We will wait outside until you are all through at Customs. We would never leave you now!"

After three hours of processing, I was finally released from the Medical Examinations Office. I was through Customs at three o'clock in the afternoon. My husband and my son were so relieved to see me walking through the gate at Customs. They had begun to worry that I might actually have the disease, that we might have to turn around and fly back to Vietnam, or that I had been sent to a medical center right in Guangzhou where the Chinese government had taken all the passengers who they suspected had the swine flu.

All of our luggage and packages and boxes were piled up high on carts my brother and sister were trying to maneuver out the door, as if they were trying to shove an elephant up a mountain.

And then, just on the other side of the gate, I saw them: there they were to welcome us: A Shia, my niece, and my nephew A Lung and his wife A Yi. They had waited for more than four hours for us all to make it through customs and the Swin Flu Scare. They had brought us soft drinks, orange juice, and a huge bag of snacks for Michael! They were so thoughtful to figure out that we would be so thirsty, having left the cool Everett breezes and landed right in the steamy heat of Asian summer. Michael and Rick couldn't wait to take a big drink before everyone could introduce himself!

My relatives were concerned about my health because of getting snatched by the Swine Flu Snatcher, but I told them that I was OK. A Shia told me that her grandma, my Auntie really, wanted to welcome us at the airport; but a trip like that—a bus ride six hours long, from Shantow to Guangzhou—would be so difficult for her, as she was an eighty- three year-old woman! I told A Shia that I felt very guilty if my Auntie was suffering just because of not being able to meet us at the airport. My husband squeezed my hands and told me not to cry, that there would be lots of times ahead for me to cry when we really arrived in Shantow.

A Shia assured me that Auntie was fine. She told me how my father's sister, my Auntie, had rushed to the temple in town as soon as they had all received the phone call from us, saying we were coming; she wanted to give her appreciation to Buddha for the reunion to come. Even though my father had passed away, his children were still coming home. And Auntie made her children get out the message to every single family in town that we were coming!

A Lung and his wife gave me a big hug with tears, as did A Shia. My older brother Ton and my older sister Chau began to sob behind me as soon as they saw our niece and nephews whom they had never met once in their lives.

Michael was fascinated by the crowded city of Guangzhou, which was so different from Seattle. It was easy to see quickly that their public transportation system was very large and so efficient, so Michael asked his father why there weren't bicycles around, as he had seen on TV. My nephew A Lung guessed that bicycles had been prohibited in the city of Guangzhou because of the city's enormous population.

Michael was very excited to see so many white people traveling in the city. Then Michael suddenly said, "We are not alone!" and he smiled that big smile on his face that made every one love him. They hugged Michael, and I could tell they were so proud about him being in their family, the family's very first American relative. The six hours bus ride was a chance to give us a good view of the part of China we were passing through.

A Shia was an architect. She said she had requested some time off from work to take care of our family while we were in China, as her parents had suggested she do. A Shia was very smart; that had been easy to see from the very beginning of our visit with her; she had planned every last detail of our trip for us and so well, as it turned out in the end. She was friendly, enthusiastic, protective, and seemed very sincere. Her fair skin and model-tall bearing made her very attractive. She made sure that we understood that she would do whatever she could to get whatever we needed at any point along the trip. What a warm welcome!

We had to hurry to get to the bus station before the last bus took off, so my nephew decided to stop at McDonald's so we could pick up something to eat quickly before the last leg of our journey was to begin. Michael whispered to me that there had been a ginger flavor in his hamburger, and he didn't like it. I told him there was just no time right now to stop for a good dinner and that we had to get to Shantow. It was going to be a long bus ride, but my Auntie had insisted that we arrive that very same day we landed at the airport for an "important reason," which A Shia didn't reveal.

My nieces and nephews wouldn't let us pay for *anything*, including our very expensive bus tickets, and Rick and I felt awkward they wouldn't allow us to help out. I guessed they must have had to get a big loan from the bank for all of us to make this trip. I vowed to myself that we would pay them back when we got to Shantow, for their parents' sakes at least!

Guangzhou was probably twenty times bigger and looked to be much more prosperous than Seattle! Beautiful and clean, the city was also very crowded and noisy, which was caused somewhat by the huge number of motorcycle riders, revving their engines up and down the streets. We boarded our bus at five o'clock that afternoon. Traffic was knotted up badly as we headed for the center of Guangzhou from the bus station, and so our bus had to work its way slowly along.

My niece A Shia had come with us for the trip, as she had been appointed our tour guide, though she did not live in Shantow. A Shia was a great guide, too, and we felt very safe and confident with her. She even spoke in English to Rick, which was great for all of us and made Rick and Michael feel comfortable and a little more a part of the family.

Each one of us had so many stories to share as we rode along. A Shia first said that we had come back to China just in time: her grandparents were trying to keep the piece of property in Shantow that my father had inherited from my grandparents for over sixty years. The Chinese government gave them a period of time to stake a claim of ownership. After August 2009, if no one–either my father or his children–had returned to claim it, then the family would lose the land forever! The story gave me goosebumps!

A Shia and I shared stories about our families, and we cried a lot because my father's last wish had been granted.

Rick told them that ever since our families had talked on the phone, I couldn't sleep at night! All I wanted to do was talk and laugh all night long, so Rick said he hadn't had any sleep either! And everybody laughed.

A Shia's eyes were red when I told her I had left Vietnam to go to America because our family was on the verge of complete ruin. They couldn't have survived any longer if I hadn't escaped. A Shia thought I was great to stand up and take on the responsibility of supporting the whole family on my bare feet, to begin with. She thought the story of my life was a perfect role model for the younger generation. She was amazed that, after all of the miseries and difficulties I had gone through to reach my long dreamed-of destination, I would then turn around and look back for her roots in China! "Who else on earth would do that?" A Shia asked.

"Nope!" agreed Rick. "Just my Julie!" And we all laughed again.

Along the way, she pointed out important historical sites and explained some of the many projects under construction that we passed on the highway, as we were working our way out of Guangzhou. The construction was another sign of how well Guangzhou was growing.

As I watched out the window, I saw people everywhere: walking on the sidewalks, going into and out of stores and restaurants, in the parks: everywhere I looked, seas of humans poured by.

Most Guangzhou residents appeared to be young, eager, and very friendly, which made the city upbeat, and they were dressed more fashionably than I had expected them to be. Thousands of trees everywhere waved their hands to fan the whole city, making it very green and cool, even though the afternoon was hot and sunny. Its handsome mix of Eastern and Western styles of architecture gave Guangzhou a resplendent and worldly feeling.

The city's stores were well stocked with goods of many varieties, each one of better quality (and more expensive) than it would have been in the United States. People seemed to like to shop more than people in my hometown did, and they seemed to have more money to spend fairly freely. Many of them were many juggling bags, parcels, and boxes as they scurried along.

'This *has* to be all a dream,' I thought: was I *actually* riding a bus in my father's own country?

Every inch of the land we passed was being used for farming, gardening, and nurseries. The bus rolled along beneath an endless, deep green canopy of trees, and it was obvious from the gorgeous, plentiful crops, plants, and growth indigenous to the land that the wet and warm weather of this tropical country was very beneficial for farming. In addition, the farmers used hydroelectricity from the rivers all year round on their farms.

The incredible hard work humans had done on this land made China look like a painting by a master. Thousands of acres, lychee, longan, and peach trees on the mountainsides had been cultivated carefully by the farmers and looked full of promise for a great harvest. Even the highway system was impressive; it was so modern. The traffic had finally eased, and we were traveling smoothly and easily, compared to terrible nightmare it was back in Seattle. Seattle, our home! I tried to grasp how far away it was from the new home we were heading toward.

I kept my eyes wide opened because I didn't want to miss a detail of our trip. My father's home. I felt sorry for my father. He had left us too soon before he had a chance to see the growth of his country. He had left China when his countrymen and women were suffering desperate starvation due to the war. He also escaped from his home village because he was so angry that the war had deprived so many and destroyed his beautiful country. If he had stayed long enough to enjoy his nation's victory with us, he would be so proud of and amazed at the transformation of his homeland.

Light purple clouds far off on the horizon looked like God's beautiful paint strokes on the canvas of dusk spread over the valley. The sun gradually slipped down behind the mountain, leaving a softening, lonely radiance in the sky; it all looked mysterious, but gorgeous. Far off in the distance, thousands of birds were migrating across the sky. The birds' families always stayed together, flying close together and heading in one direction. They followed their leader, even into storm winds and the turbulence caused by natural disasters.

We were those birds: young and lost, in a way, heading home finally after a long migration from America–but without our leader. I had become the pioneer leading our family; it had been my duty to lead us all forward for a long, long time. And on we went!

The dark had fallen like a black velvet curtain across the entire sky as our bus approached Shantow, making colorful neon lights on the Shantow city bridge shine in the dark, looking proud to welcome us. We finally entered the city of Shantow, a big city built right on the shore where my father had been born and had grown up. My heart, once again, was pricked with great pain, as I was so aware that our leader was not with us the closer we got to his home, but I also felt pride, as the rest of us were finally all together, as he had wanted us to be where he had wanted us to be.

The city appeared to be asleep, despite the bright lights, when we got off the bus at the bus station. It was about midnight. My niece, who had ridden with us the whole trip, eagerly told us the rest of our relatives were waiting for us in the parking lot. We hurried to pick up our luggage and struggled along toward the next leg of our journey that my niece had planned.

My cousin Zhi Zung Hao was waiting with his nephew in the parking lot. A Shia had called them to tell them that we were approaching Shantow. In the dark I saw my cousin smoking and watching the highway. He couldn't wait to see us: he had been the first one to answer my phone call from America. '

Suddenly I became nervous the minute A Shia said that he was her youngest uncle Zung Hao. Rick, Michael and I were all so excited. It was real: we were home.

My cousin took a little while to respond because it was the very first time he had seen an American relative, so I immediately introduced Rick to Zung Hao. Without saying a word, he shook hands with Rick and gave Michael a big hug.

Rick and Michael had learned some Chinese words to use when greeting people, and now was the time for them to us what they had learned. They both said, "Ni hao!" with their heavy American accents. That made everyone laugh, but Michale and Rick didn't mind.

Zung Hao then turned around said hi to my Brother Ton and my older sister Chau. Those two were already crying again, so they couldn't say a word yet.

Zung Hao laughed really loudly, making a very comfortable sound, just like my father's laugh. What wonderful music that laugh was for me to hear. He told them not to cry because my Auntie was waiting at home to see us, and there would be so many thing she would wanted to know about our trip.

We hurriedly got into the cars, and Zung Hao told us what to do. Our greeting at the bus station was really warm and great, though short because it was very late; but it was long enough for all of us to realize that my cousin just looked exactly my youngest brother Tai in Vietnam.

I told myself, 'I knew right away they were our Zhi family. They are our *blood* relatives! We can see and touch our connection!' We left the bus station heading home with a great happiness.

Because of Shantow city's shockingly beautiful and modern appearance, I expected we had quite a long way still to go before we would get to our destination, which *had* to be very far outside the beautiful and modern city. In my mind, I was sure my father's little village was still really poor and far behind civilization. Once upon a time, the place had been so wild that my father used to tell us he could run down the beach barefoot to catch fish to feed his family. I guessed that everyone in the village even had to share a public restroom because my friend had told me that was how it was in her relatives' hometown in China. My friend had been really shocked to find the very poor conditions her relatives were still living in.

Naturally, I imagined my experience in Shantow would be the same, as my friend's also experience matched my father's description of his home. I prepared myself for the worst. I expected we would spend the night in the dark because they had no power in the village. I had brought anti-diarrhea medication, just in case we got sick from the bad well water in the countryside. I had also packed up a suitcase full of instant food, in case we weren't close to a civilized area. I didn't care how poor they were or how bad their situation was; I just couldn't imagine it would be any other way, especially after getting my friend's report about her trip.

But Rick and Michael were Americans whose systems had never been tested before in a third world country.

My anxiety about what we would find and my excitement about what we would find competed inside me and rapidly intensified as our distance from Shantow decreased: we were about to live the most important moment in our family's history we had all–every, single one of us–waited for, for so long, and I prayed it would be the greatest moment. As my cousin's car rolled down the road, my emotions bounced up and down madly between happiness and fear.

Suddenly, I saw bright lights and unexected signs of wealth as we drove right into Shantow city! I had expected darkness! But Shantow city was wonderful, endless, and bright! The shopping mall was lit up in the middle of the night like a fireball, and thousands and thousands of people were rushing into the street to celebrate their spring festival.

Again, compared to Seattle, I found Shantow to be so beautiful and prosperous! It was absolutely nothing like my dreams of it had been. At night, Shantow turned into a crowded and bustling city, just as in Guangzhou! Shantow's residents' had a keen sense of fashion, and the luxuries and elegance they enjoyed in their lives were evident everywhere in this seaside city. I prayed my relatives didn't live too far away from this beautiful town, so I could relax a little bit more about our relatives' situation.

I knew very soon that we would see my father's poor, little village through the thick, sea smoke. I wondered how much longer we had to go until we arrived but did not dare to ask my cousin.

So far, I hadn't heard the crashing of the South China Sea's wild waves, hadn't noticed a scent of fishy salt water, nor had the sea salt that permeated the air passed across my tongue. I didn't actually see any signs that we were close to the ocean at all! The road we were on didn't turn into a sandy one, as those along the ocean often do, nor did I notice any wet rocks, which would glow in the dark on the shore, that had been washed up on the wild wave of my imagination. I assumed it would probably still take a while to get out of the city to our destination. I sat back and tried to enjoy the ride, as my husband and my son were trying so hard to keep their wild excitement about getting *home* still.

Suddenly, we hit a thick traffic snarl up ahead: the night-time public market right in Shantow's central city was alive and full of shoppers! My cousin had a hard time maneuvering the car through the crowds. Huge, remodeling projects occupied half of the city. Concrete, gravel, and construction equipment had been left overnight in random places everywhere, making maneuvering through the mess worse. But there were interesting things to see as we crawled along. And again, the construction meant growth. I became more excited and curious.

Suddenly, my cousin stopped and turned off the car right in front of an enormous, multiple-story, brick building and told us that we had arrived. I was shocked! I had never seen a building like it in my life! I had expected to see a little tiny shack with a bamboo wall in the middle of nowhere! This was a mansion!

We all jumped out, emptied the car of all of our stuff, and hobbled quickly inside. My Auntie was right there at the front door, waiting to catch us as we went into the house. More than thirty people were there inside what looked like a huge meeting room, all waiting for us! It seemed like the whole city of Shantow had waited to go to sleep until we arrived!

When we stepped into the door, I felt Michael's shock. He grabbed my hand and whispered, "Mom, look! The house is full of Chinese!"

I whispered back, "We are in China, Michael! You shouldn't be so surprised."

My Auntie was such a healthy-looking old lady. She had fairer skin than anyone else in the house. Her eyes were red from crying a lot because she had been so emotional about our great reunion. She gave us all kisses, especially Michael. Then she asked, in a very loud voice, which I took to mean she was indeed very strong and healthy, "Why did you wait so long to return home?" And then she began to cry about my father, her brother, who had not been able to be there with us right then.

I gave her a hug and apologized for our taking so long to find her and said we had so many pieces together before we could come back home, more than she could ever imagine!

I was sure that the entire Zhi family was there that night. Every single one of them mirrored each person in my family in Vietnam.

My cousin Lee Zhe Zhung, my father's oldest sister's son, with a big smile on his face, told us, "Mei mei, ni men huei lai la!"

Rick and Michael each smiled at him and then asked me what he was saying. I told them he was greeting us home. He looked exactly like father, especially when he smiled. My father had left China when Zhe Zhung turned four years old, and Zhe Zhung lived together with my father and their family before he got on the boat to escape.

Rick's and Michael's big smiles made every one cry even harder. They were so proud, not only to see us come home, but also to meet their two American relatives. I become the only interpreter for over thirty people for RicK and Michael.

Rick was thrilled and enjoying everything about this new experience in China. He felt he had never been welcomed before the way everyone here had welcomed him in all his life. My relatives' warm hospitality gave Rick a sense of belonging. He said, "It's a very valuable trip to China."

My Auntie's three sons, one daughter, and all of her grandchildren were there, too. I never thought I had so many relatives on earth! I talked and interpreted at the same time because everyone wanted to talk to Rick and Michael.

Michael loved watching all the strangers become his Aunties, uncles, cousins, nieces, and nephews. He was excited because all the grandkids called him Uncle Michael, even though they were a lot older than he was. He asked me why he couldn't call them by name, too, but could only address them as Uncle and Auntie. He was so confused.

I explained that was Chinese tradition. It didn't take Rick long at all to be getting along well with everyone in the family. He could talk without any problem, whether they understood him or not. He slowly became the center of the reunion. He started making jokes to distract my Auntie so she would not be so emotional. He talked to the grandkids in English and told them about America. That greeting was the most beautiful memory of belonging for my family in all my life.

Auntie and her children had worked hard to decorate the room for a big ceremony. This home was very beautiful and decorated in Oriental fashion. From the very expensive furniture to the curtains, from the wood floors to the kitchen appliances, everything looked almost story-book perfect!

Suddenly, my Auntie burst into tears again. We had arrived home in the early morning of June 12, 2009, our historic moment for more reasons than we even knew!

A sudden silence fell over everyone in the room. I could hear sobbing and crying. My brother, sister, and I were sobbing, as well. I hoped my father was feeling the love that his family was giving his children from their hearts, after looking forward for years to seeing him. He did. I knew he did. The feelings in the room were so powerful, he could not have missed them!

For the first time in my life, I understood–in a completely brand, new way–the very mysterious and invaluable bond of blood relationships. I realized slowly at first, but then more rapidly, that my heart was beating with the exact same blood as theirs were beating! In a single moment, I knew those 'strangers' were in and of me, were a part of my body, my mind, and my whole life, although I had never even seen them until now. There weren't enough tears among all of us to express the love, happiness, and joy that we were each feeling in our hearts at the long-lost children's returning to their family.

I bit my lips. I felt such great love from all of my Auntie's hugs and tears. I immediately loved my Auntie so much: she was the last, living elder in the Zhi family, who had tried to stay strong to be here to celebrate the reunion that had only been her–and my–dream until now.

A strange sensation came over me: we all seemed suspended in this silence forever, even though moments were passing. Then, suddenly someone remembered it was *very* late at night, and we should go up to my cousin's apartment.

As soon as we had walked through the door upstairs, my Auntie hurried us right to the dinner table and served us a special meal that she had prepared all by herself. It was a sweet meal, as is traditional to serve at a ceremony like ours: everything had been cooked with sugar and eggs. The table was laden with cakes, fresh fruits, flowers, incense, candles, meats, and seafood, and the living room had been brightly decorated in red to symbolize luck and blessings.

As we were eating, my Auntie finally explained why she wanted us to hurry and get to Shantow, even if we had to arrive in the middle of the night: we had come home on the very same day of my grandfather's memorial ceremony. This coincidence made my Auntie believe very strongly that a miracle was happening: we had come thousands of miles, 60 years after my father had left this world, to be together, each and every one of us.

Very early the next morning, my Auntie had arranged a beautiful ceremony to commemorate our reunion's occurring on my grandfather's memorial day. My Auntie instructed us to bow down on our knees in front of our ancestors' altar to receive the most important gift of our lives: our official welcome into the Zhi family. My Auntie happy eyes were full of tears because she was so proud to be the one who represented the entire Zhi family in accepting us, the grandchildren who had finally returned home to fill out our family tree, which had been incomplete for years and years. It was real and official, and I had fought so hard to make this happen.

After the ceremony, we gave them the presents we had brought for them, and our presents showed them that my father had been successful at raising and training his children, each one of whom demonstrated with gifts that he or she honored family roots.

My Auntie had borne witness to our family's entire history from the time of the war's trampling upon China. After her husband, my uncle, passed away, she took upon herself all of the responsibilities her husband had carried, and she never stopped hoping to see her little brother again, which was also her husband's—my father's brother's—last wish. This special trip had answered so many prayers.

Then my Auntie shocked us: she told us that had sent her children, my cousins, to Vietnam to look for us–and not just once, but many, many times! No one knew where we lived. She herself tried to talk to anyone who had returned to China from anywhere in the world to ask if they had seen or heard about us: no one knew a thing. Then, my sudden, short phone call across thousands of miles became the bridge for us all to cross to be a whole family.

My Auntie was so eager to tell us our family's history, as she had been holding it all inside forever. We stayed up until three o'clock in the morning every day just to listen to her beautiful stories about my father. Thanking God, I felt happy that she was still healthy and was very intelligent; she remembered everything about my father's childhood.

The very first important thing she wanted to tell us was about the property that my father inherited from my grandparents. She and her husband had claimed this property for us for so many years to the government. They tried to keep that piece of property until the day my father returned home. My father's name was still in the county registry, and we could represent him and inherit that land. She was so excited to let us know that we had come back just on time. The government had planned to confiscate my father's property in August, 2009, if the family hadn't been able to find us. I was so grateful for her kindness and faithful attitude to my father and his family.

From my Auntie's stories, our family history over 60 years came alive. In 1945, China was still suffering from the poverty and destruction of the war, in addition to their living in such close proximity to the ocean and its sometimes deadly strength. People depended on whatever they found under the ground to eat. In the small, poor village on the ocean shore, my father, a young, intelligent, and very enthusiastic man, had inherited the same destiny as the rest of the nation. He was the youngest son of a family with four older sisters and one older brother. Very talented and hard-working, he was the bread-maker of the family. He was also known in the village as a good fisherman and a good farmer. He grew vegetables to sell at the market and traded fish that he had caught to feed his family. Regardless of how hard he worked, however, their starvation didn't end. A lot of time, the only thing whole family had to share was a big pan of soup made out of a handful of rice and some sweet potatoes, and that had to last them for months.

My father was not only a gifted child but was also regarded as a kind and helpful young man who was of great support to everyone in the community. People asked him for his advice about their families, fishing experiences, or asked him to teach them a farming skill. He had never gone to school but had been taught to read and write by people in the village. His mother passed away when he was only twelve, and he helped my grandfather fight for food with the rest of the family.

Every day, he had to walk miles away from home on his bleeding bare feet in the cold weather to get to the market. He traded his fishes and produce to take home some money or things the family needed. He would go out of his way to help other people and never said 'no' to anybody. He loved his family and protected them all in the most difficult of situations without complaint. He was a role model that most parents in the village hoped their children would emulate.

When my grandfather passed away, my father's older sisters got married and moved away from home. By that time, according to government law, if a family had two sons, one son had to serve the Communist Army in the war. The family wanted to keep my father home to take care of the family because he was the youngest son of the family. The plan for my uncle, my father's brother, was to escape overseas so he didn't have to go to the army. However, my uncle suddenly decided to get married and wanted to stay home. My father, therefore, followed his brother's plan to leave his country so that his older brother could stay home with his wife.

My Auntie was five months older than my father and was a very hardworking and responsible woman. She really loved my father and treated him as if he were her own blood brother. She was so grateful to my father because he gave her husband the opportunity to remain at home with his family, and she managed the whole household: cooking, cleaning, making clothes, and raising some pigs in the backyard, while my father worked in the fields to try to grow some food for the family to eat.

When the time came, my father packed up his belongings and readied himself for the trip overseas exactly one year after my uncle had gotten married. My Auntie sold her two pigs to buy some clothes and pack up some food for my father. She gave my father some money for the long trip, knowing in her heart that she would probably never see him again.

My father left China with his oldest sister's family on a boat at Shantow to go to Vietnam in 1945, right after World War II had ended. His youngest brother left home so that his older brother's family could stay together, and so my father left behind all the love, respect, and pride his family and everyone in the community felt for him. No one knew then that was my father had left on a one-way trip to his final destination.

Auntie told us that my father had sent a lot of money home to help her family through their various difficulties and also took care of his older brother and sister's families, even though he was lonely and far away from everyone else at home.

Then, another highly devastating war exploded in Vietnam in 1954, and that war cut off my father's intimate relationship with his older brother and his wife. After that, my father lost all contact with his relatives in China. Many Chinese people had emigrated to Vietnam and then decided to return to China, among them my father's older sister and husband. They wanted to stay away from the deadly war. My father refused to return home with them, until he had become successful in a foreign country. He decided to get married and stayed in Vietnam with his family.

Any communication between the two countries became illegal. The only way for him to connect with his relatives and them to him was to go through middleman agencies in Hong Kong.

My Auntie then told us what is now my favorite and what I consider the most beautiful story about my father. A deadly flood in Southern China in 1969 had killed millions of people and washed away their whole village. People were homeless, including my uncle and Auntie's families. My uncle had not been in contact with my father for long time.

Then, all of a sudden, they received a gift from my father that my father thought would rescue them all. My father had learned about the flood, and he immediately sent money back home to help his relatives survive. Using that money, my uncle and my Auntie had rebuilt their house and fed their children during their most difficult time. My father's kindness and generosity had surprised everyone in the family because there was enough money to help *all* of them to get back on track in their lives! My Auntie had waited for so many years, hoping for a chance someday just to thank her brother-in-law, who was always with her family in spirit and always watching over her family.

My father never did return home, but instead, his descendants did: US! My Auntie finally had her opportunity to show her love and appreciation of my father through us. They took us to visit my father's friends and every single one of our relatives, some of whom were over one-hundred-years-old. Because my father had been their favorite young man 60 years ago in the village, his children now became their honored guests. They couldn't wait to see us, once they learned about that very first phone call I had made from America. My Auntie sobbed as she told us about the day she had heard my voice on the phone from the U.S., and the whole town had had a big celebration to congratulate her on her family's fortune. Relatives, friends, and neighbors filled her house full of eggs, fruits, and cakes, as was the tradition in Shantow to celebrate the return of a long-lost family member. My father had been so famous and beloved that the villagers never forgot him.

We were treated like treasures by our relatives and enjoyed the best time we ever had in our lives. They felt sorry for us, too, alone in a foreign country and receiving no support from our father's family. They felt guilty for not sharing in my father's funeral and for the difficult time my family had had when my father passed away. This splendid treatment was part of their way of paying back what they felt they owed my father for his help in the past when they were still poor. We stayed at the most expensive hotel in town and were treated to China's finest cuisine and Shantow's freshest seafood at the most luxurious, royal restaurants in the province–without paying a penny. My cousins wouldn't *ever* let us touch the bill. They probably felt sorry for our family, who had never lived one happy day in our lives, especially my two oldest brothers and sister, who still lived in Vietnam. And so, they spoiled us all rotten!

Then our family took us to visit my grandparents' old house that still stood after one hundred years. The door had been locked from the outside, so we could only see inside through a crack in one wall. The old house was just a tiny, little shelter built out of old wood and clay walls; it was moldy and about to collapse. It was dark and very messy inside, and the roofing was ancient and rotten from its years of trying to withstand nature. But the house stunned me into silence: I was actually standing outside the place in which my father had been born and grown up.

My Auntie told us the government had temporarily let the family wait for us to come back and reclaim possession of the house. I burst into tears, seeing my grandparents' little, old house standing in the middle of the big city Shantow had become, surrounded by modern skyscrapers. I thought to myself that my father had never really gone away from home over the last 60 years. His house was still waiting for him to come home. His name was still in the County Registry, and all the residents of Shantow had also waited for him to come back from his long trip away.

Standing in front of my grandparents' house, I wanted to yell out loud into the sky to make sure my father knew exactly where we were standing right then. I felt as if we were all waiting for him to unlock the door and welcome us all inside. I imagined my grandparents, still sitting on very rickety, old chairs inside and waving us into the house, too.

The furniture inside the house was ancient, too: only a small table with a few, small chairs around it for my father and his family. They slept on wooden boards that were held together while they slept by hand-fashioned "holders," similar to an American bed frame. In the dark kitchen, I imagined a few clay pots that my grandmother used to preserve her salty, dried vegetables for the winter, one of the things my father told us when I was little. I was sure I could smell dried fishes from the backyard that my grandma also preserved for the family on rainy days.

In my thoughts, I heard his voice in the air proudly telling his parents about me, his gifted child, even though I could be really stubborn. And he had always been there with me, I knew it; he had lifted me up off the ground, if I had fallen, and had given me the strength to keep moving forward, one step at a time, time after time after time.

As we stood in front of his house, I remembered stories that he told us kids so many times about his childhood. I had seen pictures of my Aunties with my grandparents and my uncle, and they all looked happy together. They all looked as if there were nice and gentle people, as my father had said they were. One looked exactly like me; she was my father's second older sister, and my father used to say we were alike in spirit, too. Everyone would have been really happy together if my grandma hadn't passed away when she was so young and the war hadn't pushed my father far away from his family.

All my life, I had told everyone that I was born into a Chinese family, had grown up according to Chinese culture, ate Chinese food, and celebrated all special Chinese holidays and festivals.

But here was the actual proof of my Chinese roots. I felt so grateful to my father: his last request of me had led us to a big gift for all of us all, even though he himself had had to go before he could enjoy it, too.

During our ten days in China, every single one of us all–from my Auntie, the elder, down to little grandchildren–were together every single day to talk, to share stories, and to laugh. They cooked all kinds of traditional foods that my father used to like a lot, and they taught us Zhi family values and paid respect to my father for his help.

Our family wanted us to move to China so they could help us with my husband's business and because they believed we would have a better life there. Something only true blood relatives would offer! The better I got to know my relatives, the more I heard and saw of the way each one talked, laughed, and acted, the more clearly I saw in what ways they were like my father. Deep down in my heart, it was hard sometimes to see my father "come alive" in one of them. My father had loved them all so much that he had named my oldest brother after one of his nephews and thereby planted some of his own roots where he had ended up.

My lovely Auntie was so sweet and so kind: she couldn't have done a better job of taking care of her nieces and nephews. Even at night, she made sure all of us were safe in bed before she returned to her house, making sure to give us many kisses and hugs every day, something she had waited to do for all her life.

My Auntie cried a lot when we told my father's family about my family's sad stories, such as when my parents went bankrupt, which caused my father to suffer a serious health condition. She was in pain and felt sorry for all of us when my father passed away, leaving us with a big financial burden. She sobbed and moaned as she listened to the adventurous trip I took to America for our family's survival.

I became not only my Auntie's little hero but also a role model for all the relatives, too. I was reliable and strong enough to do whatever it required to make my father's wishes come true. Everyone admired me for my long difficult journey leaving home and were so relieved that my mother had finally been able to come to the U.S. to live with us.

She also wanted to give us all the money that she had saved her entire life as a gift. She was concerned about my mother's health problem and wished to help my mother. And *we* had brought money to help my *Auntie*!! Instead, we had received so many gifts from her and the family. My cousins were much more prosperous than we were; they owned businesses and made tons of money from all of the rental properties they owned all over the city. They owned a sewing company, which produced thousands of dresses that were exported everywhere in the world. Many Chinese weren't suffering the poverty my friends had warned me they had seen when they had been here.

I was so proud of my relatives' successes. We were lucky we did not have to eat the instant noodles and dried food I had brought for our relatives. We didn't have to use any public restrooms, as I had been warned. Instead, I had so many wonderful experiences in China to tell my friends about when I went back. And my father and his family had surprised us in so many ways in Shantow. I wanted to share the story of my journey with everyone on earth!

After ten days in China, we had had a chance to learn about some of my father's interesting habits when he was young. Shantow's residents had a unique tea-drinking tradition. Tea is a specialty of the people in the city, and tea time was an enjoyable, relaxing, and warm time to share together. Shantow tea sets were so unique that only one place in China made and sold them. The little, tiny tea set had three little, tiny cups about a plum's size, and its small matching pot was about the size of a small orange. People sat together at the tea table, taking turns sharing a little cup of tea. They drank tea all day long without getting tired.

Today, the tea set has been modernized, compared to its first incarnation of 60 years ago. An electric pot now was used to heat water and was kept on the tea table, full of boiling water, at all times. Underneath the tea table was a drainage system, where tea waste was placed and cups washed. My cousin proudly told me the tea sets were manufactured only for Shantow people.

My parents had taught me to drink tea when I was very little, but our tea was not the tea of Shantow. Theirs had a bitter and very strong aroma, and it kept me awake all night long for the first few days I drank it with my relatives.

My cousin took us to visit a nighttime market, which was right in my Auntie's neighborhood. At five o'clock in the evening, the vendors gathered on the street to open their stands, and they were open until five o'clock in the morning. Here, I could find anything on earth I might want—name brand products, too, I thought at first, that had been imported from Europe and America: from fruit to clothing, food, and household supplies, goods were piled high on the ground, in carts, or hung on long lines along the street.

As I inspected the wares for sale, I realized quickly that the products in the market actually were really cheap and not name-brand at all but copies of name-brand products from around the world that had been made by local manufacturers and were being sold at the market. It was a crowded, noisy, and very busy place. People shopped, ate, and wandered all night long in the streets, as long as the vendors were still there. The music, the talk, and the bargaining between buyers and sellers kept the whole town up all night long. People easily negotiated an item that cost fifty yuens down to five yuens, a huge and shocking difference.

We went to the beautiful beach where my father got on the boat to leave China so many, many years ago. Shantow Beach had now become an important port in Southern China, not just a launch for small fishermen heading out onto the ocean to fish. Along this shore now, there was much exciting activity; there were lots of seafood processing companies whose products were sold everywhere in the U.S. I was shocked to find out the seafood that we ate in America had traveled thousands of miles across the ocean from Guangtong Shantow!

Walking along the shore on the cool sand, I took a deep breath to enjoy the fresh air and imagined my father being out there on his giant fishing boat, heading home to find us. I believed I would find my father's footprints somewhere in the sand, stained from his frozen, bloody bare feet. I imagined memories of my father were still everywhere in Shantow, even in the air; I know I heard the echo of his voice, talking and laughing with his fishing partners.

We walked all over my father's home village. We stopped at the little, old temple where my father and his fishing partners prayed before they headed out onto the ocean to fish. The temple was simply an ancient, concrete altar that had been built right in the middle of an intersection in town. It had an ancient, copper incense burner and a handcrafted worship stone, and the residents in town took turns putting incense, fruits, and flowers up on the altar every day. Although the temple had existed for over 100 years, the tradition of praying there had never changed. In Shantow, they still believe an angel will protect them from any of Mother Nature's dangers they might encounter on their trip. My Auntie had come here herself and prayed for our trip to go smoothly and safely a few days before we arrived; therefore, we prayed there in appreciation for her concern and love. The townspeople came here to ask for a favor or for the cure to an illness, for good fortune, and help with any difficulties they were going through.

Through those elders, I had seen an even more detailed picture of my father. If my father hadn't left home, he might have become one of the elders who had spent all their lives in poverty in China during the war, suffering starvation and natural disasters, or he might even have been killed during the war here. He might also have survived the disasters and become wealthy, as some of his family eventually had. Who *ever* knew what might be around the corner?

But now, I did understand so well that he had sent the greatest gift of all to all his friends: us, his family, living proof that he had lived, that he had been successful, and that he had always honored and had passed down his Chinese values to us.

Our seven days in Shantow were too short for our family reunion. We were supposed to go to Guangzhou for the next few days, where my nieces and nephews were planning to take us sightseeing and to try to help my husband's business.

My Auntie just about died of heartache when the day of our departure finally arrived. She gave each of us big hugs, tears, and sobs. She told us to come back as soon as possible and not to forget to bring the rest of our siblings to visit her next time. The whole town had gathered along the street to say goodbye to us, just as they had all been there to greet us the minute we had arrived. From young to old, everybody fell into silent tears, and that made our sorrowful, but grateful separation even more sobering.

Leaving Shantow, my heart was full of thankful love for my relatives and satisfied pride that I had completed my life long journey; it had all been so difficult so often, but eventually it was the most special journey–from Cu Chi to Saigon to Manila to Fargo to Seattle, and finally, at last, to Shantow and into the arms of my father's sister! It sometimes struck me as funny to think that I couldn't ever go back to where I began and repeat what I had done because I might get lost in my own puzzling maze of a life!

My father's last wish had been fulfilled, and now he would rest in peace with that beautiful, broad, Buddha smile even broader and prouder of all of the work he had been confident I could do to give his life and every member of his family honor.

CHAPTER SEVENTEEN

JUNE, 2009

"Julie! *Julie!*"

My name was being whispered from far, far away, very softly, but grew a bit closer every time it was repeated. It was Rick; I finally recognized his whispery voice. "Julie, we're *almost home* again! *Twenty minutes!*" Then, nothing.

I slowly opened my eyes, turned my head to find him, and smiled. After stretching all of my tight, 'ten-hours-locked-in-one-position' muscles free of knots, I asked him again, "*How* much longer?"

Rick still whispered, as it was still very early morning, and he didn't want to wake anyone else up, "Twenty minutes! You slept the entire way!"

"That's what "red-eye special" flights are for!" I said.

Rick laughed softly. Then he whispered, "Hungry?"

I shook my head. I wanted to watch the last leg of this journey. Outside my little round window, the dawn was beginning to wash the lightening sky with a luminous pink, adding wisps of darker pink clouds here and there. Soon the gold sun would rise in front of this amazing backdrop, working the pinks into a strong, silent blue.

As our plane descended, my heart began to thud with excitement, and just as we began to approach the runway, we passed right over a broad stand of Oregon's giant pines that seemed to be reaching high up, as if to tickle the bottom of our plane, and the wakening sky's eye was very still and clear.

Home, I smiled to myself, full of peace in every corner of my heart for the very first time in my life. Finally. Home at last.

POSTSCRIPT

JULY, 2012

At the Post Office, my first customer of the day dumped a tipsy tower of packages on the counter in front of me with a big smile on her face. "I want to send these packages to my son who's serving in Iraq." Her voice was clearly full of sheer pride and excitement about her son's being in the American Army overseas. I had heard those words and seen that look hundreds of times before.

My heart sank, and I could not return her smile right away. I could only feel sad to think about her son, struggling to survive in the war, just as I had. This mother had probably never seen a human being killed or had to walk past one on her way to school as a child. Her son, and so many, many others born and raised in America, are now faced with horrors that I know all too well, and some are facing atrocities far worse than those I had experienced.

Americans are so fortunate not to have to have been through a war on their own soil and helplessly witnessed the deaths of relatives or neighbors right on their streets at the hands of an overwhelming enemy. Lots of Americans simply have taken for granted the kind of freedom we have for over three centuries—like air, like the seasons changing. For many in the U.S., war is just something 'happening somewhere over there on the other side of the ocean,' and they go about their days as if no one would ever dare threaten them or their way of life or take and hold their children hostages—or kill their elders.

283

Goosebumps crept up the back of my neck and into my hair at the base of my skull, wondering how these proud parents would feel if they were to lose their children to the terrors of battle. I think of Michael and cringe at that thought. These parents hear of *others* who have lost their sons and daughters in a war, but it still must be difficult to *relate* to such loss. Americans' feelings are probably even more complicated because they also hate the war, at the same time, and want to dismantle the enemy, just as those of us who have experienced its bloody, firey reality do, too.

This woman's eyes expressed the innocence of the child I once was in my hometown Cu Chi, walking to school in the morning, day after day, after a deadly fight had occurred overnight, and having to step over rotting bodies to get to school and learning to pretend it was nothing. We were so innocent because we were so young and knew nothing about the realities of and the differences between death and life, just as these American soldiers' parents are: experience forced us to learn quickly to look away and hold our noses because the stench of death filled the air right in the center of our town; to huddle, as silent as if we were dead, in our underground bomb shelter; and to not sleep because our very bodies were in danger day and night. Experience is the only true teacher. Life experience truly cannot be shared: it can only be earned.

I could say nothing directly to this proud mother. Her son was already overseas; I could not help her with or change that fact, although I wanted to and although I, too, at the same time, was grateful for his willingness to be 'over there' in that madness to try to preserve the quiet, relative safety of the streets most of us enjoy here at home.

I looked up finally, handed her receipt to her, and we smiled at each other: two women, two mothers, two human beings who were metaphorically on opposite sides of the ocean, standing face-to-face inside a small-town, American Post Office.

Outside the Post Office's huge plate glass windows, I watched her walk away, head held high beneath towering pines waving softly across the silent, watchful blue eye of our American sky.

—Loan Ky Alexander